Protecting Your Microcomputer System

Harold Joseph Highland

A Wiley Press Book

JOHN WILEY & SONS, INC.
New York • Chichester • Brisbane • Toronto • Singapore

The cover photograph shows some of the equipment used by the author in the preparation of this book.

Columbia Data Products' Multi-Personal Computer (MPC Model 1600-1) is a modular desk-top microcomputer with a standard configuration containing a 16-bit 8088 processor, 128K RAM, two floppy disk drives, and a Winchester hard disk interface. Multi-Personal Computer is a registered trademark of Columbia Data Products, Inc.

The Video-300A monitor is produced by Amdek Corp.

Reproduction of the CBASIC Compiler and Personal BASIC manuals used with the express permission of Digital Research Inc. CP/M is a registered trademark and CBASIC Compiler and Personal BASIC are trademarks of Digital Research Inc.

The keyboard enclosure, TUCK-IT, available with a locking mechanism, is a product of INFODevices.

The mini floppy disks are through the courtesy of Maxell Corporation of America.

Library of Congress Cataloging in Publication Data

Highland, Harold Joseph.
    Protecting your microcomputer system.

    Includes index.
    1. Electronic data processing departments—Security
measures.   2. Microcomputers.   I. Title.
HF5548.2.H53   1983   658.4'78   83-5858
ISBN 0-471-89216-5

Printed in the United States of America

84 85   10 9 8 7 6 5 4 3 2 1

To my wife, Esther

Who has been my literary critic and
editor for nearly 50 years, starting
when we were undergraduates

Contents

Preface

Microcomputer Security in this volume is used in its broadest sense. It is the protection of a person's or a company's assets, its computer hardware, its computer programs, and its data files. It is also the assurance that the microcomputer system will operate accurately and without interruption.

This volume has been written for the home user, businessman, or professional who has purchased, or intends to purchase, a microcomputer system. It is a **security guidebook** to make the reader aware of the many problems that may arise and recommend procedures to reduce the risks faced. It covers all microcomputer environments, from a single microcomputer with one user through networks with many microcomputers and many users.

It has been written in nontechnical language. Where it is necessary to use technical computer terms, they are explained clearly in separate lists for easy reference. Even sections that may look technical at first sight will be found quite understandable when read with the accompanying text.

Among its special features, this book includes

- checklists for a quick review of what needs to be done,
- programs written in CBASIC (easily translatable into other popular BASICs) that provide software security techniques,
- step-by-step instructions to increase security through modifications of the system, computer programs, and data files (like setting up user areas on a disk to limit access to protected files, and built-in password protection in both programs and data files), and
- a list of selected sources of special software and hardware.

Most of the step-by-step instructions are illustrated using an 8-bit microcomputer and the CP/M operating system, since this configuration is widely used in business. Many of these techniques have also been tested using other operating systems, as well as a 16-bit microcomputer. The concepts are the same, and it is easy for any user to *translate* the step-by-step procedures and the programs included in the text to fit his or her system.

The book has been written in six parts, which can be read from the first through the last chapter, or may be used for specific sections in which the reader is most interested.

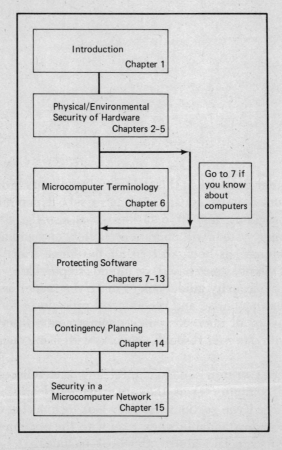

Many possible security measures are discussed and evaluated in the chapters on software protection and networks. There is more choice in this area than in providing physical security of the microcomputer system or in limiting physical access to it. Which methods are most advantageous in a particular situation will depend on the number of people involved and the technical sophistication of the users. The techniques discussed should be thought of as **layers of protection,** with each new layer adding to the value of those already in place. In software security the whole is often greater than the sum of its parts.

Harold Joseph Highland

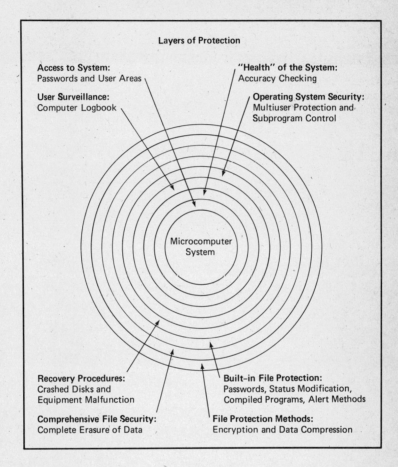

Layers of Protection

Access to System:
Passwords and User Areas

User Surveillance:
Computer Logbook

"Health" of the System:
Accuracy Checking

Operating System Security:
Multiuser Protection and
Subprogram Control

Microcomputer
System

Recovery Procedures:
Crashed Disks and
Equipment Malfunction

Comprehensive File Security:
Complete Erasure of Data

Built-in File Protection:
Passwords, Status Modification,
Compiled Programs, Alert Methods

File Protection Methods:
Encryption and Data Compression

Acknowledgments

A good portion of this book is based on my tests of software provided by various companies. Complete addresses of the companies whose software or hardware is included in this book are contained in the Appendix on page 233.

I should like to thank several individuals for their roles in the development of this book.

- Esther H. Highland, my wife, for her critical editing of the manuscript as well as her writing and testing of computer programs, and for listening to me patiently as I explored ways to improve computer security in a microcomputer environment.
- Joe Brook, Adrienne Hellman, and Harold Blathorn of Work Force, Inc. (Farmingdale, N.Y.), who provided assistance in unraveling operating systems and hardware operations.
- Adolph F. Cercula, Jr., Mary O. Jones, and Roy W. Anderson of the U.S. Geological Survey (Reston, Va.) for help in interfacing microcomputer systems and network communications.
- William F. Cosgrove of Registration Electric Supply (Linden, N.J.), who provided the technical assistance in his review of the electrical section.
- Jack Horner of Columbia Data Products, Inc. (Columbia, Md.) and the helpful, untiring support staff members, who provided special assistance in answering numerous technical questions.

- Patricia Lucas of Digital Research (Pacific Grove, Cal.), who served as a vital communications link in debugging problems in CP/M, MP/M, and CBASIC.
- Anjali Chhabra, one of my former students, who did considerable data entry, most of the text editing of the manuscript, and many of the production chores associated with the preparation of this volume.

Trademarks

The following registered trademarks have been used in this book:

TRADE MARK	COMPANY
Alertmate	Sutton Designs, Inc.
ASCOM	Dynamic Microprocessor Associates
BADLIM	Blat Research & Development Corporation
BASIC-80	Microsoft Corporation
CBASIC	Digital Research
CBASIC COMPILER	Digital Research
CB-80	Digital Research
CB-86	Digital Research
COMPRESS	Starside Engineering
CP/M	Digital Research
CP/M-86	Digital Research
Cybersoft DSS-1	CyberSoft Incorporated
DEDICATE/32	Public Key Systems Corporation
Diagnostics II	Supersoft, Inc.
Disk Doctor	Supersoft, Inc.
Encode/Decode	Supersoft, Inc.
Execuport	Computer Transceiver Systems, Inc.
FILEFIX	Digital Marketing Corporation
Formula I	Dynamic Microprocessor Associates
Hermes-4	Merritt Software, Inc.
Magnetic Media Preserver	Perfection Mica Company
MicroLIB	Advanced Micro Techniques
Microline	Okidata: Oki Electric Industry Company Ltd.

Microsoft Basic Interpreter	Microsoft Corporation
Microsoft Basic Compiler	Microsoft Corporation
MP/M	Digital Research
MP/M-86	Digital Research
MS/DOS	Microsoft Corporation
Multi-Personal Computer	Columbia Data Products, Inc.
Oasis	Phase One Systems, Inc.
PC	International Business Machines
PC LOCK II	MPPi, Ltd.
PCMODEM PLUS	Ven-Tel, Inc.
PeachText	Peachtree Software, Inc.
Powerlock	Sutton Designs, Inc.
Protector	Standard Software Corporation of America
SensAlert	Sutton Designs, Inc.
SooperSpooler	Consolink Corporation
TransZorb	General Semiconductor Industries, Inc.
TUCK-IT	INFODevices
TurboDOS	Software 2000 Inc.
UCSD p-System	SofTech Microsystems, Inc.

A Final Note

The manuscript for this book was written using the *PeachText* text editor, and the programs were written and tested using *CBASIC*, *CB-80* and *CB-86*. All the computing was performed using a Columbia Data Products microcomputer, the *MPC 1600*, which permitted the use of both 8-bit and 16-bit software on a single machine. The manuscript data files and the programs were stored on *Maxell* floppy disks and printed using a C. Itoh *Starwriter F-10* printer.

Directory of Programs in This Book

The following programs, written in CBASIC, are included with sufficient documentation to permit the reader to use them directly or to easily rewrite them into another dialect of BASIC.

NOTE: The following table is an aid to readers interested in testing any of the programs. Time needed for program entry and space required to store any program may be reduced by eliminating REM lines. Note that the programs have been copyrighted. They are for personal use and *not* for resale by themselves or as part of any program.

PROGRAM	NUMBER OF LINES	BYTES REQUIRED
DISKFILE	254	9088
PSWDPGM	152	5504
SNOOPCK	60	1920
FILEPRO	63	2048
H007	142	4736
E007	86	2944
KEYPASS	121	3840
CLOBBER	109	3840

Index of Special Features

CHECKLISTS

EQUIPMENT PROBLEMS AND BUYING GUIDES

BASIC TERMINOLOGY

SECURITY AND PROGRAMMING AIDS

List of Figures

CHAPTER 1

An Overview of Computer Security

You are now, or will soon be, the owner of one or more microcomputers. The promise of this new equipment—increased efficiency, reports and summaries that were never available before, speed of operation, and other benefits—has been well advertised and will be yours if the system is properly run. Less well advertised, however, is the problem of computer security, which comes with the new equipment.

Computer security has a narrow definition to many. It is taken to mean primarily the protection of the equipment from natural hazards, like fire, and unauthorized use of the computer system. In this book we have used a much broader concept: *computer security is the protection of a company's assets by ensuring the safe, uninterrupted operation of the microcomputer system and the safeguarding of its computer, its computer programs, and its data files.*

Failure to recognize the risks involved can be costly. Not long ago, in a suburb of the nation's capitol, an employer, who had recently installed a microcomputer system, notified one of his three office employees on a Tuesday that her employment would be ended at the close of the week. She was permitted to continue her work in the office and collected her check on Friday. When the owner and his staff arrived the next Monday morning and went to use the microcomputer, they found that every floppy disk had been neatly cut in half with the paper cutter. Backup copies of disks with the previous week's work were normally made on Monday. All the work of the last week had to be redone, as well as the new week's work, and by a reduced staff. The owner did not know one of the basic security rules that is followed in a major computer center: "Any employee who is notified about the termination of employment should immediately be denied access to the computer and any of the related files."

The owner of a fuel oil firm who had purchased a microcomputer system for his office set up the system in the corner of the office with large glass block walls, where one wall faced the street and the other the driveway. After several months of use, one of the truck drivers parked his truck with the motor running just outside the office wall while he went to pick up some forms. Because it was still early he took some coffee and doughnuts, which were available to employees. After 10 minutes of chatting and drinking his coffee, he left. Later it was discovered that the information stored on the disks that had been placed next to the computer for use that morning had been destroyed. The company was not aware of emissions caused by "noisy" electrical systems of trucks and cars.

A doctor who had purchased a microcomputer for his office was told by his dealer that all he had to do was plug the machine into any outlet. He set up the equipment, and his office assistant entered a complete patient file to maintain medical records and a record of accounts receivable. Normally, the assistant did the computer work when the doctor was not in the office because she was needed for other tasks when he was in. One day, while she was updating her records and making a backup copy, the doctor returned with an emergency patient. When he used the x-ray machine, the microcomputer was "zapped" and both disks in the machine were rendered useless. Six months of patient records were wiped out in 2 seconds. The doctor had never been told about the dangers of using the x-ray equipment concurrently with the microcomputer, *and* he had never been told that only one backup copy was insufficient.

BASIC DATA SECURITY MEASURES

Large or small, any business that relies on a computer information system needs *data security*. The lack of such security can cause irreparable damage or long-lasting adverse effects to the business. No single data security technique can guarantee total security at all times. Therefore, any program for data security must be an ongoing, evolutionary process that requires periodic reappraisal.

Data security is primarily the protection of information, the data files, and the computer programs from accidental or intentional illegal disclosure, modification, and/or destruction. To be effective, data security should provide the necessary protection with minimum interference to normal, everyday operations and with minimum inconvenience to the user.

There are four broad attributes of effective data security. They are

1. *Secrecy*, which implies no unauthorized release of company information (data files) or computer programs;

2. *Integrity*, which involves no unauthorized modification of data or programs;
3. *Availability*, which includes the ability to react and recover from the effects of a failure in computer security when it happens; and
4. *Auditability*, which is the capability of a company to monitor and discriminate between normal and abnormal computer system operation and thereby detect a breach in computer security.

The computer security specialists recognize four layers of security that protect the software (data files and programs) and hardware (the equipment) of a computing system (see Figure 1). The first layer, *legal and societal*, consists of the protection provided by national and local laws and the accepted mode of behavior within society. The second layer, *company policy*, is the protection provided by the company through its policies, its methods and procedures involving microcomputer system use, and its personnel structure and policies. The third layer, *physical*, refers to the use of such means as theft- and fire-protection techniques, protection of floppy disks, and special methods used to limit physical access to the microcomputer system. The fourth layer, *electronic and programming*, refers to the protection provided by both the hardware devices and the software techniques within the operating system, data files, and applications programs.

Absolute data security is impossible to attain even with large mainframe computer systems. It is even less attainable with microcomputer systems. Therefore, in planning and implementing a computer security system, it is necessary to (1) minimize the probability of the occurrence of a loss or security breach and (2) minimize the damage that could result if it happens.

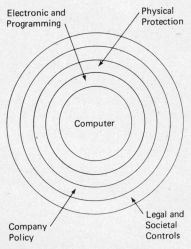

FIGURE 1

Four layers of computer protection.

WHAT THREATS DO YOU FACE?

Just as an illustration, try putting a price tag on

- the loss of a list of active customers, including names, addresses, and the record of purchases over the past 5 years;
- the destruction of an accounts-receivable file that has been kept on the computer for the past year;
- the disclosure of a patient's or employee's medical history and record to an unauthorized source, such as an insurance company;
- the distribution in the office of all payroll information listing salaries and other benefits paid to each employee;
- an entry clerk's modification of an order, so that the customer receives the number of units ordered but is billed for only half the amount;
- destruction of the microcomputer's power supply system by an electrical power surge, which will take at least a week to replace;
- an employee playing a computer game periodically during the day on a system that is being used near its capacity level.

WHAT THIS BOOK OFFERS

This book is an introduction to the problems of computer security and contains information for the protection of both hardware and software. It has been written for the *nontechnical reader*. The security procedures, which are explained in step-by-step detail, can be followed by anyone who has learned how to start the microcomputer and run a prepared program.

Many of the recommendations for protecting software and the microcomputer system *will not cost you anything* to implement. A few, which add to the security of your microcomputer system, are inexpensive compared to the security they offer. The cost in actual expenditures and/or the time needed to implement the many techniques may be viewed as a form of insurance. The cost to protect the company's data files and programs is trivial compared with the loss that may result from files that have been illegally exposed, modified, or accidentally or intentionally destroyed. To achieve high security with a microcomputer system, it is essential to build *layers of protection*, combining individual software security techniques into an effective barrier to disaster.

The security measures are designed to assist you in

- taking measures to minimize interruptions to data processing operations caused by electrical power irregularities and interruptions,
- protecting your hardware from theft,
- reducing the risks of fire, smoke, and water damage,
- providing a safe operating environment that avoids accidental destruction of your data files and reduces employee error,

- safeguarding the stored programs and data files on floppy disks,
- preventing unauthorized personnel from using the microcomputer system,
- preventing persons authorized to access the system from obtaining copies of information, modifying data already stored in the system, or making illegal entries into data files,
- establishing and maintaining an acceptable level of security in a micro-computer network,
- ensuring that vital information is not accidentially or intentionally removed from floppy disks,
- developing increasing levels of security through software techniques to protect the information you have stored in your microcomputer system, and
- planning to meet your computing needs if your computer system fails and cannot be repaired within a reasonable time.

COMPUTER-RELATED CRIME

Many security experts agree that small businesses are particularly vulner-able to computer-related crime because the elaborate security systems employed in large installations are either impossible for them to use or too costly. It is also true that many small-business owners and professionals

---

PLAYING COMPUTER GAMES

Any study of the home computer market reveals the strong fascination for computer games; they are big business. But what about playing games on a business computer system?

Recently, when meeting with several of the nation's top computer security specialists, we discussed computer game playing by em-ployees on business microcomputer systems. It was generally agreed that it would be almost impossible and too expensive to attempt to prevent employees from using the system to play these games. Many users add the games to their own user areas, where their computer programs and data files are stored. The only way to police this activity is to search each individual's programs to see if any games are hidden there, and this is time-consuming and therefore costly.

The final conclusion at that informal meeting was to put all com-puter games in the public area of the microcomputer system, since it would save storage space. It's better to have only one copy of "Adven-ture" or other computer games in storage than to have ten or more. All that can be done is to *discourage* too much play.

install computers with little knowledge of how they work and with the unfounded belief that everything that appears in a computer printout is correct and to be relied upon. The computer, it is true, does not lie, but the computer is subject to manipulation.

That does not mean that you should expect or accept the possibility of computer-related crime in your office or factory. Your best protection, perhaps, is just being aware that you can be ripped off. In the words of Fred Carlson (that's an alias for a computer thief who embezzled $1 million before being caught): "The question you have to keep asking yourself is, How vulnerable are we?"

Because almost all users of microcomputer systems are new to the computer field and have never been involved in the management of a computer center, they are unaware of the problems of computer security. Furthermore, at this stage of their development, microcomputers do not have many of the built-in security features that the large mainframe systems have. The first step in the area of computer security is to recognize that the problem exists and after some analysis determine what action you feel is necessary and cost effective.

Computer-related crime is only a small part of the subject of computer security. Because it is sensational, we have included it in our overview of security. Most businesses using microcomputers are not in the same class as banks from which individuals have stolen millions of dollars by using the computer system fraudulently. Stealing $2 million from a bank by fraudulent computer action will make headlines, but stealing $1000 from a small business in the same way will undoubtedly be ignored by the newspapers. Yet, that $2 million in a bank with a volume of $5 billion is 0.04%; the $1000 from a company with a $2.5 million volume is also 0.04% and is just as important to that company.

Computers are engendering a new type of crime. New occupations have extended the traditional categories of criminals to include computer programmers, computer operators, and tape librarians. The methods of committing the crimes are also new, and a jargon has developed to identify automated criminal methods. The names given to these criminal methods tend to make them sound adventurous and romantic, like Trojan horse, rather than criminal. Adding to the problem is that many of these criminals

---

FOUR CATEGORIES OF COMPUTER-RELATED CRIME

1. Introduction of fraudulent records or data into a computer system
2. Unauthorized use of computer facilities
3. Alteration or destruction of information or files
4. Stealing, by electronic means, money, property, financial instruments, services, or valuable data

A MATTER OF DEFINITION

The U.S. Department of Justice provides the following definitions in the area of computer crime.

Computer abuse: Any incident associated with computer technology in which a victim suffered or could have suffered loss and a perpetrator by intention made or could have made gain.

Computer-related crime: Any illegal act for which knowledge of computer technology is essential for successful prosecution.

Data leakage: Unauthorized, covert removal or obtaining copies of data from a computer system. This is a deliberate act, whereas in **data seepage** the removal of data is accidental.

see themselves as *only* defrauding an impersonal organization rather than individuals. In one case, the criminal stated that he never took more than $20,000 from a single bank account because he knew that the accounts were insured up to that amount and "no one" would suffer. This attitude has even been given a name—"the Robin Hood syndrome."

Computer-related crime has been portrayed fictionally in several novels, motion pictures, television dramas, and comic strips. Unfortunately, the public interest and sensationalism associated with it have made folk heroes of the criminals and caused significant embarrassment to the victims.

The targets of computer-related crime are also sometimes new. Electronic money, as well as paper money and plastic money (credit cards), now represents assets subject to theft. Money in the form of electronic signals

ANALYSIS OF COMPUTER ABUSE CASES

Only a small portion of computer-related crimes and cases of computer abuse are actually reported. The U.S. Department of Justice in its latest study reports the following:

TYPE OF COMPUTER ABUSE	PERCENTAGE OF TOTAL	AVERAGE DOLLAR LOSS
Physical destruction	14	$ 836,000
Intellectual property (data and programs) stolen	28	$3,322,000
Financial manipulation	43	$1,462,000
Unauthorized use of computer services	15	$ 32,000

and magnetic patterns is stored in and processed by computers; money is debited and credited to accounts inside computers. In fact, the computer is rapidly becoming the vault for the business community. Many other physical assets, including inventories of products in warehouses and materials leaving or entering factories, are represented by documents of records inside computer systems.

The timing of crimes may also be different. Traditionally, the time of criminal acts is measured in minutes, hours, days, weeks, months, and years. Today some crimes are committed in less than 0.003 seconds (3 milliseconds). Nor do geographic constraints inhibit these new criminals, due to the prevalence of networking and advanced communications.

Computer-related crime and computer abuse methods have been defined and given names in many of the studies and articles intended for the professional reader. We describe them briefly here, although not all are applicable to microcomputers or micronetworks in a small business. They will, however, serve to familiarize you with terms commonly used and to indicate the extent and variety of possibilities that must be considered in making a system secure.

Data Diddling: This is the simplest, safest, and most common method used in computer-related crime. Any size of business with any computer system is vulnerable to it. It involves changing data before or during input to computers. The changing can be done by anyone associated with, or having access to, the processes of creating, recording, transporting, encoding, examining, checking, converting, and transforming data that ultimately enter a computer. Examples are forging or counterfeiting documents, exchanging valid computer tapes or disks with prepared replacements; source entry violations, and neutralizing or eliminating manual controls.

A typical example is the case of a timekeeping clerk who filled out data forms of hours worked by 300 employees. He noticed that all data forms were entered into the computer with the employee's name and number but that the computer actually used only the number. He also noticed that manual controls outside the computer used only the employee's name, since no one thought of the people as numbers. He therefore entered overtime hours for employees who frequently worked overtime but used his own number for the computer. He thus increased his annual earnings by several thousand dollars, until an auditor noticed the unusually high earnings for a clerk.

Trojan Horse: This method is the covert placement of computer instructions in a program so that the computer will perform an unauthorized function but will usually still allow the program to perform its intended purpose. This is the most common method in computer program-based frauds and sabotage but requires more technical knowledge than data diddling. A programmer could, for example, instruct the computer to place the names of all new customers in a special, unauthorized file whenever it lists the name in the legitimate file. The programmer would thus acquire a potentially valuable list of names without anyone knowing.

Salami Techniques: An automated form of crime involving the theft of small amounts of assets from a large number of sources is identified by this picturesque name, which indicates taking small slices without noticeably reducing the whole. Not applicable to small businesses that do not have a sufficient number of accounts to make it profitable, it could be illustrated by a banking system in which a program could be changed (using a Trojan horse method) to randomly reduce a few hundred accounts by 10 or 15 cents and to transfer the money to an account from which it could be withdrawn by normal methods.

Superzapping: Superzapping got its name from Superzap, a macrocomputer utility program used in most IBM computer centers. Computers sometimes stop, malfunction, or for other reasons need attention that normal access methods do not allow. In such cases, a universal access program is needed, making the system vulnerable to tampering. It is the master key to the system and a powerful and potentially dangerous tool if kept in a program library instead of secure from unauthorized use.

A classic example of superzapping resulted in a $128,000 loss at a New Jersey bank. The manager of computer operations was using a superzap program when he discovered how easy it was to make changes without the usual controls or journal records. He made changes, transferring money to three friend's accounts, and continued long enough for a customer to find a shortage.

Trapdoors: Trapdoors are usually intentional points of entry into a large application or operating system program intended to allow access to the program during debugging, modification, or restart procedures. However, trapdoors may also be introduced inadvertently through a weakness in

---

MICROCOMPUTER COMPUTER-RELATED CRIMES

Although microcomputers have been with us for only a few years and their use in business is only in its initial stages, several types of microcomputer-related crime have already surfaced. Those that appear to be most common are

- unauthorized use of computer time by authorized personnel,
- manipulation of computer input,
- theft of data files,
- copying (stealing) of computer programs, and
- unauthorized modification of computer programs.

design logic or in the electronic circuitry of the computer. When included intentionally for debugging, trapdoors are normally eliminated in the final editing, but they are sometimes overlooked. During the use and maintenance of computer programs and circuitry, ingenious programmers invariably discover some of these weaknesses and take advantage of them for either legal or illegal purposes.

In one computer-related crime, several automotive engineers in Detroit discovered a trapdoor in a commercial time-sharing service in Florida that allowed them to search uninhibitedly for privileged passwords. They discovered the password of the president of the time-sharing company and were able to obtain copies of trade-secret computer programs that they then used free of charge.

Logic Bombs: This method has also been called a time bomb; the phrase logic bomb could apply because it is code inserted into a program (a Trojan horse), and it could be called a time bomb because the code is only executed at a specific time or under specific conditions. In one case, a payroll system programmer put a logic bomb in the personnel file so that if his name was ever removed from the personnel file, indicating termination of employment, the secret code would have caused the entire personnel file to be erased.

Scavenging: This is a method of obtaining information that may be left in or around a computer system after the job is finished. Simple physical scavenging could be the searching of trash barrels for copies of discarded computer listings or carbon copies—even the carbon paper from multiple-part forms. More technical methods may involve searching for residual data left in a computer after job execution.

For example, a computer operating system may not erase buffer storage areas used for the temporary storage of input or output data. Some do not erase magnetic disk or magnetic tape storage media because it requires too much computer time. New data are simply written over old data. It may be possible, therefore, to read the old data before they are replaced by new data.

One case of industrial espionage was detected by an alert computer operator in a time-sharing service that had a number of oil companies as customers. He noticed that a particular customer always "read" from a temporary storage tape before "writing" on it, and he reported the fact to management. The customer was obtaining seismic data stored by various oil companies on the temporary tapes and selling these highly proprietary, valuable data to other oil companies.

Browsing: Similar to scavenging, this hunt for information is a search through storage for something that may be interesting or potentially valuable. The browser does not necessarily know that anything of value is there or in what form it is stored. Legitimate access to part of the system is used to access unauthorized files.

Data Leakage: A wide range of computer-related crime involves the removal of data or copies of data from a computer system or facility. There is considerable danger to the criminal because, although the technical act may be well hidden in the computer, the data must be obtained from the system in order to convert it to economic gain.

Several techniques have been used to leak data from a computer system. The sensitive data may be hidden in otherwise innocuous-looking reports. Many of the other methods of leaking data are rather exotic and might be used only in high-security, high-risk environments. It has been reported that hidden in the central processors of many computers used in the Vietnam War were miniature radio transmitters capable of broadcasting the contents of the computers to a remote receiver. They were discovered when the computers were returned to the United States.

Piggybacking: Piggybacking can be done physically or electronically. Physical piggybacking could be illustrated by an individual with his hands full of computer-related objects, such as tape reels, who stands by a locked door until someone authorized to enter comes along. The individual, although unauthorized to enter the area, goes in with the authorized person.

Electronic piggybacking can take place in an on-line system where individuals are using terminals and identification of the terminal is verified automatically by the computer system. Compromise of the verification system can occur if an unauthorized terminal is connected to the same line as a legitimate terminal through the telephone switching equipment and used when the legitimate user is not using his terminal. The computer will not differentiate between the two terminals.

Impersonation: In this process, also called masquerading, one person assumes the identity of another. An example of a clever impersonation occurred when a young man posed as a magazine writer and called upon a telephone company, indicating that he was writing an article on their computer system. He was invited in and given a detailed briefing, with the result that he was able to steal over $1 million worth of equipment from the company.

An electronic impersonation involves claiming the identity of an authorized user after obtaining passwords or other authorization items through wiretapping or other means.

Several other criminal methods have been described and named, but these require considerably more technological sophistication and equipment and as yet may not impact microcomputers.

WHO ARE THE CRIMINALS?

It has been often stated that most computer-related crime goes undetected or unreported, but from a small group of criminals caught and tried a set of characteristics has been identified. These are, of course, not conclusive or complete because of the small number of people included, but they are supported by the fact that there appears to be little difference between modern, amateur, white-collar criminals who do not use computers and those who do.

- They tend to be young; the median age was 25 years and the range was 18 to 46 in the group surveyed. Younger people in data processing occupations have often received their education in colleges and universities where manipulating campus computer systems is not only condoned but often encouraged as an educational activity.
- They are among the most skilled and knowledgeable technologists. One of the greatest risks comes from employees who are overqualified and easily bored with their routine work.
- They frequently hold positions of trust that give them easy access to the system while apparently doing their own work. Among the occupations in the group surveyed were an accountant, a systems programmer, a systems manager, a sales manager, and the president of a firm.
- Collusion is more frequent in computer-related crimes than in other types of white collar crimes. Collusion usually involves a computer specialist who can perform the technical part of the act and another individual at the periphery or outside the organization who can convert the technical act to profit.
- The *differential association syndrome* refers to the criminal's use of small deviations from the accepted practices of his associates. Groups of people working together may engage in unauthorized acts that escalate to serious crimes. The competitive nature of computer specialists and their often elitist attitudes can result in a one-upmanship in performing pranks. In one case it was found to be common practice for the programmers of two competing service bureaus to access each other's systems for the purpose of playing games or obtaining customer names and the type of work they were doing.
- The Robin Hood syndrome was exhibited by most of the criminals in the group interviewed. They differentiate strongly between harming people, which is highly immoral within their standards, and harming organizations. They would become quite disturbed if the interviewer implied they were crooks in the sense of causing individual people to suffer loss.
- Some computer specialists believe that using an idle computer does no harm and that they have a right to use it for challenging intellectual exercise. All but one of the criminals interviewed indicated that think-

ing of their computer-related crimes as games played a significant part in motivating them to continue their fraudulent activities.

The summary profile of the potential criminal, based on those who have been caught, is young and intelligent, with varying degrees of computer expertise. But there are always exceptions. One computer operater had access to a repeat button on the printer that was meant to allow for repeat printing if a payroll check was unusable. When his check came through he kept pressing the repeat button, thus printing multiple checks for himself. He then took the batch of checks with identical information on them— name, number, date, amount, and so on—at the same time to one bank teller, who understandably became suspicious. The technology involved was pushing a button.

CHAPTER 2

Electrical Power Protection

Your microcomputer is very sensitive to the quality and the continuity of the electrical power it receives. We think of the electrical power supply as we do of the water supply. Turn on the faucet, and the water flows; press the light switch, and the electrical current flows. But sometimes there are particles of dirt in the water, or a heavy chemical smell, or the water flow is reduced to a trickle or doesn't flow at all.

We encounter similar problems in the electrical power supply, and these can have disastrous effects on computer hardware and the data being processed. On the average, some four to five times each day, the electrical power supply is dangerous to the "health" of your computer system. This danger can take the form of

- erasing an information file,
- logic errors in the operation of a program,
- destruction of an operating program,
- erroneous data transfer between the central processing unit (CPU) and the peripherals,
- misreading input data,
- time spent in needless debugging of a program,
- wiping out a program or data that are being entered,
- faulty data transfers between one disk and another, and
- physical damage to the CPU itself, the disk drives, or other parts of the system.

Protection is available in many forms and at a cost of as little as $10 to $2000 or more. To determine which devices are needed to protect *your*

HOW SECURE IS YOUR MICROCOMPUTER'S ELECTRICAL SYSTEM?

	Yes	No	N/A
1. Do you have spare fuses for your CPU and other computer components?	___	___	___
2. Is the amperage on the electrical line sufficient for your existing system and possible expansion?	___	___	___
3. Have you installed emergency power cutoff switches at all exits in the room in which your microcomputer is housed, as well as at the computer itself? Are the switches protected from accidental activation?	___	___	___
4. Do you have an uninterrupted power supply for your microcomputer, or are the time and cost of data reentry unimportant to you?	___	___	___
5. Have you a separate, or "clean," power line for your microcomputer?	___	___	___
6. Are all components of your system connected to the same power line?	___	___	___
7. Have you checked on the reliability of the electrical power supply from your company to determine the equipment you need?	___	___	___
8. Does your microcomputer have a separate ground?	___	___	___
9. Are the computer, components, and wiring shielded from interference by electromagnetic and radio frequency waves?	___	___	___
10. Is there a separate on-off switch for each of your microsystem components?	___	___	___

Score Analysis

- 10 "Yes" answers: Great! You have a safe electrical system for your microcomputer setup.

- 8 or 9 "Yes" answers: Good! You have some protection, but there is need for improvement.

- 6 or 7 "Yes" answers: You are probably asking for trouble, depending on the efficiency and reliability of your system's power supply, the response time of protective devices in your CPU, and the quality of the local power utility.

- Less than 6 "Yes" answers: You need help unless you enjoy living dangerously!

GLOSSARY OF ELECTRICAL TERMS

Blackout	Total loss of commercial electrical power.
Brownout	Below-normal voltage over a prolonged period. The nominal reductions are usually 3, 5, or 8%. This voltage reduction is instituted intentionally by the power utility to meet a high demand for power, such as exists on very hot days or with a sudden rainstorm during the day.
Clean power	Electrical power free of all noise and all voltage fluctuations.
Common-mode noise	Unwanted, high-frequency interference transmitted between the "hot," or energized, conductor and the ground line of an electrical circuit.
Fault	A momentary power outage.
Ground	A connection from a circuit or an object, such as a microcomputer CPU or printer, to the earth.
Inrush current	Initial current surge required before a load resistance or impedance adjusts to its normal operating value; the "extra" power required to start equipment, similar to that needed when starting an automobile.
Magnetic field	Pattern of magnetic lines surrounding a magnet or an energized conductor, circuit, or piece of electrical or electronic equipment.
Noise	Any unwanted random disturbance that tends to interfere with the normal operation of a device.

microcomputer system, we will examine individual power situations, indicate the scope of the problem, and then explore possible solutions.

How much you wish to spend for electrical protective equipment depends upon your assessment of the "cost of the damage." We all recognize that physical damage to the microcomputer system is costly. But what is the cost if your accounts-receivable records are destroyed by electrical interference? What is the cost of having a program wiped out?

MAJOR TYPES OF ELECTRICAL INTERFERENCE

Electrical power-related computer problems are now commonplace. According to studies made by the federal government, utility companies, and IBM, the average computer is subjected to 110 to 140 error-producing power disturbances each month. These can result in simple data processing

Orderly shutdown	The sequential shutting down of the units of a micro-computer system to prevent the garbling or loss of data, or damage to components within the system.
Power line monitor	A device that detects and indicates changes in power line frequency and voltage amplitude.
Regulator	A unit designed to condition a power line and keep the voltage level steady; may act as a noise filter.
Sag	Lower-than-normal voltage for a short time.
Sealed battery	A battery containing a gelled or liquid electrolyte, but having no access for water replenishment.
Shielded line	A line or circuit that is shielded from external electric or magnetic induction by a shield of magnetic or conductive material that encloses the transmitted energy.
Spike	Momentary, higher-than-normal voltage.
Surge	Higher-than-normal voltage for a moderate time.
Transient	Disturbance or noise along an electrical line; usually, a high-amplitude, short-duration pulse that is super-imposed on the normal voltage.
Transmission line	Conductors or wires used to carry electrical current from one location to another.
Traverse-mode noise	Unwanted, high-voltage, high-frequency interference created between the "hot," or energized, conductor and the neutral conductor of an electrical line.
UPS	Uninterruptible power supply to provide clean power even during a power outage; duration of this power depends upon size of the battery of the system.

errors, or be powerful enough to burn the CPU and possibly the peripherals of an unprotected computer.

Electrical problems and/or interference can be classified into three major categories:

1. power line and ambient noise,
2. voltage fluctuations, and
3. power outages

Power Line and Ambient Noise

Practically everyone has seen or heard electrical noise. It generally appears as snow on the TV screen or static on the radio. In technical terms, these disturbances are known as **transients**, and if they are especially strong, as

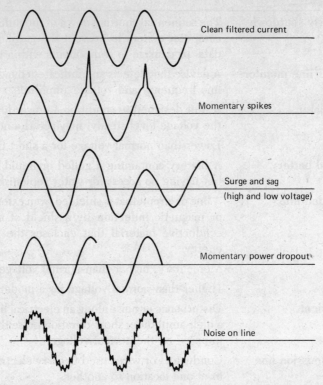

Clean filtered current

Momentary spikes

Surge and sag
(high and low voltage)

Momentary power dropout

Noise on line

FIGURE 2
Illustration of electrical power line disturbances.

spikes. In a typical community, they account for almost 90% of power line noise disturbances and are estimated to cause about 50% of computer errors. (All figures are national averages.)

Noise in an electrical system is created by random, unwanted disturbances that interfere with the normal operation of a device or system. It is the most disruptive power problem for microcomputer systems. It is generated by the electrical power lines themselves or by man-made electronic and electrical equipment, even by the electrical line transformers. There are two types of noise: (1) electromagnetic interference, **EMI**, generated within the electrical wires, and (2) radio frequency interference, **RFI**, created by the components of the electrical system.

In the common three-wire electrical supply system, one wire is the "hot," or energized, conductor, another is the "neutral" conductor, and the third wire is the "ground." Electromagnetic noise is created by the difference, or potential, between two of these three wires. The first type, *common-mode noise*, is created by the potential between the energized conductor and the ground. The other type of electromagnetic noise, *traverse-mode noise*, is generated between the energized conductor and the neutral conductor. Within the microcomputer system, the electronic components connected directly to the ground provide a path for noise to travel and are said to be sensitive to common-mode noise. Those components wired to the "hot," or energized, conductor and the neutral conductor are sensitive to traverse-mode noise.

Electromagnetic noise is often caused by the utility company during network or load-leveling operations. It may be caused in the office or home by the starting and stopping of the motors of air conditioners, photocopy equipment, and refrigerators, or by any electrical machinery used in an industrial plant or a medical or dental office. Electrical storms and lightning may cause line noise. Noise can even be caused by turning the printer on and off while the computer is running. Although power line noise is only annoying on TV or radio, it can cause data logic errors or the loss of data that have been entered, and may even damage components of the CPU and peripherals.

Lightning-caused transient voltages are induced on buried as well as exposed, long-run electrical power lines, and on the data lines that interconnect computer equipment, such as the line between the CPU and terminal. Both the electrical line to the computer and the communication line, if you use one, must be protected from lightning. In areas that experience lightning strikes, transient surges up to 20,000 volts are not unusual. Proper grounding of the microcomputer equipment and shielding and grounding of communication lines will help reduce and virtually eliminate any lightning-caused failures. With a multimicrocomputer system, where the CPU and terminal are separated by more than 30 feet, a protective device between these components is advisable. Such a device is also recommended if your microcomputer is, at times, interconnected with a major computer mainframe in a time-sharing network.

The extent of the danger of being struck by lightning depends on the part of the country in which the computer is located. Lightning, present in rainstorms, is also present at times in dust storms and snowstorms and can even come as a "bolt out of the blue." If you are located on the Gulf side of central Florida, for example, Tampa, you can expect thunderstorms and lightning during some 100 days of the year; the number drops to about 50 days per year in St. Louis, Missouri, and to less than 10 days a year in Honolulu, Hawaii.

Radio frequency interference creates magnetic waves similar to those used to transmit TV pictures and sound and can affect the operation of your computer. Even a truck warming up outside a wall where a computer is located can cause ambient noise, as can placing the microcomputer against a wall through which many electrical cables have been installed. The magnitude of such noise can be quite small, but when discharged near a microcomputer, it can create enough interference to cause a memory "crash," shutting down the computer. Ambient noise, such as that created by fluorescent lighting, may even damage EPROMs (Erasable Programmable

Read-Only Memory) in the computer, unless these chips are properly covered with protective shielding material.

When wires (both electrical cable, carrying 110 volts, and interconnecting cable between the CPU and peripherals) are used in a "noisy" environment or are run over long distances, it is essential that they be shielded with special materials. Various types of shielding materials are available. There is EMI-suppressant tubing, which can be used to cover existing cables. Also available are special shielding tapes and foil. These are generally available through distributors handling ham operator and other communications equipment.

You can protect your CPU from ambient EMI or RFI by placing sheets of aluminum on the walls or even using heavy aluminum foil. In extreme cases, you can put the CPU in an aluminum cage, which provides access and adequate ventilation.

Protecting storage media, such as floppy disks, is covered in a section in Chapter 7 on floppy disks and storage media.

Voltage Fluctuations

Voltage fluctuations are common phenomena that often make lights dim momentarily or even cause fuses to blow. They can be classified in two ways: (1) variations above and below normal voltage levels and (2) the time or duration of the upper or lower voltage level. Momentary disturbances of short duration usually last between 0.004 second up to a second. Longer disturbances can last for hours.

On the one hand, if the voltage is higher than normal for a long time, it is referred to as a **surge**. If it lasts for a short time and is of extremely higher-than-normal voltage, it is known as a **spike**. On the other hand, if the voltage is lower than normal for a long time, it is called a **brownout**, but if it is of short duration, we refer to it as a **sag**.

Fluctuations in voltage occur normally in the transmission line between the power utility and the building and even within the building itself. It is estimated that these sags and surges account for more than 25% of electrical power line disturbances, and are estimated to cause about 30% of computer errors.

The ANSI (American National Standards Institute) standards allow a normal line loss of about 8% between the utility power plant and your electric meter. Another drop of about 3.5% is permitted between the meter and your computer system. The permitted total loss of power between the utility's station and your computer can be as high as 11.7%, but most microcomputers are designed to operate within 10% of the normal power rating. In periods of high demand for power, utilities initiate **brownouts**, and in severe cases they may reduce the voltage by as much as 10% at the source.

The voltage required to run your microcomputer is normally 110 volts. If the voltage drops to 105 volts for 0.004 second or if the voltage rises to 125 volts for 0.016 second, there is excessive fluctuation in the computer's DC power supply. These power surges and sags may cause errors in data manipulation and transfer, and if prolonged, may result in physical damage to the microcomputer system itself.

Power Outages

When the voltage flow is interrupted, a power outage results. A momentary loss of power is known as a **fault** or **dropout**; a longer power outage is termed a **blackout**. In recent years we have encountered an increasing number of brownouts and some serious blackouts. Blackouts may be caused by the high demand for electrical power at certain times of the year, malfunction of the utility's generators or switching systems, or damage to equipment by lightning or accidents. Blackouts account for about 5% of the electrical difficulties faced by a microcomputer. Outages can last for as little as 2 seconds to as long as days, depending upon the cause. Many blackouts are corrected by the power utility company in less than 6 seconds, but are sufficient to cause microcomputer "damage." The average blackout, however, lasts about 5 to 10 minutes.

A blackout not only means you are inconvenienced by the lack of power to run the computer, resulting in downtime, but the sudden loss of power during computer operations may result in the loss of the files being processed, the loss of a program being entered, and even physical damage to the computer system itself.

POWER PROBLEMS AND THEIR SOLUTIONS

PROBLEM	FREQUENCY OF OCCURRENCE	SOLUTION
Electrical noise or transients	Continual throughout the day	Power line filter
Power surges or faults	Continual throughout the day	Spike suppressor
Brownouts	During peak operating hours: air conditioners on hot days, afternoon thunderstorms	Voltage regulator
Blackouts	On a national basis, about eight times a year, lasting about 5 to 10 minutes	Uninterruptible power supply

PROTECTIVE MEASURES TO REDUCE ELECTRICAL NOISE

There are several steps you can take to help reduce line and ambient noise, as well as possible physical damage to your microcomputer system. Power line noise is generated and transmitted along the electrical wires, whereas ambient noise is "found" within the air surrounding the microcomputer system.

1. Unless you use an uninterruptible power supply unit, use a *dedicated* electrical power line for the microcomputer system, that is, an electrical line not used by any other electrical equipment that can create noise, even an electric clock. A 15-ampere line with its own fuse or circuit breaker is a start. A dedicated line will *not* solve the problems, but it will help to reduce or isolate them. (See "Possible Dedicated Line Difficulties" later in this chapter.)

2. All units of the microcomputer system should be plugged into the same electrical line or power source. This will help reduce noise between the units caused by different-phase electrical cycles and will provide a common ground.

3. Do *not* switch all your equipment on simultaneously, even if you have a single on-off switch for the system. It is far safer to switch on each unit independently to avoid a power surge that might damage the delicate electronic circuits. There are multiple plug-in strips that have individual on-off switches for each of the outlets, in addition to the master on-off switch. Also, as a basic rule, do **not** turn on the power with a floppy disk already in the drive. Some manufacturers suggest you do so, but many professionals recommend against doing so.

4. If it is necessary to run long electrical cables from the outlet to the microcomputer, be sure to sure to use special shielded wiring, available from electrical distributors. Additional protection is provided by a totally shielded cable assembly in which the connector as well as the cable are shielded.

5. If your wall outlet is made for a two-prong plug, you may use an adaptor into which you can place the three-prong computer plug. However, many outlets designed for two-prong plugs are not grounded or not adequately grounded. Therefore, it is essential that the pigtail of the adaptor be well grounded to a water or heating pipe, using 16-gauge wire (at minimum) and a clamp. If there is any doubt, secure professional help.

6. Connect a 16-gauge wire to the ground of each component of the system. (If in doubt, have your dealer do this.) Join all the wires and connect them to at least a 16-gauge wire that is properly clamped to a ground (water or heating pipe) in the building.

7. Keep the telephone away from the CPU, disk drives, and terminal. There is an electromagnet in the phone, and ringing and dialing create electromagnetic noise. If you use an acoustic coupler, the telephone must be near the computer, but the risk is eliminated if you use a direct-connect modem.

8. Keep all magnets, no matter what their size, out of the computer area. Even a large magnetic bulletin board near the microcomputer or on the wall behind it may invite trouble. Remember that many of the new paperclip dispensers contain a magnet. Also, the paperclips from such dispensers retain some of the magnetism.

9. Avoid the use of fluorescent lights near the microcomputer since the ballasts used are "noisy." The lights are also harmful to EPROMs, which may be among the chips used in your computer. Constant exposure to room-level fluorescent lighting could erase a typical EPROM in approximately 3 years, but it would take about a week to cause erasure if the CPU is exposed to direct sunlight. This danger is reduced if opaque labels have been placed over the chip's window by the manufacturer or dealer.

10. Prohibit employees from using a portable radio or TV set near the computer. Even an office intercom may present a problem. If it must be nearby, consult with a communications specialist who can incorporate an EMI-RFI suppressor into the system.

11. Note if any electrical motor equipment is on the other side of the wall against which the microcomputer is placed, or if there is electrical equipment within 25 feet of the system. Sheets of thin aluminum on the walls adjacent to the computer will help reduce ambient noise, or an aluminum shield or cage might be needed around the equipment, especially the CPU, disk drives, and terminal.

12. If you have x-ray equipment or very high energy machinery on the premises, it is best to secure professional assistance in blocking this type of ambient noise.

13. If you are in a "sensitive data" business, avoid using microwave detectors to make a sweep for "bugs."

SPECIAL GROUNDING FOR THE MICROCOMPUTER SYSTEM

A microcomputer system, especially the CPU, should have a well-connected ground in addition to the normal electrical ground in the three-wire plug. A ground is needed to

- Reduce the level of "noise" caused by the electrical power supply and possibly by components of the computer itself.

- Provide a "fault-current path" in case of lightning or high-power surges. This will avoid fire hazards by eliminating all high-point impedance ground points within the equipment.
- Provide for employee safety by minimizing the chance of arcing and electrical shocks.

Run a heavy-gauge wire from the ground connection of the CPU, or the chassis if there is no external ground connector, to a professional grounding clamp (available at electrical supply stores) attached to a water or steam pipe. The other components of the microcomputer system should be similarly grounded to the ground wire from the CPU.

In addition to grounding the microcomputer itself, you should also protect your carrier or communication lines if there are any very long interconnecting cables between the components of your system, if your microcomputer is part of a network, or if you interface your microcomputer with a large mainframe time-sharing system. This is done by providing spike protection and grounding connections to your transmission lines.

Spike protection should be part of your telephone communication lines. If a special unit has not been installed by the local telephone company, it is best to have it installed by the telephone company, a licensed electrician, or a communications specialist. There are units to protect individual stations (phone interconnecting boxes) or the entire telephone system in a shop or office.

HOW TO DETERMINE THE "HEALTH" OF YOUR POWER LINE

It is unfortunate that we are unable to obtain precise information about the reliability of the electrical power supply coming into our office or shop directly from the local power utility. The utility has information for the lines in general but does not monitor each specific meter location. There are two ways in which you can determine the "health" of your power line. One is by using the services of a professional electrical or communications specialist who has the proper equipment for monitoring the power line. The second is to purchase a power line monitor, which can be used not only to test the electrical system but can also act as an alarm. A power line monitor identifies disruptive or dangerous line disturbances that can cause electronic equipment malfunctions. True, such an alarm would provide information "after the fact," but it would indicate the nature of the electrical disturbance.

Line monitors are simple units that plug into the electrical outlet. The simpler monitor has indicator lights and an audible alarm that is triggered by

Power failure, indicating a utility power failure, a power distribution failure, or a tripped circuit breaker or a blown fuse

Low line voltage, resulting from an overloaded power circuit, the starting of a heavily loaded motor, or an intentional brownout by the power utility for energy conservation

High line voltage, which would detect an error in power wiring, a power utility malfunction, or the internal power generation from heavy electrical equipment

Voltage spike, caused by lightning, a static discharge, or a switching malfunction by the electrical power utility

Voltage drop, which would result from an error by the power utility, starting an electric motor, or the addition of a heavy load to the power network (for example, the increase in electric use for lighting during a thunderstorm), or

High-frequency noise, indicating amateur or commercial broadcast interference, bad brushes in small electrical motors, or arcing in electrical switches

The more advanced models not only monitor these conditions but also monitor high and low line frequency and provide a printout of the time and nature of each occurrence on paper tape. With these models it is possible to deactivate the printer and/or the alarm.

POSSIBLE DEDICATED LINE DIFFICULTIES

Electrical power that appears to be adequate for other electrical equipment can be totally unacceptable to a microcomputer. To compensate for this "dirty power," using a separate electrical line for the microcomputer and its

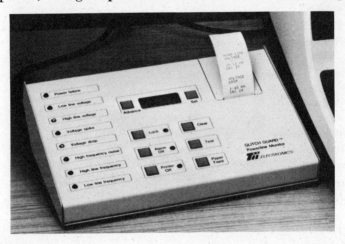

FIGURE 3

Power line monitor with printer (also available without printer) detects power failure, low and high line voltage, spikes, high-frequency noise and high and low line frequency variations. (Courtesy of TII Electronics, Inc.)

peripherals is often recommended. This practice has merit, but it does not always work.

The internally dedicated line to provide "clean power" to the microcomputer system may eliminate the noise caused by motors and other electrical items within the user's building if it is properly routed and shielded. But the inherent electrical difficulties that originate at the power utility source have not been eliminated. The "clean power" line, even properly shielded, cannot protect the user from brownouts, transients, spikes, and power outages; additional protective devices are needed. Some specialists note that the cost of establishing a dedicated line would be better spent if it were part of the price paid for an uninterruptible power supply, which can be installed anywhere in the normal power line. In this way, there would be "clean power" between the unit and the microcomputer and other components of the system.

ELECTRICAL POWER PROBLEM-SOLVING GUIDE

	TRANSIENT VOLTAGE SUPPRESSOR	AUTOMATIC VOLTAGE REGULATOR	TRANSIENT SUPPRESSOR/ VOLTAGE REGULATOR	UPS[1]
Power line noise				
Lightning strikes	*		*	*
Spikes caused by switching	*		*	*
Transients caused by motors	*		*	*
Voltage fluctuations				
Sudden over-voltage		*	*	*
Sudden under-voltage		*	*	*
Brownout		*	*	*
Chronic low voltage		*	*	*
Power outage				
Blackout				*
Momentary power loss				*

[1]Uninterruptible power supply; same characteristics apply to a standby power system.

ELECTRICAL POWER PROTECTIVE DEVICES

Various types and makes of electrical power protective devices are available to guard against the three threats: (1) power line noise, (2) voltage fluctuations, and (3) power outages. Four types of devices and their protective abilities are shown in the accompanying table.

The amount you wish to spend, the reliability of your local power utility, and the nature of your microcomputer operations will determine which protective devices to purchase. As a minimum, you should protect your investment with a quality transient voltage suppressor (spike suppressor). For moderate security, purchase a comprehensive voltage regulator. For maximum safety, an uninterruptible power supply is needed.

HOW TO BUY A SPIKE SUPPRESSOR

A spike suppressor between the power line outlet and the CPU provides the most elementary form of protection. These units are designed solely to suppress abnormally high voltages, or spikes, and are available in three forms.

1. *Absorption type:* This is a small circular or rectangular unit that is plugged into the same wall outlet as the microcomputer.
2. *Plug-in type:* This is similar to a three-way plug used in many homes to provide additional outlets from the wall outlet. It plugs directly into the wall receptacle, and the microcomputer is then plugged into this unit.
3. *Multiple plug-in strip:* This is similar to the three-way plug but provides for several electrical devices to be connected to it. This

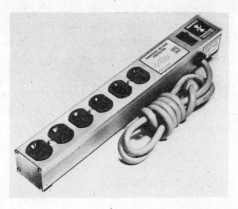

FIGURE 4

Transient or spike suppressors come in different forms. The Transient Voltage Protector shown here uses a *TransZorb* suppressor and filtering network to provide both transient protection and EMI/RFI suppression. (Courtesy of General Semiconductor Industries, Inc.)

unit generally contains an on-off switch for all the outlets. Only some of the multiple plug-in strips are made with noise or spike suppressors.

What to Look for When You Buy a Spike Suppressor

- When selecting a spike suppressor, look for one that has a high energy dissipation. A unit at the level of 50 to 100 joules, or over 500,000 watts for at least 100 microseconds, should be sufficient for most medium-size microcomputer systems.
- A pilot light should be part of the unit. However, the light should indicate that the protective circuit is working, *not* that the unit is connected to the current. If the pilot light on a good unit is not on, it will indicate that the internal circuit is not protecting your microcomputer.
- The use of a circuit breaker with a reset button on the suppressor is of secondary importance in a well-wired electrical system. A high current surge will trip the line's circuit breaker or fuse. A circuit breaker on the spike suppressor will act only as a backup later in the line, just as the fuse will in your microcomputer.

CLASSIFICATION OF LINE VOLTAGE REGULATORS

Automatic voltage regulators come in two forms.

1. *Terminal style:* These require installation by a licensed electrician since they are connected in line with the electrical power, connecting the unit's terminal block to the meter supply line. Some units have a receptacle outlet to accept the microcomputer's plug, but others do not and must be wired to the wall outlet into which the microcomputer can be plugged.
2. *Line cord or receptacle:* These units come with a wire and plug, which is connected into the wall outlet, and an outlet into which the microcomputer can be plugged.

How to Buy a Line Voltage Regulator

Line voltage regulators have different characteristics as well as different advantages and disadvantages. Some voltage regulators accept the input from a normal electrical power line and maintain the voltage output at a relatively constant level, regardless of variations in the input voltage. A better unit, often called a power, or line, conditioner, not only performs the

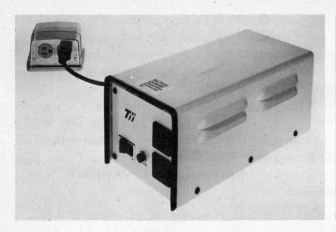

FIGURE 5

Line conditioners or isolation regulators filter noise, clip spikes and quickly and automatically regulate output voltage. (Left: courtesy of TII Electronics, Inc.; right: courtesy of Gould, Inc.)

function of a voltage regulator but also includes an isolation transformer to minimize common-mode noise. In selecting a unit, make certain that it can handle the load you require and is produced by a reputable manufacturer. The following list of "things to do and check" will help you and the dealer make the correct selection for your system.

1. Prepare a list of the power requirements of each of the units to be included in the circuit. Generally, this information is found on the nameplate with other information, or in the equipment manual. If in doubt, check with the dealer from whom you purchased the computer system.

2. Remember that the wattage figures are "static data" and do not take into account "inrush current," which provides what is called "dynamic loading data." That is, when you first turn on the CPU or any other device, such as a printer, there is a current surge. A microcomputer system with a total of 5-ampere static capacity may take over 6-ampere dynamic capacity for a fraction of a second.

3. All voltage regulators correct for low voltage by increasing the current drain. This means that the power line must be able to handle both the load and the regulator drain. A 15-ampere voltage regulator requires more than a 15-ampere power line.

4. Consider the ambient temperature in your computer facility. Higher ambient temperatures reduce the effectiveness and life of voltage-regulating equipment. Therefore, provide adequate ventilation for such equipment.

5. Make certain that the transformer of the unit is adequately shielded. In better units each coil of the transformer is enclosed in a wrapped foil box shield.

6. Whether you buy a single-phase or three-phase power line conditioner or regulator depends upon the current output (amperage) you require. High-output units are three-phased. In the case of most microcomputer systems, you can use a quality-made, single-phase unit without encountering any difficulty.
7. Be sure that the regulator is rated high enough not only to support your existing system but to allow for future expansion as well. With a normal electrical voltage of 110, you would need a unit with about 600 VA (volt-ampere) rating for a 5-ampere system. If you plan expansion of the system in the future, then a 1 kVA (1000 VA) rating would be advisable.

Most medium-sized microcomputer systems (a CPU, two disk drives, a monitor, and a printer) require about 5 amperes or 600 VA of "static power." Unless you purchase a quality unit, a 6-ampere unit should be used to absorb higher "dynamic power." If you purchase a UPS for only a single-user microcomputer and a monitor, with no disk drives or printer, a quality 200 VA unit should be sufficient.

HOW TO SELECT AN UNINTERRUPTIBLE POWER SUPPLY

The most sophisticated electrical power protection you can obtain is an uninterruptible power supply (**UPS**). Three factors must be considered in the selection of an uninterruptible power supply.

1. You have to determine the optimal battery time required for your system. This can range from as little as 2 to 5 minutes, enough time for an orderly shutdown of the system, up to several hours, if you wish to continue operating during the power outage.
2. You also have to decide the type of battery to be used in the UPS.
3. The final factor concerns the mode in which backup power is provided. Some UPSs are standby units that switch the batteries on when the electrical power fails. Others provide power directly from the batteries at all times; the microcomputer uses battery power continually, but the electrical line power is used only to charge the batteries.

Battery Backup Power

The batteries used in microcomputer UPS systems come in a variety of forms with different advantages and disadvantages. To be effective they must be rechargeable, whether they are dry, wet-cell, or sealed wet-cell (also called absorbed electrolyte). Dry batteries are not recommended because they are unable to sustain the electrical load required by a computer system during a blackout.

Sealed batteries offer many advantages for installations where there is no secure, thoroughly ventilated area in which to locate the battery bank, and to users who do not want to perform regular maintenance, as is required for wet-cell batteries. Although the sealed batteries have pressure-relief vents, they can be located in offices, stores, or small industrial plants with no worry about corrosion or gas.

The following descriptions explain the characteristics of several types of batteries available for use with UPS.

Lead-calcium: These batteries are generally not sealed but are available in sealed units. They have about a 30-year life expectancy and provide excellent discharge rates whether they are operating over 5 minutes or 24 hours. They are the most popular of the lead-acid batteries used in UPS backups. However, if not sealed they do generate hydrogen and oxygen, increasing the danger of fire and explosion, although at a much lower level than the lead-antimony cells. It is necessary to mount these batteries in a secure area in open-frame racks. The terminals must be cleaned, and specific gravity checked, and water must be added at regular intervals, generally every 6 months.

Lead-antimony: These batteries are the old standard. In terms of current availability and support times their performance is equal to that of lead-calcium variety but are not as frequently used in UPS. Their life expectancy is about one-half that of the lead-calcium batteries, maintenance is necessary at about 3-month intervals, and both oxygen and hydrogen gas are generated in the unsealed units.

Nickel-cadmium: The advantages of this type are its relatively small size and light weight for a given electrical capacity and its excellent low-temperature properties. They are expensive but generally cost-effective for short-time use, up to about 5 minutes. They have a long life and are designed for reliability with minimum maintenance under strenuous operating conditions. However, the sealed units are not considered industrial grade and are not preferred for computer backup systems.

If you select the unsealed wet-cell, it is necessary to provide regular maintenance. Furthermore, several safety precautions are needed.

- The walls and ceilings of the room in which these batteries are stored should be made of noncombustible material.
- There should be a portable carbon dioxide extinguisher located near the entrance of the room.
- Smoking should be prohibited in the area.

- It is advisable to have a fire alarm on the outside of the door to the room.
- The batteries should be located in a low-traffic area, preferably behind a locked door.
- Many power distribution systems operating at 600 volts or less are particularly susceptible to dangerous and destructive arcing faults. It is therefore imperative that proper grounding of the backup battery system be done professionally.

The true cost of a battery system must take into account the life expectancy, physical size, maintenance required, personnel safety, effect of temperature on performance, and power delivery, as well as the initial cost. The sealed wet-cell battery (whether lead-antimony or lead-calcium) is most cost-effective. Most of those currently used come in rectangular packages, but in the past year a newer cylindrical form has become available. It is reported to be far more efficient in power output and to require approximately 25% less storage area than the rectangular form. Although they are higher in price, it is possible to use a lower-amperage (power)

FIGURE 6

Uninterruptible power supply unit not only suppresses spikes and regulates power but also provides battery power backup when there is a power failure. (Courtesy of TII Electronics, Inc.)

cylinder to obtain the same effective output as a higher-rated rectangular, so that the costs would be approximately comparable.

NOTE: All UPS systems require adequate ventilation. The smaller units are convection cooled, whereas the larger ones are fan (incorporated within the unit) cooled. UPS systems should be placed in an air-flowing area, not in a cabinet or behind file cabinets.

What to Look for When Purchasing a UPS Unit

There are five important factors to consider when purchasing a UPS unit.

1. A unit that supplies battery power continually will provide greater protection than one that switches to battery power when the utility's power supply fails. The former units cost very much more. A microcomputer can tolerate a total loss of power for up to 15 milliseconds. Unless the switching type can react within this short time, it will not provide the safety you need. Better units of both types have a visible signal that indicates when the utility's power has failed and that the system is working on batteries.
2. Batteries are rated in ampere-hours. In a UPS backup the battery must be capable of providing repetitive discharges for short periods of time and a condition of standby readiness for many years. Ampere-hours should not be the prime consideration when purchasing a battery backup. Also consider such factors as load profile, voltage window, and operating temperature range. This technical information is available from the battery producer or from a reliable distributor or producer of UPS backups. Select a battery system that is maintenance-free and compact, one with sealed wet cells sufficient for the power needs of a microcomputer system.
3. Both the rectifier, which is used to charge the batteries, and the inverter, which is used to convert direct current from the batteries into alternating current for the microcomputer, are critical components. Some rectifiers continue to charge the batteries even when the voltage falls as low as 90 to 95 volts; others do not charge the batteries until the current returns to normal. The inverter must be capable of delivering automatically adjusted voltage to the microcomputer during the life of the batteries.
4. Because of the complexity of construction of UPS units, as well as their cost, it is advisable to obtain a unit made by an established, reliable producer and from a dealer who can assist you if anything needs adjustment.
5. Check how long the batteries will last at the required output level during a power interruption and how long it will take to recharge

them if they are completely run down. Both will affect the cost of the system. The longer the battery lasts, the higher the cost; the shorter the recharge time, the higher the price. The backup time supplied by these systems varies from about 5 to 90 minutes. Even the minimal time would be adequate to shut down the microcomputer system in an orderly way and prevent the loss or alteration of data.

CHAPTER 3

Protecting Equipment from Theft

Most businesses have some sort of burglar alarm system, but the addition of a microcomputer system and its ancillary components often represents a sizable investment to be specially protected. In major computer installations, a "fortress concept" has become standard; there is a perimeter, or outer shell, of protection and concentric inner shells surrounding the EDP assets. This concept has undergone some modification with the advent of terminals and the establishment of computer networks. With the growing popularity of the microcomputer system in businesses, we have returned to the early days in techniques of security for a computer. Whether you have a single microcomputer or a microcomputer network, the basic principles of equipment security are the same.

BASIC SECURITY EQUIPMENT

Most simple burglar alarm systems are designed to prevent intrusion through doors and windows. In more advanced systems, these are supported by other technological means of determining access to or occupancy of critical areas when those areas should be vacant. If you are now protecting only the doors and windows, you may wish to consider a support protection system. Because most support systems are sophisticated, it is advisable to obtain assistance from professional installers of burglar alarm systems.

There are different types of space-protection devices. They employ many diverse technologies, ranging from photoelectrics, through ultrasonics, to new concepts like passive infrared. Let us consider four basic types.

35

1. *Photoelectric:* In a photoelectric system, a transmitter generates an invisible beam of infrared energy, which is detected by a receiver. If that beam is interrupted (broken) by any moving object, the unit triggers an alarm. Units can be used with mirrors to "bend" the beams around a corner of a hall or even along exterior walls.
2. *Ultrasonics:* A transmitting transducer generates ultrasound energy, which is above the level of human hearing, and that sound bounces off the floor, walls, and objects in a room. The receiving transducer, which functions like a microphone, "listens" to the sound. If there is an intruder, there is a change in the bounced sound signal the receiver detects, and since the signal is different, it

HOW EASILY CAN YOUR MICROCOMPUTER BE STOLEN?

	Yes	No	N/A
1. Do you have a burglar alarm for your office or shop with all exterior doors and windows alarmed?	___	___	___
2. Are there special locks on the door(s) to the room in which the computer is kept? Do you keep track of who has keys? Do you make certain that employees who are no longer with the company return their keys?	___	___	___
3. If there are emergency exits, are they monitored with special devices to prevent unnoticed exits?	___	___	___
4. Does the microcomputer have a key-switch to prevent unauthorized users, including cleaning personnel, from turning the equipment on or off?	___	___	___
5. Is each component permanently "labeled?"	___	___	___
6. Is each component locked in place or connected to the burglar alarm system?	___	___	___
7. Are disks and documentation locked away at night?	___	___	___
8. Are the microcomputer and components unable to be seen through a window by a passerby?	___	___	___

Score Analysis:

• 8 "Yes" answers: Great! You are well protected.

• 6 or 7 "Yes" answers: Good—but why take even a small chance? It may not even cost more to reach a perfect score.

• Less than 6 "Yes" answers: Review and correct the situation. Your microcomputer system is a valuable asset.

sets off an alarm. Drafts and air turbulence can create false alarms with these units.

3. *Microwave:* The microwave generator, known as a Gunn diode, is placed inside an enclosure, the dimensions of which precisely determine the exact frequency of the microwave. Unlike the ultrasonic unit, the energy wave does not require air as a transmission medium and is unaffected by air turbulence and noise. The size and shape of the protected area is determined by the microwave antenna or horn and by energy waves bouncing off the walls, floors, and objects. The receiver diode picks up both the transmitted and bounced energy

FIGURE 7

Four passive security devices (clockwise from top left): infrared detector, photo-electric sensor disguised as electrical outlet, microwave detector, and ultrasonic unit. (Courtesy of ADEMCO.)

waves, and if these are different (caused by the presence of an intruder), it will activate an alarm.

4. *Passive Infrared (PIR):* Every object radiates infrared (IR) energy, also known as heat. The amount of energy radiated by any object depends upon its temperature, color, and surface texture. Because this IR energy is always present in an area, and because its level changes very slowly, any abrupt change means that an object (or person) has moved into or out of the area. The passive infrared detector "captures" and measures the IR in an area, and any drastic change in the IR level will result in an alarm alert.

For interior security monitoring, the passive infrared is one of the most effective and trouble-free types of equipment that can be used. In areas free of excessive air motion, the ultrasonic units provide large-area security cover. Photoelectric units are highly effective for "passage protection" because of the beam. Microwave protection units present more problems and should be installed only in those locations considered suitable by a professional installer. For example, since microwaves penetrate walls, passersby outside an exterior wall could trigger an alarm unless adequate shielding is provided.

TECHNIQUES FOR PREVENTING THEFT

Any firm that has experienced the loss of a calculator or a typewriter will easily recognize the need to secure the microcomputer system. There are two types of microcomputers. One is integrated with CRT, CPU, and disks in one physical housing. The other consists of individual components, generally a CRT and keyboard, joined to separate CPU and disk drives. In both types, a printer is joined to the CPU. Although an integrated microcomputer may appear to be too big and clumsy to remove from an office without detection, many such units have "walked away." Individual microcomputer components are much simpler to remove.

Here are several ways to secure your microcomputer from theft; some also help prevent unauthorized use during the work day. Additional procedures are discussed later under "User-Protect Control."

- Each component of your microcomputer system should be "labeled." Some companies use an identification label and number to keep an inventory of all items. These are metal and are adhered with a special cement or glue. In other cases, a decal is used. Both are really ineffective, since the cement can be dissolved with lacquer thinner and the decal removed with a special spray available in automobile supply stores. The most effective way to label is to use a *diamond-tipped pencil or engraver.*

This pencil costs about $2.50 and is used like an ordinary pencil; it cuts your name and address directly onto the surface of the equipment. In many communities, the local police department lends heavy-duty, electrical mechanical engravers to citizens as part of their property protection program.

- You can use an alarm alert to prevent anyone from disconnecting the electric plug and removing the computer. Several devices on the market connect to the power supply into which the computer is plugged. Removing the electric plug of the computer causes a buzzer to sound. This technique works well during the day, but after hours it is ineffective, since there is no one to hear the buzzer. (See Figure 8.)
- Emergency exit doors, used in the case of fire, should be wired into the burglar alarm system, if possible. Some units are combination burglar-fire systems on 24 hours a day. The better units have zone protection; that is, the alarm circuits are subdivided into segments. Although entrance door and window alarm devices may be deactivated during daytime hours, the remaining protective circuits can be used for the emergency exit doors and the "traps" noted in the next item.
- You can have total security if you interface the microcomputer with your burglar alarm system, and if it is active 24 hours a day, as the better units are. There are two ways in which this can be done.

   1. A wire cable can be attached to the equipment in the same way as an electrical power cable, and can be disguised as a communications link if desired. The accompanying diagram illus-

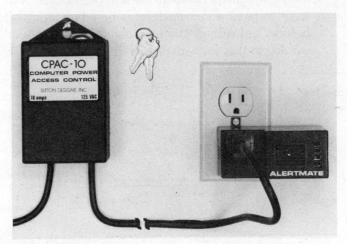

FIGURE 8

(Left) Computer Power Access Control is a key-operated switch that prevents anyone without the key from using the microcomputer. The Alertmate (right) sounds an alarm if anyone attempts to steal the computer by disconnecting the unit or the plug inserted into the unit. (Courtesy of Sutton Designs, Inc.)

trates how the cable connection is made. It does, however, require a hole in each component. If you cannot do this, your dealer can assist. Removing this cable plug from the outlet on the wall will trigger the burglar alarm system. (See Figure 9.)

2. If you do not wish to add more wires or make holes in the cabinets of the microcomputer and its components, you can use various tamper switches sold by burglar alarm companies. The switch is installed in the surface on which the unit being protected rests. The weight of the equipment is sufficient to depress the push-button switch and prevent the alarm from sounding. However, this system presents a problem, since an inadvertent shifting of any piece of equipment during the day will cause the alarm to sound. At night, you must be certain that each component is set carefully over its switch.

• Another method of securing the computer and its components is an anchor lock. To install the unit, it is necessary to remove the outside cover of each piece of equipment and then bolt the mechanism directly to the surface on which it rests. A key is necessary to remove the equipment from the secure pad. Such devices have been used for a long time with typewriters.

• You can reduce the potential for theft and protect the microcomputer from unauthorized use in two ways.

1. Some computers come or can be equipped with a key-lock switch to control power to the microcomputer. A burglar would have to have a key made or a new key-lock switch installed before "unloading" the merchandise; no reputable locksmith would do this for a person walking in off the street. An em-

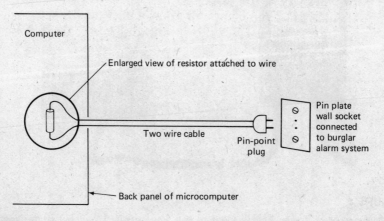

FIGURE 9

A simple two-wire cable with a 1K ohm, ¼ watt resistor in series can be used to protect the microcomputer from theft by interconnecting it with a quality burglar alarm system.

FIGURE 10

TUCK-IT, a space-saver unit, has a sliding drawer that can be locked. When the drawer is opened, the keyboard is available for use. Microcomputer sits on top of space-saver unit. (Courtesy of InfoDevices.)

ployee would be hesitant to take the microcomputer for his own use because he too would face the same problem. Keys should be provided to only a limited number of authorized individuals in the office.

2. If the microcomputer does not have a key-lock or you do not want to make a hole in the microcomputer's cabinet, there are two alternatives. First, a separate key-contolled power switch, which is mounted near the microcomputer, could be used. The switch's cord should be connected to the electrical power outlet and the microcomputer's power line connected to the switch. It would then be impossible to disconnect the microcomputer

FIGURE 11

SensAlert is a battery-powered portable intrusion alarm that can be used to protect confidential disks stored in a drawer or file from unauthorized use. Any movement or light level change will trigger a built-in 90-decibel alarm. (Courtesy of Sutton Designs, Inc.)

without removing the special plate on the locked power switch with a special tool (see Figure 8). The second alternative is to purchase a special sliding drawer unit to store the keyboard unit under the microcomputer or monitor. The drawer is pulled out to use the keyboard and may be cantilevered from the work surface; when the drawer is closed it can be locked, making the keyboard inaccessible (see Figure 10).

• Use a special door lock on the office in which the microcomputer is kept. It is also advisable to have the microcomputer key-lock switch replaced with a special unit as well. There are locks on the market available with keys that cannot be replicated except by an authorized locksmith. The lock manufacturers require that their special authorization code, which came with the lock, be provided at the same time as a duplicate key request is made. In some cases, only the manufacturer will issue a duplicate key upon receipt of an authorized signature.

• Keep a special list of individuals to whom door and/or computer keys have been issued. This list should be kept in a secure location. When any person to whom a key has been issued leaves the company, a checkout procedure should be followed so that no final paycheck is issued until all keys have been returned.

• It is possible to provide workday protection of the system by using closed-circuit TV. A camera can be mounted in the room with the microcomputer system, with monitors placed where constant supervision is possible. This technique not only offers protection against theft during the day but can also be used to protect against use by unauthorized company personnel.

JUST IN CASE . . .

If you are unfortunate enough to have equipment stolen, you will need a detailed description of each piece of equipment and its identification number from the manufacturer. Although such data may be retrievable from records, it is better to keep the data in a readily available emergency file. Also, keep the telephone number of the local police department with these data. Here is an example.

1. **CPU #1**
   Multi-Personal Computer by Columbia Data Products, Inc.
   Model 1600–1. Serial number 1683; Size 22 × 15 × 6;
   CRT controller (1604) S/N 1866,
   Z80 card (1603) S/N 142
2. **Keyboard**
   Columbia Data Products, Inc. (1616) Serial number 0773;
   18 × 8 × 2; white metal; keyboard + 10 function keys
   LED number and caps locks; FT02–51
3. **Monitor**
   AMDEK Video-300. Serial number 250031; 14 × 12 × 12 (1615)—12″ bw screen
4. **CPU #2**
   NOBUS-Z80 by EXO Electronics. Serial number 1268;
   7 × 17 × 18; white metal cabinet—vents in back;
   Shugart disk drives (A) K12910 (B) K12967;
   Power supply number 8389; Board number 484
5. **Terminal**
   MIME-2A by Micro-Term, Inc. Serial number M2A80371342;
   22.5 × 14.5 × 17; white plastic cabinet—12″ bw screen;
   Keyboard plus 14 keypad and 16 control keys
6. **Printer**
   C. ITOH FP-1500–25 Starwriter. Serial number 800723;
   24 × 14.75 × 11; light gray metal + plastic
7. **Spooler**
   SOOPERSPOOLER by Compulink Corporation. Model SS-1000;
   Serial number 0227032; 10 × 8.5 × 3; black top and sides,
   silver face with two-digit display screen.
8. **Two-Way Switch Box**
   A/B-C Centronics switch unit.
   Switch type TRW 77–40360; beige unit with gray face;
   HH:ID on bottom—(HJH13)
9. **Cables**
   Assorted cables to interface equipment:
   Shielded units with TRW 77s and 37-pins.

Fifth Precinct Police
825–5500

CHAPTER 4

Protection from Fire, Smoke, and Water

The danger from fire is probably no greater to your microcomputer than to your TV set at home, but when you compare the costs of the two and the need for a computer in your office, it is apparent that there should be special protection for your microcomputer investment. Basic housekeeping and common sense are normally sufficient to prevent many fires, but a definite program for fire safety should be a key part of your security program.

Experience has shown repeatedly that prompt detection is a major factor in limiting fire damage. Typically a fire goes through three stages.

1. Some event, such as a failure of electrical insulation, causes ignition. An electrical fire will often smolder for a long period of time.
2. When an open flame develops, the fire spreads through direct flame contact, progressing relatively slowly, with a rise in the temperature of the surrounding air. The duration of this second stage is dependent on the combustibility of the materials at and near the point of ignition.
3. Finally, the temperature reaches the point at which adjacent combustible materials give off inflammable gases. At this point the fire spreads rapidly, and ignition of nearby materials will result from heat radiation as well as direct flame contact. Because of the high temperatures and volumes of smoke and toxic gases associated with the third stage, fire fighting becomes increasingly difficult, and often people cannot remain at the fire site.

Given the objective to discover and deal with a fire before it reaches the third stage, one can readily see the need for detection devices and the need to train personnel in the proper way to combat possible fires.

FIRE DETECTION EQUIPMENT AND ALARMS

The better burglar alarm systems are adaptable to act concurrently as fire alarm systems. If your system is not suitable for expansion, then it would pay to have a combination burglar-fire alarm system installed professionally. A less expensive approach is to install self-contained smoke and combustion detectors, but these alarms are effective only when someone is in the building to hear them. For greater security, an alarm system that provides both an interior and exterior bell or siren should be installed.

A Four-Way Fire Alarm System

A good fire detection and alarm system should be capable of handling a four-way alarm system. This would include

1. a number of thermostats, which monitor the temperature in a given area,
2. photoelectric smoke detectors,
3. ionized-air combustion detectors, and
4. a manual pull station alarm.

The use of these four items is discussed below.

Selecting a Thermostat

There are two types of thermostats you can use in a fire detection system:

Fixed-temperature thermostats, generally about 2½ inches in diameter, are designed to be activated once the temperature exceeds either 135 or 190 degrees Fahrenheit. These units protect an area of about 20 by 20 feet, or some 400 square feet. The 135-degree units are used in the office; the 190-degree units are usually reserved for furnace or other high-heat areas.

A more sophisticated and expensive unit is a rate-of-rise, fixed-temperature sensing unit, which protects a 50- by 50-foot area. The element within the unit measures the rate of temperature increase, as well as the fixed-temperature setting, and responds accordingly.

Photoelectric Smoke Detectors

This type of unit provides excellent response to smoldering and flaming fires. When smoke enters the chamber in the unit, the light from a nearby LED (light-emitting diode) is reflected off the smoke into the "smoke

HOW SAFE IS YOUR MICROCOMPUTER FROM FIRE

Building and Area Design

	Yes	No	N/A

1. Is the building in which the computer is located constructed of modern, fire-resistant, and noncombustible material? ___ ___ ___

2. Are the furniture, fixtures, shades, and/or drapes made of noncombustible materials? ___ ___ ___

3. Are combustible materials (e.g., paper and other supplies, rags and cleaning materials, and photocopy and duplicator chemicals) stored well away from the computer and separated by a fire-rated wall? If the wall is of questionable quality, is a fire detector mounted on the wall? ___ ___ ___

4. If you have air conditioning and/or heating ducts, are there easily closed dampers to shut the ducts? ___ ___ ___

5. Are major disks not in use and documentation stored in a fireproof safe within the computer area? ___ ___ ___

6. Are backup disks and/or tapes made periodically during the day and stored in the safe or in a remote area? ___ ___ ___

7. Are emergency phone numbers (fire department, hospital, doctor, and others) posted in a visible location near the telephone? ___ ___ ___

Electrical

1. Has all electrical wiring been done by a licensed electrician? ___ ___ ___

2. Has the computer system been properly grounded? ___ ___ ___

3. Is the use of electrical extension cords or multiple-outlet plugs prohibited in the computer area? ___ ___ ___

4. Is there emergency battery backup lighting for the computer area? ___ ___ ___

5. Is there a main power switch near the door(s) to shut off the computer system, air conditioner, and other electrical items in the room? ___ ___ ___

Detectors and Equipment

1. Are there fire detectors and smoke detectors in the vicinity of the computer and the peripheral equip-

ment (e.g., printer), as well as in the air-conditioning and/or heating ducts leading into the room? ___ ___ ___

2. If there is any space below the floor (basement or another floor) and the floor is not fireproof, do you have a fire detection device on the floor? ___ ___ ___

3. Do you periodically test the fire and smoke detectors? ___ ___ ___

4. Are there fire extinguishers strategically located in the computer area and clearly marked? Do you have a Halon extinguisher to use on computer equipment? ___ ___ ___

5. Are the fire extinguishers recharged on a regular basis? ___ ___ ___

6. If there is a sprinkler system, is the cutoff value clearly marked, and do the employees know how to shut off the valve? ___ ___ ___

Personnel

1. Are employees prohibited from smoking within the computer area? ___ ___ ___

2. Have employees been trained in the use of fire-fighting equipment? Have they been assigned specific duties in case of a fire? ___ ___ ___

3. Are unannounced fire drills practiced periodically? ___ ___ ___

4. Has the area been designed to permit quick evacuation of personnel and ready access by fire-fighting personnel? Are exits and evacuation routes clearly marked? ___ ___ ___

Score Analysis

You can come close to a perfect score by using sensible procedures which cost little. *Minimum scores* should be

- 6 "Yes" answers for Building and Area Design
- 4 "Yes" answers for Electrical
- 5 "Yes" answers for Detectors and Equipment
- 4 "Yes" answers for Personnel

That would be 19 of 22, but all other safety measures should be implemented wherever possible.

chamber" in the unit. The "smoke cell" in the smoke chamber "sees" the light, changes its electrical resistance, and activates the alarm. Better units in an alarm system also include a 135-degree Fahrenheit heat detector to provide for double coverage.

Ionized-Air Combustion Detectors

Older units of this type were often unreliable in that they sent false alarms. The newer units are not as susceptible to humidity and atmospheric changes. The newer units have two chambers of ionized air; one is a "sensing chamber," exposed to the surrounding environment, and the other, a "reference chamber," which is sealed from the outside. The current output of both chambers is constantly analyzed and compared; if the outputs do not agree, the alarm system is activated. A good detector can monitor up to 900 square feet when placed on a smooth ceiling with a minimum amount of air movement. Where there is active air movement (for example, when air conditioning is in operation or sunlight through a window heats one part of the room) or uneven ceilings, the area monitored is reduced accordingly.

Manual Pull Station Alarm

In large offices or factories, pull station alarms should be placed in critical areas. Even in a smaller office, particularly where the fire alarm system is interfaced with an automatic telephone dialer to the fire department, it is advisable to install a manual pull station in the vicinity of the microcomputer system.

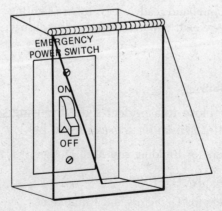

FIGURE 12

Master electric power switch to cut off power in case of emergency. This should be located in an easily accessible place, clearly marked but protected by a clear plastic shield from inadvertent misuse. Unit is hinged at top for quick access.

FIRE-FIGHTING EQUIPMENT

Most business firms have some type of fire-fighting equipment, but your microcomputer is best protected by a special extinguisher. The National Fire Protection Association (NFPA) has identified three classes of fires and has recommended the type of fire extinguisher to use with each. The three classes are

A. fires caused by paper, wood, fabrics, and other solids;
B. burning liquids (e.g., gasoline and oil); and
C. fires in energized electrical circuits.

Four types of fire-fighting extinguishers (water, CO_2, dry chemical, and Halon 1211) have been evaluated by the NFPA for use in combating the different classes of fire. The accompanying table contains a summary of the effectiveness and characteristics of these four.

	WATER	CO$_2$	DRY CHEMICAL	HALON 1211
Type of fire	A	BC	ABC	ABC
Chance of incorrect use	High	Moderate	None	None
Equipment (i.e., micro-computer) damage	Some	None	Considerable	None
Range	Good	Poor	Good	Good
Visibility	Good	Good	Poor	Good
Effectiveness on obstructed fire	Poor	Moderate	Poor	Good
Light-weight hardware	No	No	Yes	Yes
Required cleanup later	Some	None	Extensive	None

Halon 1211

Halon 1211 is the ideal agent for portable extinguishers to provide fast, clean, efficient fire-fighting capability, especially for electronic and other high-value equipment. It is recommended by the NFPA for electronic computer and data processing equipment.

Halon 1211 has the following advantages over water, CO_2, and dry chemicals.

- The long, concentrated throw of the liquefied Halon 1211 gas makes the extinguisher highly effective, even in the hands of an inexperienced fire fighter.
- It is fastest in smothering fires, particularly electrical ones, since it is five times heavier than air.
- It does not shock the sensitive electronic components with a cold discharge, as does CO_2, which is at −110 degrees Fahrenheit.

- The chance of a dangerous flashback is minimized with Halon 1211.
- It will not corrode metals, connectors, or wiring in the microcomputer, nor will it damage magnetic disks or tapes.
- As a liquefied gas, it flows around obstructions in fires that are hard to get at.
- There is no cleanup necessary after the fire is out because the gaseous agent has evaporated.

Halon 1211 comes in extinguishers of varying sizes depending upon the area you wish to protect. The units range from small, 2½-pound hand extinguishers to 14-pound units. Also available are ceiling-mounted automatic units, which operate when the temperature reaches 160 degrees Fahrenheit. The ceiling units come in various sizes, covering an area as little as 2½ square feet, to as much as 64 square feet.

FIGURE 13

Halon 1211 should be used to combat a microcomputer fire. The extinguishers come in varying sizes and are either hand-held or mounted on the ceiling. The area to be protected determines the size unit required. (Courtesy of Permall Fire Extinguishers Corp.)

THINGS TO DO

In addition to protecting your microcomputer system with an adequate fire alarm system and a Halon 1211 extinguisher, you can help reduce the danger of fire and reduce the damage if it occurs by following some common-sense steps.

1. Make certain that there is adequate ventilation for the micro-computer system. Do not place units flush against a wall.
2. Don't let lots of papers accumulate around the equipment or allow the paper to cover the ventilation grills of components.
3. Enforce a *No Smoking* rule in the computer operating area.
4. Keep cloths and rags away from the equipment.
5. Prohibit the use of extension cables or multiple electric outlets.
6. If the computer is near a window, keep the draperies away. If you use draperies, make certain that they are fire-resistant or fire-retardant.
7. Provide battery-powered backup lighting in the computer area. This is essential if the computer is located in a windowless room and will be helpful at night in any area, since it will provide lighting to combat the fire and/or leave the area safely.
8. Keep the phone number of the local fire department posted near the telephone.
9. Assign and train employees to act as fire fighters to combat small or smoldering fires. Run fire drills periodically.
10. Keep the office free from obstructions that may impede the ability to fight a fire or to leave quickly.
11. Test shutoff vents of the heating and air-conditioning system regularly to be sure they can be readily closed in case of a fire elsewhere in the building.
12. Test fire detection equipment and the fire extinguisher on a periodic basis, and keep a written report of such tests. Have the Halon 1211 extinguisher recharged as required.

PROTECTION FROM WATER AND SMOKE DAMAGE

Water and smoke are additional dangers from which microcomputer systems should be protected. A major company in New York City was recently struck by both within a period of 4 months. The computer was located in an office in a multistory building shared with other companies. The first incident was a fire in an office two floors above. A large amount of water used to combat the fire came through the ceiling, "raining on" the computer and flooding the floor. Four months later, smoke from a fire in the office below left a soot deposit, not only over the computer but also over the disks, making them unusable.

Proper planning in locating the microcomputer, as well as use of detection devices and planned procedures for office personnel, can greatly reduce the hazards from water and smoke.

Location Planning: Avoid placing the computer in a room that has water and/or steam pipes passing through the ceiling. Do not, if possible, place the computer in the basement or in a room that is below grade. If there is a water or cooling tower on the roof directly above the computer's location, it is essential to use water-sensing protective devices. If the roof is directly above the computer, make periodic checks of the roof for possible weak spots that might result in leaks.

Detection Devices: There are a number of water sensors on the market. These are generally small units that sound an alarm when they become wet. It is advisable to place one or more units below a raised floor, if you use one, or in an out-of-the-way spot in the office. If possible, you may wish to have such a unit interfaced with your burglar-fire alarm system.

Another protective device is a waterproof cover for each of the components of the microcomputer system. They are available in vinyl to fit most units. The better ones are made of waterproof nylon, which are extremely sturdy and can be made to order for any piece of equipment. These protective covers should be placed over each piece of equipment at the end of the working day, as well as during the day in case of emergency.

Personnel Procedures: At least one person in your office should be assigned the task of verifying that each piece of equipment is covered once the system is shut down at the end of the day. The cover of each unit should be stored during the day near that unit. In the case of a fire emergency, some individuals should be assigned the task of covering the units before leaving the premises if there is safely time to do so. If there is an automatic sprinkler system in your office or shop, make certain that each employee knows the location of the cutoff valve and can use it if required. Check periodically that the valve is easily available and not blocked by furniture or cartons, and that it is in working order.

Finally, as an added safety measure, if the room in which your microcomputer is located does not have a drain, purchase a sump pump or a special water pump to remove floor water quickly in the event of a flood. These units are readily available from a number of different outlets.

CHAPTER 5

Protecting the Environment and the Workplace

The environment in which the microcomputer system resides has a critical impact on the accuracy of its operation and its availability. The protective measures noted previously are completed during the installation phase, and most do not require continued attention on a regular basis. Other aspects of security, however, influence operation regularly and can seriously affect the continuous operation of your system.

The loss of microcomputer use during *downtime* (the cessation of all computer operations) can quickly result in the disruption of the orderly operation of your business and financial loss. Many of the recommendations discussed in this chapter are neither time-consuming nor costly, but will help prevent errors and downtime. They are essentially common-sense decisions and actions that are often overlooked by those unfamiliar with a computing environment.

ENVIRONMENTAL FACTORS

In general, the room in which your microcomputer system is located should

1. have adequate ventilation and air conditioning,
2. include protective devices against static electricity, and
3. be free of dirt and dust.

More specific factors concerning the environment are discussed in detail below.

Temperature Control

Because microcomputer systems are small compared with mainframe computers, it is often assumed that no added environmental protection is necessary. In fact, while I was recently browsing through a popular microcomputer magazine I found a short piece by one of the editors that indicated there was no need to consider air conditioning a safety factor. This may be true if you are using a small, personal home-type computer (a keyboard with a CPU chip enclosed) attached to the home TV set. It is even true for some terminals, if they are not in the same room as the microcomputer and disk drives. However, as a basic rule, always provide adequate ventilation for the dissipation of heat from any electrical equipment. In a microcomputer system it will reduce the danger of damaging the sensitive components and help prevent fire.

The microcomputer system I use in my office has the following characteristics:

EQUIPMENT	AMPERES	WATTAGE
CPU	0.85	100
Monitor	0.25	28
Spooler	0.20	25
Printer	1.5	180

This 333-watt system generates about 1200 BTU, and even with the most adequate normal ventilation, it generates enough heat to raise the temperature in that portion of the room in which it is located by about 1 degree Fahrenheit per hour.

Not only is it strongly recommended that there be sufficient air conditioning to afford a comfortable workplace for employees, but there must be added air conditioning to dissipate the heat generated by the microcomputer system. This is particularly true in warmer areas of the country, as well as on hot days in any part of the country.

Some manufacturers note in their technical literature that a small microcomputer can operate in temperatures ranging from 40 to 115 degrees Fahrenheit. However, heat is hazardous to the health of your microcomputer. The high temperatures can adversely affect the operation of many power supply systems and seriously damage the computer's memory and logic circuits. High temperatures cause the microcomputer's transistors and chips to overheat, and this in turn causes them to malfunction. This then makes them generate even more heat, causes even greater malfunctioning, and may eventually cause severe damage and a shutdown of the computer system. With many computer systems, temperatures above 80 to 85 degrees

IS YOUR MICROCOMPUTER SYSTEM IN A SAFE ENVIRONMENT?

	Yes	No	N/A
1. Are the temperature and the humidity of the room in which the microcomputer system is located monitored on a regular basis?	___	___	___
2. Is there adequate air conditioning in the room in which the computer system is located?	___	___	___
3. Are the air conditioner filters cleaned or changed regularly?	___	___	___
4. Are the terminals, CPU, and other equipment protected from damage by static electricity?	___	___	___
5. Is the room, particularly the area in which the microcomputer is located, kept free of dust and dirt?	___	___	___
6. Are all pieces of equipment covered with dust and waterproof covers at the end of the workday?	___	___	___
7. Are eating, drinking, and smoking prohibited in the computer area?	___	___	___

If you have answered "No" to *any* of these questions, you are inviting computer problems.

Fahrenheit increase the chances of data dropouts in memory, logic and calculating errors, and even the addition of extra bits in storing data on disks.

Humidity and Static Electricity

A static charge, accumulated on personnel, can play havoc with your computer. Indoor relative humidity is a significant factor in building up a static charge. During the winter, the heat in the office dries the air. In the summer, a similar dry air condition develops because the air conditioner dries the air as it cools it.

If the relative humidity in the room is too low, below 40%, the danger of static electricity is greatly increased. If the humidity is too high, above 60%, there is an increased danger of condensation resulting in poor electrical contacts and even corrosion. These in turn could lead to dangerous short circuits of the power system and the electronic components.

You can generate more than 12,000 volts of static charge by walking across a carpet. With very low humidity, a static electricity charge of 20,000 volts can occur with certain floor surfaces. Even within the normal range of humidity, a 4000-volt buildup is common when one walks across a vinyl floor. It has been reliably established that as little as 40 volts of static electricity can cause a microcomputer malfunction: memory loss or alteration (bit dropin or dropout), faulty data entry, video wipeout, disk errors, and program damage.

The accompanying table indicates the level of impact on a microcomputer by varying static charges.

CHARGE (VOLTS)	POSSIBLE REACTION
40	May damage logic circuits and sensitive transistors.
1000	If CRT is touched, may wipe off the screen and crash the buffer.
1500	If disk drives are touched, it will attract airborne contaminants to disk surface and may cause data loss and head crash.
2000	May shut down the microcomputer system.
4000	If printer is touched, it can cause a paper jam.
17,000	May shock entire system out of parity.

The most effective way to combat static electricity is to use antistatic carpeting or static-control floor mats. Some carpets, made by combining nylon with electroconductive carbon elements, do not have to be grounded if they are laid on a well-grounded floor. For smaller areas, static-control mats made of the same materials come with a grounding wire and should be connected to a water line or an established building ground.

Dust Control

Dust is an enemy of all your equipment—not only your floppy disks and disk heads. Many units have *dip switches* (exceedingly small switches) on their back plates to set various controls. Dust accumulating between the contacts will eventually affect the electrical signal. Recently, an associate of mine found that his CRT had developed a double cursor after the system had been used for about 30 minutes. Turning the CRT on and off did not solve the problem. A bench check made in the repair shop indicated that the switch contacts had been covered with dust. After the contacts were cleaned, the

FIGURE 14

Rigid static-control floor mats can be used at the CRT to prevent static electrical discharges. Soft mats with an antifatigue feature can be used where the operator would normally stand. Each mat comes with a 15-foot ground cord, as shown in upper right corner of mat. (Courtesy of 3M.)

CRT no longer malfunctioned. However, it did result in system downtime for the 4 hours needed to take the CRT to the repair shop.

Some microcomputers have filters built in to protect the floppy disk drives. If your unit contains filters (check your manual or with your dealer if you are not sure), make certain that these are replaced on a regular basis.

Another source of dust and dirt is the paper used in the printer. The cutouts of the holes used by the tractor feed are not always removed but at times find their way between the pages. These accumulate in the printer and can interfere with the operation of the machine. A portable, small vacuum cleaner can be used with a lint-free cloth to clean the inside of the printer on a regular basis. The frequency of cleaning needed depends on use. In some cases it may be advisable to clean the printer daily, but a minimum of once a week is recommended in the average business environment.

PROTECTING THE WORKPLACE

In addition to the control of temperature, static electricity, and dust, other actions should be taken to provide a suitable workplace in order to reduce input and operations errors. Adding a microcomputer system to the office is not the same as adding another typewriter or a bookkeeping machine. Whether you plan to introduce a single, multiuser microcomputer or a multitasking, multiuser system with several terminals, the work station should provide sufficient privacy to permit an employee to concentrate on

---

RECOMMENDATIONS TO PROTECT THE ENVIRONMENT

- Place a temperature and humidity indicator near the CPU so that it can be observed throughout the day. Take appropriate action—use an air conditioner and/or dehumidifier—when indicated.
- If the temperature near the CPU rises above 80 degrees Fahrenheit, use an air conditioner to maintain the room's temperature at an efficient operating level. Opening the windows will not only raise the noise level but will usually result in a greater flow of dust into the area.
- Use a dehumidifier when the humidity is above 60%. Although manufacturers note in their technical literature that equipment can be used in atmospheres from 20 to 80% humidity, you will find it more efficient and safer to maintain the humidity within the 50 to 60% range.
- If your microcomputer system is located in an office subject to the flow of dust from a shipping room or a plant, use an air purifier with a dust remover in the room.
- Use lint-free cloths when cleaning computer equipment, such as the CRT, printer, and the doors of the disk drives.
- Prohibit smoking, eating, and drinking in the computer area.
- Cover all components with dustproof and waterproof covers at the end of the workday.
- Make certain that papers and other materials do not cover the vents of units at any time.
- Clean or replace the filter in the air conditioner regularly.
- If there is a hot-air heating system, wipe the intake vent covers daily to prevent dust buildup. If possible, use a filter at the vent, and clean or replace it on a regular basis.

the work being done and at the same time maintain enough openness to allow supervision.

Human Factors and the Workplace

A few years ago, a United States government agency, the National Institute for Occupational Safety and Health (NIOSH), conducted a study of workers using CRTs because of the concern over the hazards of radiation emission by the CRTs. It was discovered that the real danger lay not in radiation but in simply adjusting to what is novel in a new work situation.

When CRT operators were matched with a control group of nonoperator office personnel, the NIOSH study found that "the CRT operators experienced a number of health complaints, particularly related to emotional, optical and gastrointestinal problems, more so than nonoperators." The study concluded that a greater level of emotional stress was being suffered by the operators, which could have potential long-term health consequences.

The NIOSH study stressed the importance of *ergonomic* solutions, that is, design arrangements adaptable to a variety of individual users. Although no fixed criteria to cover individual situations were set, it is nonetheless helpful to consider certain factors in attempting to reconcile the design requirements with the real health and emotional needs of the operators. These factors are

- the CRT and terminal hardware,
- optical considerations,
- legibility of the screen display,
- environmental lighting, and
- working positions required to operate the equipment.

The CRT and Keyboard Hardware

The input-display portion of the microcomputer system, the CRT and keyboard, can be divided into two types.

1. *CRT with integrated keyboard:* In some cases the CRT and keyboard form a single piece of equipment and cannot be independently positioned. This often makes it difficult to position the keyboard at a comfortable working level and have a proper, convenient viewing position of the TV screen.
2. *CRT with separate keyword:* In other cases, the CRT and keyboard are completely separate units joined by a flexible cable. This sytem is more adaptable to individual use.

Optical Considerations

The NIOSH study found that of the three problems most commonly reported by CRT users, two—eyestrain and burning eyes—were due to inappropriate working environments. Obviously, the quality of vision depends on the individual, but if the work station is properly designed it is possible to adjust for

- the distance between the eye and the CRT monitor,
- the distance between the eye and the work material, and
- the distance between the eye and the keyboard.

Legibility of Screen Display

Viewing a CRT in a microcomputer system is similar to, but not the same as, watching a program on a home TV set. The latter is a continuous story with changing scenes and sounds. While working at the CRT the operator is faced with a static screen of text composed of letters and numbers that are less than half the size used on a home TV set.

The contrast of the CRT, that is, the difference in brightness between the letters and numbers displayed and the background, is adjustable. The NIOSH study found that "excessive contrast within the operator's field of vision can lead to difficulty in reading the display and to visual fatigue due to the repeated need for light/dark adaptation." Employees should be encour-

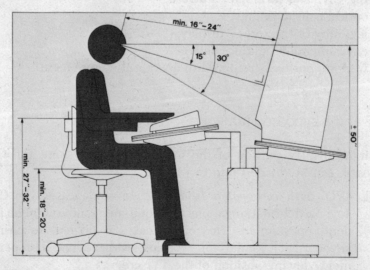

FIGURE 15

Engineering the workplace for user comfort increases worker productivity, reduces data entry errors, and improves employee morale. (Courtesy of Systems Furniture Company.)

aged to use the minimum contrast level to meet their needs and to avoid setting controls for maximum contrast.

With color monitors employees should be encouraged to test different color combinations of foreground and background colors to find the combination with which they are most comfortable. They should also test various color intensities because the level of "brightness" is a critical factor.

Ambient light falling on the screen can also lead to employee problems, causing faulty reading of information being recovered or incorrect verification of data being entered. Provisions must be taken to reduce screen glare. This can be done by proper location of the CRT and keyboard, changes in room lighting fixtures, or the use of special glare filters made of polarizing materials that fit over the screen.

Environmental Lighting

Lighting in most offices has been designed for overall office use and not for specific work stations. Hanging or ceiling-mounted lighting fixtures may provide overall office illumination but may also cause glare on the CRT screen. Recessed lights or dropped ceiling lights create less of a problem for users of microcomputers.

The NIOSH study makes six general recommendations regarding room lighting in and around the microcomputer work station.

1. Drapes, shades, and/or blinds over windows should be closed, especially when windows are exposed to direct sunlight. Remember that direct sunlight on your microcomputer may also be harmful to EPROMs.
2. Position the CRT terminal properly with respect to windows and overhead lighting so that glare sources are not directly in front of the operators or reflected on the CRT screen.
3. In some instances, hoods over the CRT top and along the sides may be desirable to shield the screen from reflections.
4. Antiglare filters may be installed on the CRT screen.
5. Direct-lighting fixtures should be recessed and baffles used to prevent the light from acting as a glare source. Generally, the lights should be directed downward within the room.
6. Where possible, use indirect lighting to illuminate the office and desk lamps, when necessary, to illuminate work areas within the office.

Work Positions for Equipment

Several human engineering factors influence the proper installation of the CRT and keyboard. These include

- height of the seat from the floor,
- position of the operator's arms when using the keyboard, and
- placement of the CRT screen in relation to the operator.

The height of an operator's chair should be set so that both feet can be placed flat on the floor. The operator's thighs should be supported by the seat but not obstructed by the front edge. Better office chairs can be adjusted so that the seat is 17 to 20 inches from the floor.

The position of the forearms when operating a keyboard should be horizontal, generally 27 to 33 inches from the floor. This angle and height lessen fatigue, which in turn reduces data-entry errors. Similarly, the CRT screen should be placed so that it is about 16 to 24 inches from the operator and tilted so that the operator looks directly at the screen. Some computer furniture is made so that both the height of the keyboard and the screen can be set independently and the angle of each is adjustable.

Protection of Cables

Because it is necessary to run cables between different components of a microcomputer system, steps must be taken to protect these cables, to

FIGURE 16

The split two-level desk, UFO 2000, adjusts to the operator's physical and psychological levels. Each section can be independently raised or lowered and may also be tilted. (Courtesy of Systems Furniture Company.)

prevent employee accidents. Cable bridges are easily installed along the floors when it is necessary to run cables from one part of the office to another. The cables are placed into a precut slit in the underside of the cable bridge, making it unnecessary to remove any of the connectors.

CHAPTER 6

Microcomputer Systems Terminology

For a better understanding of the different software security techniques that follow, it is necessary to explain some microcomputer systems terms. In addition, the detailed instructions on how to perform a few necessary operations will show you that the "black boxes" are not the mystery they may seem to be and you do not have to be an expert to handle them. If you are thoroughly familiar with microcomputer terminology, you can skip this section. However, if when reading about the security techniques you encounter an unfamiliar term, you can use this section as a reference.

THE MICROCOMPUTER SYSTEM

A microcomputer system consists of a collection of electronic devices, each of which performs one or more specialized functions. In its simplest form the system consists of

- an input device,
- a central processing unit, and
- an output device.

The input device may be a *terminal* that consists of a CRT (cathode ray tube or screen) with a keyboard or a *monitor* that is a special type of CRT and a separate keyboard. The *central processing unit* (CPU) contains at least one microprocessor chip and memory. In most computers the memory is "wiped out" when the electrical power is turned off, but special memory units are available and will retain all data even after the power is turned off. The

DO YOU SPEAK MICROCOMPUTERESE?

In this chapter we define a number of terms you will encounter in this book, but here are a few of the more elementary terms.

Binary digit (Bit)	An electronic signal represented by 0s and 1s used by the microcomputer to indicate the "on" and "off" states of hardware elements.
Byte	In most microcomputers it consists of 8 bits, the "space" needed to hold one character (a letter or a number) or a special symbol, such as a period.
Dumb terminal	A terminal that has no internal processing ability.
Field	A set of consecutive storage locations used to store a single item of data, such as a name, amount of a check, social security number, or date.
File	A collection of individual records that are treated by the computer as a single unit. Any program or data file consists of a set of records, and the term *file* used in this book refers to either.
Intelligent terminal	A terminal that has built-in processing hardware to perform logic functions, such as copy editing, prior to transmitting data to the CPU.
Microprocessor	An electronic chip that acts as the CPU's brain. It processes data but does not store it, which is the function of other chips called memory.
Program	A series of steps or instructions to be executed by a computer, enabling it to read, process, and store input data and display or print output data.
Record	A set of related fields treated as a single unit.
Word	Composed of 1 or more bytes; size is determined by design of the microprocessor within the microcomputer. Most microcomputers today utilize a design in which one word equals 1 byte.

output device may be the terminal's CRT or the monitor's screen, which displays data for you to read but which cannot be filed away, or a *printer* and/or *plotter*, which will produce *hard copy*.

In addition to the CPU's memory, most business computer systems also contain *mass*, or *secondary*, *storage* used to store data for a longer period; the data do not disappear when the power is turned off. *Hard disks*, *floppy disks*, and *magnetic tape* are all forms of secondary storage.

Several other electronic devices are sometimes used in a business microcomputer system. These include

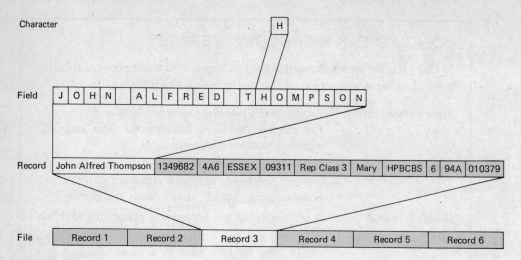

FIGURE 17

Structure of a file.

- *Spooler:* This device is interfaced (connected between) the CPU and the printer. It is a stand-alone unit with its own power supply, cabinet, and internal hardware, which includes a microprocessor. Its purpose is to free the CPU for use during lengthy printing.

For example, using my own system with some 2500 words (14,380 characters) of text for this book prepared under PeachText, it took 9 minutes and 35 seconds to print 266 lines of copy (about 6½ pages of 40 lines) using a 25-characters-per-second bidirectional daisy wheel printer. Using a spooler it took about 22 seconds to transmit copy from the CPU to the spooler, and the CPU was then available for my use while the spooler controlled the printer output.

- *Modem:* If your computer is to "speak with" another computer over the telephone line, you must use a modem. There are two basic types. The acoustic coupler is lower in price and requires that you place the telephone mouthpiece and earphone into specially designed sealing cups. The direct-connect modem directly connects the microcomputer to the telephone line and can be used in noisier environments. (See Chapter 15 for more information about data communications devices.)
- *Multiport switch:* These "black boxes" eliminate redundant hardware by permitting multiple microcomputers to use one printer, one computer to use multiple printers, or switch input/output (I/O) communications among different components. They are made in different styles, depending on their use. Some connect one piece of equipment to either of two others; others permit the connecting of up to five components, such as terminals, to a single modem.

FIGURE 18

Typical business microcomputer system. Multi-Personal Computer 1600-1 is interfaced with the switch box and spooler, which is connected to the Microline 93
matrix dot printer, which can be used at 160 cps in data processing mode and 40 cps
in correspondence quality mode. The switch box is used to connect the microcomputer to the modem for transmission or to the printer. (Computer courtesy of
Columbia Data Products, Inc. Modem courtesy of Ven-Tel. Spooler courtesy of
Consolink Corporation. Printer courtesy of Okidata.)

Business microcomputer systems can be classified by the number of users who can access the system.

- In the simplest form, we have a *single-user system,* in which each person has his or her own CPU and terminal and may also have a printer.
- Some of the single-user, stand-alone systems are, however, used by more than one person. These are classed as *multiuser, single-unit systems.*
- Within the past year, *multiuser, multitasking systems* have become more common in the business office. These are single-unit microcomputers capable of processing multiple jobs from one terminal simultaneously or permitting several users with individual terminals to use the microcomputer concurrently. *Multiprogramming* and *time-sharing* are other terms for multitasking.

Variations of this last classification are considered later under *microcomputer networks.* The multiuser, multitasking single unit is the simplest form of a network.

MAGNETIC STORAGE MEDIA

Programs and data files are stored on some form of magnetic media. Floppy disks are the primary software medium used in microsystems, and it is estimated that there are more than ten million in use today. Magnetic media in the form of magnetic tape date back to the early days of computing, the 1940s. The rigid magnetic disk for mainframe computers made its appearance in the commercial field almost 20 years ago. Since those early days, the cost of storing data on magnetic media has dropped sharply, from more than $50 to less than $1.50 per megabyte (one million bytes, or almost 750 pages of double-spaced, typewritten copy).

The Anatomy of a Floppy Disk

The floppy disk, so called because it is thin enough to bend or flop, was invented in 1972. The recording surface is made of a fine, computer-grade magnetic powder, which is formed into a "paste" and used to coat a thin mylar surface. This magnetic coating must be applied with the proper dispersion and density over the base material. The extraordinary precision needed in this process is evident when one realizes that the magnetic coating is about 2.5 micromillimeters thick (about one-millionth of an inch), with a tolerance of plus or minus 0.1 micromillimeter.

The coating process takes place in a "clean room," in which the air is filtered to remove dust, humidity, and other contaminants. During the

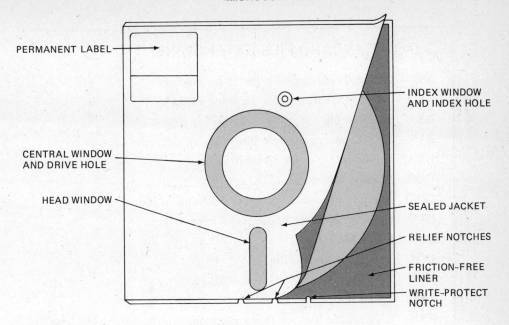

PERMANENT LABEL

INDEX WINDOW
AND INDEX HOLE

CENTRAL WINDOW
AND DRIVE HOLE

HEAD WINDOW

SEALED JACKET

RELIEF NOTCHES

FRICTION-FREE
LINER

WRITE-PROTECT
NOTCH

FIGURE 19

Anatomy of a floppy disk.

calendering process the coated mylar sheets are run through a "rolling-pin" machine under very high pressure to produce a surface that is smooth, ultraeven, uniform, and free of any oxide coating flakes. During this process a special lubricant is applied; this lubricant is designed to reduce wear of the reading/writing head of the disk drive when the disk is used.

The rolls of magnetic material are then cut and punched into precise size. A misalignment of even a fraction of a millimeter will result in a defective disk. The cut disk is placed inside a black polyvinyl chloride cover that has an interior nonwoven rayon fabric liner. Finally, this entire package receives an antistatic treatment before it is permanently sealed.

Types of Floppy Disks

A disk is like a phonograph record; it stores information. The record contains music or voice information, and the disk stores data. They are both round and have a hole in the center, but there the analogy stops. A record has grooves that are in the form of a spiral; the disk has a series of concentric circles. The record cannot be erased, whereas the disk can be. Information stored on a disk can be written over and effectively erased.

Data are recorded on the disk in concentric circles known as *tracks*, and each track is divided into a number of *sectors*. There are the same number of sectors on each track on a disk. Each track can contain thousands of characters of data. The mechanism used to read and write on a disk is known as a *disk drive*, which contains a *read/write head*. This head is positioned over

QUASI-STANDARD FILE EXTENSIONS

.A86   Assembly language file for 16-bit machine

.ASM   ASseMbly language file for 8-bit machine

.BAK   BAcKup file

.BAS   BASIC program source file

.CMD   CoMmanD files for 16-bit machines

.COB   COBOL source file

.COM   Directly executable program (COMmand file)

.CTX   Encoded file uses Public-Key Cryptosystem

.DAT   DATa file

.DOC   Text (DOCument) file

.EDX   Text file called by COM or EXE file

.ERL   Pascal relocatable file

.EXE   EXEcutable files for 16-bit machines

.FOR   FORTRAN source file

.GML   File called by COM or EXE file

.HEX   Intel HEX format object code file

.HLP   HELP file to be read by user on CRT

.INT   CBASIC INTermediate language file

.IRL   Indexed ReLocatable file

.KEY   Encryption KEY file: private or public

.KLP   Help file in OKARA

.LIB   Extension for LIBrary file

.MAC   MACro file (subroutine used in assembly language programs)

the disk by the disk drive, which determines how far out across the surface of the disk the head will go and which track or sector will be read or written over.

Floppy disks can be classified by four different methods: (1) sector control, (2) number of magnetic surfaces, (3) size or diameter of the disk, and (4) data storage density.

- *Sector control:* Using this classification system, there are two types of disks, *hard sectored* and *soft sectored*. To assist the read/write head of the disk drive to locate a particular sector on a track, the hard-sectored disks have a series of equally spaced holes along the outside perimeter, either 16 or 32. These holes mark the sectors of each track. Soft-sectored disks have only one hole. This hole and one selected hole on

.OBJ	OBJect code file in machine language
.OVL	PL/I Compiler OVerLay
.PAS	PAScal source file
.PC	Personal Computer file
.PGM	Sample or demonstration program
.PLI	PL/I-80 source program
.PRL	Page ReLocatable MP/M file
.PRN	Printable file displayable on the screen or printer
.PUB	PUBlic key file for communications
.REL	RELocatable object code program
.SL5	Forth or Stack Language 5 source program
.SPR	System page relocatable file
.SUB	Command file for a SUBmit run
.SYM	Symbol table file
.SYS	System file for CP/M 3 and PC-DOS
.TEX	Source file for TEX-80
.THE	THEsaurus file
.TQT	Compressed file, see note below
.TXT	TeXT file
.WPM	Word Processing Module
.XRF	Cross-reference file produced under XREF
.$$$	Temporary file or an improperly saved, unusable file

NOTE: Some file extensions may include the letter Q in the file extension, e.g., DQC or AQM. The Q is used to indicate that the file has been compressed or "squeezed" by a special program. A file of this type must be "unsqueezed" using a special program before it can be printed or executed.

the hard-sectored disks are timing holes used by the disk drive to determine the beginning of any track.

- *Number of magnetic surfaces:* Floppy disks are produced with either one side or both sides suitable for recording data. It is obvious that with two surfaces available we would be able to store more data on a single disk. Whether one uses one-sided or two-sided disks depends on the microcomputer's disk drive mechanism.
- *Size of disk:* Until 1982, floppy disks were available either in 5¼-inch or 8-inch sizes. Usually the 8-inch disk was called a floppy disk, and the 5¼-inch disk was often referred to as a diskette, or minifloppy. In 1982, several companies, using new improved technology, introduced a smaller disk, which is capable of storing more data than the 5¼-inch disk.

- *Data storage density:* The number of tracks placed on a disk determines its density. A *single-density* disk may have 25 to 40 tracks on its surface, whereas a *double-density* disk may have 70 or more tracks within the same space. The density of the disk determines how many characters can be stored. *Quad density* disks are two-sided, double-density disks.

PROGRAM IDENTIFICATION

When using CP/M or most other operating systems, there is provision for what is technically known as "file extension." This consists of the three characters that follow the period or decimal point after the filename. By using a common ID set, it is possible to immediately identify the type of file listed on the CRT when anyone requests a printing of the disk's directory.

Unfortunately, because microcomputers are a recent addition to the computer world and to some extent because of the diversity of applications, no official standards have been established. It should be noted that CP/M is the de facto (but not the only) operating system for 8-bit microcomputers; the list is shown on pages 70 and 71 based on CP/M, MS-DOS, PC-DOS, and others commonly used. Many packaged programs use these extensions, and it would be good operating practice to use them and make them commonly known to all personnel using your microcomputer system.

THE OPERATING SYSTEM

The electronic components of a system constitute *hardware*; the programs that operate the system or perform various business tasks are known as *software*. Software is divided into two types. First, there are programs that operate the microcomputer system and must be in the computer before any other program can be used. They are known as the *operating system*. Second, there are programs used to perform specific business tasks; these are known as *applications programs*.

The operating system is the means of communication between the user and the hardware components and applications programs. CP/M, developed in 1973, has become the quasi-standard operating system for 8-bit microcomputers. PC-DOS, MS-DOS, and CP/M-86 are among the more popular operating systems for 16-bit microcomputers. Other operating systems have been developed for multitasking, multiuser systems, such as MP/M. The manufacturers of microcomputers modify parts of the operating system to meet the specific requirements of their own equipment.

We will use CP/M to explain the structure and operation of an operating system for microcomputers. CP/M has three functional modules, as well as a series of utility programs; the latter is discussed later in this chapter under "CP/M Housekeeping Utility Programs."

The three functional modules of CP/M are as follows.

1. *Console command processor* (**CCP**): Enables the user at the keyboard to communicate with the computer and interacts with the other two modules. It is the "brains" of the operating system and is discussed more fully later in this chapter in "Elements of an Operating System."

2. *Basic input/output systems* (**BIOS**): Contains a series of utility routines to enable the CPU to communicate with the other devices, such as the CRT or printer, of the system.

3. *Basic disk operating system* (**BDOS**): Consists of utility routines to manage the disk files and perform various functions when the system's disks are used.

Loading the Operating System

After the power is turned on, it is necessary to "load" the operating system into the computer. Some systems have the *cold start loader* built into the hardware; others require either pressing a button or turning a switch. The cold start loader, if it has been placed on a disk, is then read into memory with the operating system. This process is sometimes called *IPL,* a term borrowed from large mainframe computers, standing for "initial program loading."

Once the system is IPLed using CP/M, the computer responds with a *prompt,* A>, and waits for you to type some command.

Formatting a Disk

Soft-sectored disks have to be *formatted,* unless this was done by the disk manufacturer. To format a disk, reply to the machine prompt, A>, by typing the word **FORMAT** if you use CP/M 2.2 or an earlier version, and pressing the return key. With CP/M 3, the **COPYSYS** command is used. The operating system asks a series of questions to which you type the responses and press the return key after each answer.

During the formatting, the operating system "marks" the sectors on each track and stops only if the system encounters a difficulty with a specific portion of the disk. With a quality disk and a read/write head that is aligned and in working order, there should be no difficulty. If problems do arise, try to format again once or twice. If there are still problems, see the section "Prior the Formatting a Disk" in Chapter 13 on page 191.

Elements of the Operating System

Some of the security procedures described in detail later require an understanding of the components or subprograms that form the operating system. Every disk used to IPL the system must contain the *SYSGEN* part of the CP/M or "boot portion" of the operating system.

In microcomputer terminology, a file refers to any program or any data file. Unless specifically referred to as a data file, the term *file* in this book includes programs and data files.

With an operating CP/M disk in drive A, insert a formatted disk in drive B and IPL the system. Type SYSGEN after the prompt, A>, and press the return key if you are using an early version of CP/M. With CP/M 3 it is necessary to enter CPM3.SYS after the disk has been formatted using COPYSYS. The computer will respond with a series of questions; after you answer each, remember to press the return key.

SYSGEN transfers seven subprograms of the operating system from the CP/M master disk to the new disk. These seven subprograms are explained below.

PROGRAM NAME	PURPOSE
DIR	Displays the *directory*, a list of filenames contained on the disk.
ERA	Erases a filename from the disk's directory and releases the storage space occupied by the file.
REN	Enables you to rename a file on the disk.
SAVE	Saves the contents of the computer memory on the disk.
TYPE	Displays the file named on the CRT.
USER	Followed by a number, changes the currently logged user number. USER 0 is common and is used when the disk is IPLed. It is possible to use any number from 0 through 15 as a user number.
[letter:]	A letter followed by a colon will change control to the disk drive identified by the letter.

Any time you transfer the operating system onto a disk, all these subprograms are automatically included. In Chapter 8, "How to Create a User-Protect Disk," we discuss how to remove some of these subprograms in an effort to promote greater security.

CP/M HOUSEKEEPING UTILITY PROGRAMS

CP/M also contains a series of utility programs that are helpful in writing and debugging programs, and in using the system in general. In many cases you will find the following four programs helpful. Each has to be copied from the original CP/M master disk to the disk you have just SYSGENed.

NOTE: In the following copy, as well as elsewhere in this book, the underlined characters are those that are typed by the operator at the keyboard and that will appear on the screen. The system prompts and any responses by the computer are not underlined. A "carriage return," a special key on the keyboard, is shown as <CR>.

PIP for Copying of Files

One utility on the CP/M master disk is PIP.COM, the peripheral interchange program, used to copy a program or data file from one disk to another. Its formal structure is

```
A> PIP B:=A:PIP.COM    <CR>
```

The entering of PIP causes the utility program to be loaded into the computer's memory. The B:=A: is the notation to take a program from disk A and move it to disk B. The name of the program or file, in this case PIP.COM, follows the second colon. It is good practice to place [V] after the name of the program; this causes the computer to verify the copy on disk B with the original copy on disk A. If an error in transmission has occurred during copying, the computer will let you know.

Entering the letter E within the brackets will echo (display on the CRT) the copy while it is being copied. Thus, if you wish to verify and see the copy on the screen, type:

```
A> PIP B:=A:PIP.COM[E V]    <CR>
```

If you wish to copy an entire disk, type:

```
A> PIP B:=A:*.* [V]    <CR>
```

STAT for the Display of Status Information

STAT.COM, short for statistics, is a housekeeping utility with several uses. First, it displays the amount of unused space in bytes that is still available on all disks in drives or a specific disk. Second, it can be used to obtain the number of *records* (a 128-byte unit as stored under CP/M) and the *file size* (length of the file or program in bytes or characters) taken by a group or a single file or program. Third, it can be used to prevent a user from writing over a specific file or program.

ED for Writing and Editing a File

ED.COM with a number of built-in commands enables one to write and/or edit a specific program or file that is stored on the disk. When called, it creates an edit buffer in the memory and allows the user to modify a file or program.

You can write the original copy of a program by using this utility, called a *Context Editor* by Digital Research. This editor is both character- and line-oriented (a line is any group of characters ending with a carriage return). Therefore, when using this utility you can enter or make changes by individual characters or entire lines.

DDT for Testing and Debugging Programs

DDT, Digital Research's Dynamic Debugging Tool, has a number of uses. Among these are

- PDUMP (displays or prints) part or all of memory,
- modifies the contents of the memory, and the internal registers of the CPU,
- makes corrections to or updates the software, and
- traces the execution of a program so that you can observe what is happening to memory and internal registers of the CPU.

It is invoked by typing DDT and the name of the program after the prompt, A>. With CP/M 3, DUMP is used instead of DDT to display the memory; to modify the memory as will be done later, the SID utility is used. The following is an illustration of using DDT with a program, CREATE.BAS.

```
A> DDT CREATE.BAS    <CR>
```

The computer responds with the following display on the CRT:

```
DDT   VERS   x.x
NEXT    PC
0300   0100

-
```

DDT prompts the user with the character "_" and waits for an input command. What has appeared on the CRT is the identification of DDT and the version of the program in use. The 0300 under NEXT is the address in hexadecimal value of the next free location that follows after the file or program, which has been loaded into the computer memory. The 0100 under PC is the hexadecimal location at the start of the program that has been loaded.

In this illustration, we enter D followed by a carriage return. The D command requests the computer to display memory by storage location in hexadecimal and ASCII code, which is shown in Figure 20.

To exit from DDT after a prompt, "_", is shown, enter G0, that is, the letter G followed by a zero, as shown.

    -G0   <CR>

The system will go back to command mode and display A>. Making changes in the program using DDT is explained in detail in Chapter 8, "How to Create a User-Protect Disk."

To save the program that has been modified under DDT, it will be necessary to convert the hexadecimal value under NEXT into a decimal value.

HOW TO CONVERT HEXADECIMAL TO DECIMAL VALUES

All number systems—decimal, binary, hexadecimal, and others—are related to each other by means of a set of symbols or characters that stand for

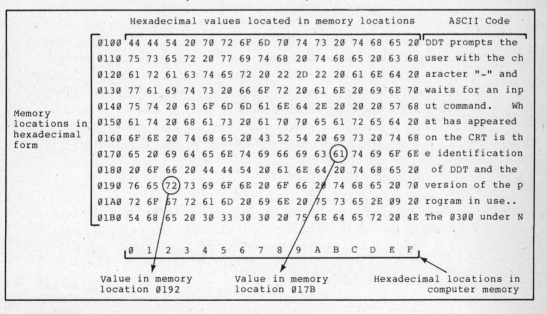

FIGURE 20

A computer dump showing hexadecimal values stored at specific addresses in the microcomputer and the corresponding ASCII values, which are human readable.

numbers. The place occupied by these symbols in a positional number system determines how large or how small the number is in value. Thus, the decimal values 692, 269, 926, and 629 all have different values but contain the same symbols or digits.

Number Systems

Systems of numbers are identified by their base, or *radix*. The base is a number indicating how many characters or symbols the system uses, including zero.

- In the decimal system we have 10 symbols or digits: 0 through 9.
- In the binary system, we have only two symbols or digits: 0 and 1.
- In the hexadecimal system, we have 16 symbols, which include the digits 0 through 9 and the letters A through F, where (in base 10 values):

$$A = 10 \quad B = 11 \quad C = 12 \quad D = 13 \quad E = 14 \quad F = 15$$

Positional Value and Counting

A car's mileage indicator, or odometer, will be used to illustrate some very basic rules common to all number systems. As your car moves along the highway, the odometer also moves, and each digit is advanced in a certain order. In the decimal system, for example, advancing the digit 0 means replacing it by the digit 1, advancing digit 1 means replacing it by digit 2, and so on, until the cyclic action begins to repeat itself. At this time the digit at its adjacent left place is advanced; advancing the digit 9 replaces it by 10.

The place value chart for the decimal system, or base 10, is formed by writing the base in columns and then assigning exponents to the base of each column in ascending order, from right to left starting with 0; that is,

$$\ldots \quad 10^3 \quad 10^2 \quad 10^1 \quad 10^0$$

The column with value 10^0 is the first column to the left of the decimal point, which we call the units column. (Any number to the zero power equals 1.) Thus, if we write 926 in decimal form, we have

$$9 \times 10^2 + 2 \times 10^1 + 6 \times 10^0$$

which is

$$900 \quad + \quad 20 \quad + \quad 6 \quad = \quad 926$$

The same is true of the hexadecimal system, where the positional values would appear as

$$... \quad 16^3 \quad 16^2 \quad 16^1 \quad 16^0$$

The hexadecimal number A6F would therefore be:

A   6   F

$$(10 \times 16^2) + (6 \times 16^1) + (15 \times 16^0)$$

which is

$$10 \times 256 + 6 \times 16 + 15 \times 1$$

or

$$2560 \quad + \quad 96 \quad + \quad 15 \quad = 2671$$

in the decimal system.

Conversion When Using the DDT Program

In some illustrations we have used the DDT program of the operating system in order to determine the size of the program or file we wish to transfer and save on another disk. On the CRT you would see, for example,

```
DDT VERS xx.xx
NEXT    PC
5A00    0100
```

The hexadecimal value printed under NEXT is 5A00. Although this is technically the next free memory location that follows the program that has been loaded into memory, we may use this as the size of the program. If the last two digits are 00 we may ignore them and use the 5A, which would be converted as:

5   A
$$5 \times 16^1 + 10 \times 16^0$$

which would be

$$5 \times 16 + 10 \times 1 \quad = 90$$

in decimal form.

If the last two digits are *not* **00**, increase the third value from the right by one. For example, if the hexadecimal value under **NEXT** was **5A40**, we would first increase the **A** by one to equal **B** and then follow the same procedure, now converting **5B00** and disregarding the two zeros.

$$5 \qquad\qquad B$$

$$5 \times 16^1 + 11 \times 16^0$$

which would be

$$5 \times 16 \;+\; 11 \times 1 \qquad = 91$$

in decimal form.

Powers of 16

To assist you in converting, we have noted some of the powers of 16:

$$16^0 = \qquad 1$$
$$16^1 = \qquad 16$$
$$16^2 = \qquad 256$$
$$16^3 = \quad 4096$$
$$16^4 = 65,536$$

CHAPTER 7

Basic Disk Security

Security as defined in this book is the protection of a company's assets. If you are a typical microcomputer user, you probably have, or will have, more money invested in software — programs and files — than in computer hardware. In this section we cover the physical protection of software media and the programs and files stored on them. In later chapters we discuss the software protection techniques to protect your programs and files from unauthorized access, wrongful or illegal modification of data, intentional destruction, and other related topics.

PROTECTING DISKS FROM DAMAGE IN THE DISK DRIVE

The floppy disk drive is probably the part of a microcomputer system most likely to fail or at least present the greatest difficulty to you in operation. Even if you use quality disks and handle them with care, there is no guarantee that you will not encounter difficulty. This is also true, but to a lesser extent, of the drives for other magnetic media.

The read/write head of the disk drive is the most sensitive element. In operation the disk travels at speeds between 60 and 140 miles per hour. The head in some microcomputers actually touches the disk at all times. In other microcomputers, the head will fly over the surface at about 20 to 100 thousandths of an inch and touch the disk only during the read or write cycles. A fingerprint smudge on the surface of the disk, a smoke particle, or a piece of dust will be sufficient to cause the head to crash, losing data and possibly the disk. Figure 21 illustrates the sensitivity of the disk head to

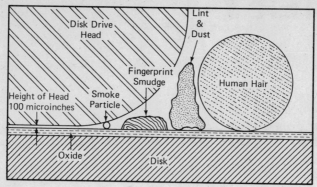

FIGURE 21

Magnified view of ceramic read/write head "floating" over the surface of a floppy disk.

foreign particles. Under extreme conditions, you may even lose the use of the drive because of a damaged head.

BACKUP COPIES OF DISKS

Most individuals just starting to use microcomputers think of backups only when they receive a message on the screen that a read or write error has been encountered on the disk. They may also remember a backup immediately after they have inadvertently erased a file or program. It may be possible to recover the erased information (see "How to Unerase Programs That Have Been Erased" in Chapter 13), but having backup copies of your disks will prevent wasted time and a rise in blood pressure.

The Need for Backup Copies

Prior to the advent of microcomputers, companies maintained their records in books that were stored safely away at the close of the business day. Valuable records were placed either in a safe or in a fireproof, locked cabinet. These records had to be protected only from fire or theft. This is not true of information stored on floppy disks. Electrical malfunctions of the system and even dust can damage disks. *Backup* copies are a necessary protection.

When you bought your microcomputer system, the dealer probably made a backup copy of the operating system, or urged you to do so as soon as the system was operating. When you purchase a packaged program, you find instructions to make a backup and *save the original*. Of course having a second copy is protection, but what procedure should you follow? How many copies should you make? Should you store all the originals together? What is a safe location for storing disks?

Save the Original?

When working with mainframe computers, it is axiomatic that no data stored on magnetic media should be held indefinitely or even for a "long" time. In some companies, backups are produced several times during a day; in others, backups are produced daily. In two computer centers of which I was director we did not keep any magnetic disk or magnetic tape for more than 6 months. If the stored data had not been rewritten onto another disk or tape within that period, we automatically made a copy and saved the new copy, reusing the tape or disk on which the original had been stored. One of the major computer network services follows a similar 6-month procedure.

There is a growing awareness in the microcomputer field that storing an original disk for a prolonged period is unwise. A floppy disk that has been unused for many months may become completely unusable or cause a head crash, resulting in the loss of data on the disk. As a result, I recommend a policy that is at variance with what is usually written in the instruction manuals that come with software packages.

Most packaged programs come in single-density format, and it is *strongly recommended* that you prepare backup copies of the purchased programs. You will also want to make backup copies of your data files periodically. The frequency of these backups will depend upon several factors: their importance to your business operation, the frequency of use, and the cost of their replacement (reentry of the data).

> **NOTE:** Some companies selling packaged programs today have designed their programs so that they cannot be copied onto another disk and instead sell backup copies at an additional small fee. If you purchase one of these (check with your supplier if you are not certain), then you cannot follow the procedure outlined above. Do *not* attempt to copy a self-destruct disk if you have purchased one; instead, purchase the backup from the supplier.

How to Make a Backup Disk

Whether you are making a backup of a packaged program, a program written in house, or a data file, the same procedure should be followed.

First, start by formatting a new disk and adding the operating system (under CP/M) as well as the utility programs for copying a disk, PIP.COM. and COPY.COM. If you are making backup copies of a purchased program, remember to use single-density even if you use double-density or quad-density in daily operations.

Second, with this new disk in drive A, place the disk to be copied in disk drive B and copy it onto the disk in drive A. This can be done in one of three ways; each has different advantages.

1. You can use the COPY utility that comes as part of most operating systems; in CP/M this is the utility, COPY.COM. Following the convention noted earlier that *underlined copy* is what you enter following a systems prompt and <CR> is a carriage return, you would first "call" the program by typing COPY and then respond to the questions on the screen.

```
A> COPY <CR>

Enter Source drive B <CR>
Ready Source disk in B: and hit return <CR>

Enter Destination drive A <CR>
Ready Destination drive in A: and hit return <CR>
```

Depending upon the modification of the operating system by the manufacturer of your computer, you will receive either of two responses once the disk has been copied:

```
Press Return to reboot
```

or

```
Copy complete. More? (Y/N)
```

In the first instance, all you need do is press the carriage return, <CR>. In the second case you would probably enter N followed by a carriage return <CR>. You now have a copied disk that has been automatically verified by the program.

2. You might wish to use the PIP utility. This is often slower than using the COPY utility, but is useful in making a copy of selected portions of a disk. It is also possible to have the computer verify the copy as it is read from one disk and written on the other. To copy an entire disk, you would enter after the prompt:

```
A> PIP B:=A:*.*[V] <CR>
```

This command instructs the computer to copy from the disk on drive A to the disk on drive B, B:=A:, all the material on the disk, *.*, and at the same time verify the read/write operation, [V]. When using the PIP utility the computer displays the name of each module as it is copied from one disk to the other.

3. There are other packaged utilities to perform the same function as the PIP utility; one of these is "COPYV," which is part of FILEFIX. The source file from the original disk is read entirely into memory, and a new file is written from memory onto the new disk. As the new file is written, it is compared to the original and an error message is printed if the new file does not match the old.

Finally, whether you have used the COPY utility, the PIP utility with the verification modifier, or the COPYV program, you have a backup disk of the original and the copy has been verified to make certain that both files are identical.

How Many Backup Copies Should You Make?

Many producers of packaged programs permit you to make anywhere from three to five backup copies. How many copies you need depends on how well you protect your disks, but at a minimum you should make two copies. You will then have three copies of the program.

1. One copy should be kept in a special file at the microcomputer work station.
2. Another copy should be stored either in a fireproof safe or other safe location in the office, but not in the same room as the computer.
3. The third copy should be kept off-site. This copy may be stored in a safe manner at home or in another office in a different building.

The following sequence of copies should be used. The backup copy at the microcomputer is used to make the everyday working copies of the program on single-density, double-density, or quad-density disks. If the backup is found to have an error, then the other copy in the office may be used, and finally the copy stored off-site.

NOTE: The number of backup copies you need applies not only to packaged programs that you have purchased, but also to the files you have created and use in your business and any programs written by you or your staff.

It may seem costly to use so many disks for backup. However, when compared with the price of purchased packaged programs, the cost is negligible. In addition, consider the real value of a disk that contains files of data vital to your business. According to the Data Entry Management Association (DEMA), a data entry clerk is capable of about 11,100 strokes per hour—that is, three strokes per second. For example, using a double-density, 8-inch disk with a capacity of 600,000 bytes, the data entry clerk would take about 54 hours to fill the disk. With a national average hourly rate of $8.50 an hour, the cost of entering all the data would amount to $459. Even with a 5½-inch, single-sided, single-density disk, with a capacity of 164,000 bytes, the cost would exceed $125.

Rotation of Original Disks

It is highly recommended that every 2 months, if not more frequently, a new copy of the original be made and the existing three disks be rotated.

1. Using the procedure for copying an original noted earlier, make a new original copy. This copy should be stored off-site.
2. The first off-site copy should be returned to the office and placed as the second backup in the office in a location other than the computer room.
3. The original second on-site copy should be taken and used at the microcomputer if additional work copies are needed.
4. The original single-density copy at the microcomputer should be erased. It can then be reused for other programs and/or files.

In this way there is always a "freshly made" backup available, and no backup copy remains unused for more than 6 months. One way to avoid possible mix-ups of these source disks is to use color or color/symbol coding with your disks, as shown in Figure 22.

DISK STORAGE TECHNIQUES

Floppy disks are subject to damage and must be stored carefully. A system should be established for maintaining the disks during daily operations and protecting them at the day's end. The box in which the disks are purchased is not the best container for storing disks. Several more convenient methods are available.

- Most popular is the *disk library case*, with a pop-up feature that puts a maximum of ten floppy disks in full view for instant access. When not in use, the closed case is small enough to be placed on a bookshelf. It is designed to hold the disks firmly in a vertical position, the way a hi-fi enthusiast stores records, to prevent warping. The closed box also reduces exposure to dust.
- A variation of the library case is the *disk file tray*, a plastic box with a clear, removable plastic top. The tray is capable of holding 80 disks at one time but unless the number of disks stored is near capacity, the disks will not be stored compactly and upright. Some trays are divided into sections with vertical dividers to provide this protection.
- A *rotary stand* gives easy access to more disks at one time. Two disks

FIGURE 22

Two disks produced for backup. Note disk identification numbers (upper left corner of disk) and coded symbols and dates to assist in keeping a record of the age of the backup disks.

are stored in each divided vinyl file, and it is possible to have as many as 150 disks available at once. Although the disks are stored upright, they are not protected adequately from dust unless a sheet of plastic or a special custom-made cover is used at the end of the day to cover the entire unit.

- Another method of storing disks is in *clear vinyl protective covers* that are kept in a ring binder. One advantage of this type of storage over the others previously noted is that there is more space for disk information and it is more clearly readable. (See Figure 23.)
- A *disk storage case* is made to hold floppy disk *file folders*. The sturdy vinyl case has a flap cover providing instant access to the stored disks. (See Figure 23.)
- Two products used together make it convenient to work with programs requiring step-by-step instructions or for which documentation must

FIGURE 23

Two ways to provide protective storage for floppy disks: (left) in clear vinyl protective sleeve, which is kept in a ring binder, and (right) in special vinyl folder within a plastic case. (Courtesy of 20th Century Plastics, Inc.)

be available while running. An *easel binder* holds the instructions or documentation. It looks like an ordinary ring binder, but can be folded and placed in an upright position to permit reading of copy while working at the terminal. If the disk has been stored in an *adhesive-back floppy disk pocket*, the cover can be attached to a page in the binder, where it is easily found but out of the way.

Using Special Color-Coded Files

No matter which of the previous disk storage techniques you use, it is advisable to color-code the storage units to distinguish among the types of disks. For example, if you use disk library cases, you might consider using different color cases. Master copies of purchased disks—the single-density originals—as well as in-house programs and files, could be stored in a case that is distinctly different in color from others, and only special personnel would have access to disks stored in that particular case.

A similar method can be used when disks are stored in individual clear vinyl protective covers. The master copies can be kept in a binder that is different in color from the rest. In some cases it is also possible to label the edge and front cover of the binder to ensure their protection.

Magnetically Shielded Cases

At least one set of backup copies should be protected from electromagnetic interference (EMI) and radiofrequency interference (RFI). This interfer-

FIGURE 24

Copies of manuals, documentation, and disks should be kept in an orderly, secure fashion. Individual binders that are clearly and easily identified should be used. (Courtesy of Wilson Jones Company.)

ence is commonplace, produced by power-generating equipment, power lines, transformers, lightning, and magnets. The security detection systems used in libraries, airports, and even some commercial stores can also result in disk degradation.

Special units made of a magnetic-shielding alloy with heliarc-welded seams ensure optimal shielding. These portable cases come in different sizes to accommodate a varying number of floppy disks. For additional security, most models have a key lock or hasp that will accept a padlock.

Although these units were designed primarily for transporting sensitive magnetic media, they are highly recommended for storing original disks and vital programs and data files, particularly in off-site locations.

Insulated Safes

As noted earlier, computer users cannot rely solely on traditional fire protection measures, such as fireproof buildings, sprinklers, and fire-insulated products designed for protective storage of paper records. The conventional commercial safe does not provide the protection from heat and humidity necessary to protect magnetic media. Humidity protects paper documents but can actually destroy magnetic media. Temperatures above 125 degrees Fahrenheit will also destroy these media.

FIGURE 25

Magnetic-shielded case used to protect and store original, key backup, and vital data disks when not in use. (Courtesy of Magnetic Shield Division, Perfection Mica Company.)

A special safe designed for the protection of magnetic media is necessary if you wish to provide full protection. It is recommended that at the close of a workday you place a copy of all vital files stored on floppy disks inside the safe. The safe should also be the storage location of one set of the backup disks and all master copies of programs and data files.

HOW TO CARE FOR YOUR DISKS

At a recent computer conference I met an old friend who teaches microcomputing at one of the Big Ten universities in the Midwest. We discussed the

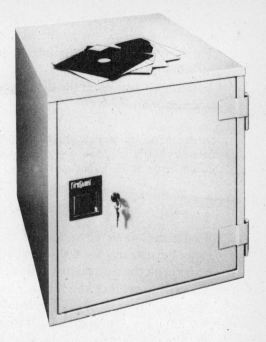

FIGURE 26

For secure overnight storage of master and vital data disks a special fireproof safe designed for computer media, such as the *Fireguard Diskette Safe*, should be used. (Courtesy of Schwab Safe Co., Inc.)

care and feeding of floppy disks, and he told me about his students who carry their disks slipped in between the pages of a textbook exposed to rain and snow. Others bent their disks slightly so that the disks could be slipped into a coat pocket. One of these students would place her disk under a pile of books for a half hour to make certain that it was flat again. Another student stored his disk under his shirt against his body as he jogged 5 miles to school. What surprised my friend most was that rarely did a disk fail to work.

When I hear tales like these I wonder if most of us are not overcautious, but I am brought back to reality when one of my disks that has been given tender care causes the system to crash. Although it is possible to violate disk-handling rules now and then without resulting disaster—my mother-in-law used to say that God protects fools and children—I feel that proper disk care is essential. Here are some common-sense rules for the care and storage of floppy disks.

DO . . .

- Keep the floppy disk in its protective envelope or in a special vinyl sleeve when it is not in the disk drive.
- Store the disk in an upright position in a dustproof case, box, or special plastic sleeve.
- Use a felt-tipped pen, and write lightly if you must write on the label of the disk.

- File one copy of vital disks in magnetically shielded containers and/or specially insulated fireproof safes at the end of the workday.
- Turn the power on for the microcomputer *before* you insert any disks into the disk drives.
- Remove all disks from the disk drives *before* you shut off power to the microcomputer.

NOTE: Some microcomputer manufacturers instruct the user to insert disks before turning on the power and to remove the disks after the power is off. Most professionals advise users against doing so.

DON'T . . .

- Touch the magnetic surface of the disk. A fingerprint, even if you cannot see it, can cause the loss of data and possibly a head crash. The fingerprint contains oil that will attract dust and/or other contaminants.
- Attempt to remove the floppy disk from its sealed protective cover. The nonwoven rayon lining inside is there to protect the delicate magnetic iron oxide surface. It permits the disk to revolve freely and attracts the dust that might have gotten on the disk.
- Attempt to clean or apply any liquid to the magnetic disk.
- Fold or flex the floppy disk.
- Bring a magnet or magnetic object near the disk, or use a magnetic bulletin board anywhere near the microcomputer or the disks.
- Use rubberbands to hold several disks together.
- Erase writing on the label. Remove and replace the label instead. A buildup of labels can jam in the disk drive.
- Use a paperclip to attach a note to the disk. Be careful when using paperclips from a magnetic dispenser, since they may be magnetized and affect the disk.
- Place a disk flat at a workstation when not in use. This precaution will prevent anyone from putting heavy objects on it.
- Place two disks without their protective covers against each other. Disks rubbing against each other build up static and attract dust.
- Eat, smoke, or drink at the workstation when using disks.
- Force a disk into a disk drive. If it doesn't go in easily, start over again.
- Expose disks to excessive heat or direct sunlight, or to extreme cold and humidity. Floppy disks can be stored in temperatures ranging from 40 to 120 degrees Fahrenheit and in areas with relative humidity between 20 and 80%. However, the disks should be allowed to come to room temperature and humidity before being used.

NOTE: Take extra precaution when traveling with disks. Avoid the protective devices used in libraries, airports, and some stores. Also be very careful if you buy packaged programs and disks in stores, which use special detectors to foil shoplifting. Recently a friend purchased a game package to which a sensing metal had been attached. The sensing metal was removed by the salesclerk, but the disk was damaged when carried through the electromagnetic field of the detector.

A DISK DIRECTORY FOR YOUR DISKS

Keeping a list of the programs and data files on your disks is not only a good housekeeping practice, but is also an essential part of a security program. You should know what resources you have and on which disks they are. If you are just beginning to implement the system, you may have only a few programs and files, and the list can be kept with paper and pen. However, you will find that as the list gets longer, the microcomputer will be as valuable for this task as for other applications.

Diskfile

There are commercially available packages to create and maintain a directory of all the programs and files you have on disks. At the end of this chapter, there is, however, a program, DISKFILE, with which you can do the same job. To use the program, you must first number each disk. The number is placed on the label showing the contents of the disk.

There are seven parts in the menu for the DISKFILE program. Part 2, create a file, is used only when you start the file and is never used again. You can search for a program using the CRT, or you can have a printed copy of the entire file in alphabetical order. If a disk is destroyed, you can search by disk number to determine which programs have been lost. You can also display (on the CRT) or print a list of the keywords. The keywords are major classifications.

Any program or data file entered by DISKFILE requires four items of information:

1. name of the program or file,
2. number of the disk on which the file or program is located,
3. the keyword or its major category, and
4. a description of the program or file.

A copy of the **DISKFILE** program is included on the following page.

```
REM ***********************************************************************
REM
REM        PROGRAM:     DISKFILE.BAS            FILE: DISK.FIL
REM
REM        PURPOSE:     PROGRAM IS TO CREATE A DIRECTORY OF PROGRAMS
REM                     BY DISK NUMBER, KEYWORD AND DESCRIPTION
REM
REM        PROGRAMMED IN CBASIC BY ESTHER H. HIGHLAND
REM                  PROGRAMMED:     DECEMBER 20,1981
REM                  LATEST UPDATE:  AUGUST    13,1982
REM              * COPYRIGHT 1982,  HIGHLAND + HIGHLAND *
REM
REM ***********************************************************************
        REM
        REM        HOUSEKEEPING FOLLOWS AND BASIC INPUT
        REM
        REM ***************************************************************
        REM
        CLEAR$ = CHR$(126) + CHR$(28):       REM CLEAR SCREEN
        PRINT CLEAR$:   INPUT "ENTER TODAY'S DATE..."; DATE$
        PRINT:      INPUT "NAME OF FILE..."; NOF$
        REM
        REM ***************************************************************
        REM
        REM        DISPLAY OF PROGRAM MENU AND SWITCH ROUTINE
        REM
        REM ***************************************************************
        REM
10      PRINT CLEAR$:    PRINT "WHAT WOULD YOU LIKE TO DO?":    PRINT
        PRINT "1     END EXECUTION"
        PRINT "2     CREATE FILE"
        PRINT "3     ADD TO FILE"
        PRINT "4     MODIFY, DELETE OR SUBSTITUTE A RECORD"
        PRINT "5     PRINT FILE SORTED BY NAME"
        PRINT "6     SEARCH FILE BY PROGRAM NAME, DISK NUMBER OR KEYWORD"
        PRINT "7     DISPLAY / PRINT ALPHABETIZED LIST OF KEYWORDS"
        PRINT
        PRINT "-------------------------------------------------------------"
        PRINT "NOTE: TO ESCAPE ANY ROUTINE EXCEPT 5 PRESS 0 ON FIRST INPUT"
        PRINT "-------------------------------------------------------------"
        PRINT
        PRINT "NOTE:     MUST END EXECUTION WITH #1 WHEN FINISHED":   PRINT
20      INPUT "ENTER CHOICE BY NUMBER... ";NO%:     PRINT CLEAR$
                IF NO% < 1 OR NO% > 8 THEN 10
                IF NO% = 1 OR NO% = 2 THEN 25
        OPEN NOF$ RECL 128 AS 1
        READ #1, 1; INDEX%, START%
25      ON NO% GOTO 95, 40, 45, 50, 70, 80, 60
        REM
        REM ***************************************************************
        REM
        REM              ROUTINE TO CREATE OR ADD TO FILE
        REM
        REM ***************************************************************
        REM
40      CREATE NOF$ RECL 128 AS 1
        START% = 0:    K% = 1:    GOTO 46
45      K% = INDEX%
46      PRINT CLEAR$
        PRINT "IF ALL ENTRIES HAVE BEEN MADE ENTER   QUIT   FOR NAME"
        PRINT:    PRINT:    INPUT "NAME......... ";NAME$:    PRINT
                IF NAME$ = "0" OR UCASE$(NAME$) = "QUIT" THEN 47
        INPUT "DISK.......... "; DISK$: PRINT
        INPUT "KEYWORD......."; KEY$:  PRINT
        INPUT "DESCRIPTION ..."; DESC$: PRINT
        INPUT "IS ENTRY CORRECT ... (Y/N) .... "; AN$:    PRINT
                IF UCASE$(AN$) <> "Y" THEN 46
        PT% = 0:    K% = K% + 1:    INDEX% = K%
        PRINT #1, K%; NAME$, DISK$, KEY$, DESC$, PT%
        PRINT #1, 1; INDEX%, START%:    GOTO 46
47      CLOSE 1:    GOTO 10
```

```
        REM
        REM *****************************************************************
        REM
        REM          ROUTINE TO MODIFY, DELETE OR SUBSTITUTE A RECORD
        REM
        REM *****************************************************************
        REM
50      PRINT CLEAR$
        PRINT "TO DELETE A RECORD ENTER   ZZZ   FOR PROGRAM NAME":  PRINT
        INPUT "RECORD NUMBER ..................... "; K%
                IF K% < 2 OR K% > INDEX% THEN 55
        READ #1, K%; NAME$, DISK$, KEY$, DESC$, PT%
        PRINT NAME$, DISK$, KEY$, DESC$:      PRINT
        INPUT "CORRECT RECORD? ... (Y/N) .... ";AN$
                IF UCASE$(AN$) <> "Y" THEN 50
        PRINT: PRINT
52      INPUT "NAME ............ "; NAME$:  PRINT
        IF NAME$ <> "ZZZ" THEN 53
        DISK$ = "":     KEY$ = "":    DESC$ = "":     GOTO 54
53      INPUT "DISK NUMBER ..... "; DISK$:  PRINT
        INPUT "KEYWORD ......... "; KEY$:   PRINT
        INPUT "DESCRIPTION ..... "; DESC$:  PRINT
        PT% = 0: INPUT "IS ENTRY CORRECT? ... (Y/N) .... ";AN$:   PRINT
                IF UCASE$(AN$) <> "Y" THEN 52
54      PRINT #1, K%; NAME$, DISK$, KEY$, DESC$, PT%:     PRINT
        INPUT "ANOTHER CHANGE? ... (Y/N) ...... ";AN$
                IF UCASE$(AN$) = "Y" THEN 50
55      CLOSE 1:     GOTO 10
        REM
        REM *****************************************************************
        REM
        REM             ROUTINE TO PRINT SORTED KEYWORD LIST
        REM
        REM *****************************************************************
        REM
60      DIM KW$(100), LGTH%(100)
        FILL$ = "XXXXXXXXXXXXXXXXXXXX": PRINT CLEAR$
        INPUT "DO YOU WANT TO DISPLAY/ PRINT KEYWORDS? ... (Y/N) .... "; AN$
                IF UCASE$(AN$) <> "Y" THEN 66
        PRINT:     PRINT "GOING THROUGH SORT ROUTINE":    PRINT
        C% = 1:    READ #1, 2; NAME$, DISK$, KEY$
        KW$(1) = LEFT$ (KEY$ + FILL$, 20)
        LGTH%(1) = LEN (KEY$)
        FOR K% = 3 TO INDEX%
                READ #1, K%; NAME$, DISK$, KEY$
                FOR J% = 1 TO (K%-2)
                        KWT$ = LEFT$ (KEY$ + FILL$, 20)
                        IF KWT$ = KW$(J%) THEN 61
                NEXT J%
                C% = C% + 1:    KW$(C%) = KWT$:    LGTH%(C%) = LEN (KEY$)
61      NEXT K%
        J% = C%
62      J% = J% - 1
        FLAG% = 0:     M% = 0
63      M% = M% + 1
        IF KW$(M%) < KW$(M% + 1) THEN 64
        SAV$ = KW$(M%):    KW$(M%) = KW$(M% + 1):    KW$(M% + 1) = SAV$
        SAV% = LGTH%(M%):     LGTH%(M%) = LGTH%(M% + 1)
        LGTH%(M% + 1) = SAV%:     FLAG% = FLAG% + 1
64      IF J% > M% THEN 63
        IF J% > 1 AND FLAG% <> 0 THEN 62
        PRINT:  INPUT "DO YOU WANT THE PRINTER ON? ... (Y/N) .... ";AN$
                IF UCASE$(AN$) = "Y" THEN \
                        LPRINTER WIDTH 80\
                ELSE \
                        PRINT CLEAR$
        PRINT "KEYWORDS", DATE$: PRINT
        FOR J% = 1 TO C%
                PRINT LEFT$ (KW$(J%), LGTH%(J%))
        NEXT J%
        PRINT
        INPUT "PRESS SPACE BAR AND RETURN KEY TO CONTINUE .... "; AN$
65      CONSOLE
66      CLOSE 1:     GOTO 10
```

```
        REM
        REM ***********************************************************
        REM
        REM                    ROUTINE TO SORT AND PRINT A FILE
        REM
        REM ***********************************************************
        REM
70      INPUT "DO YOU WANT TO PRINT THE SORTED FILE? ... (Y/N) .... ";AN$
            IF UCASE$(AN$) <> "Y" THEN 79
        PRINT:    PRINT:    PRINT "MAKE CERTAIN PRINTER IS ON.":    PRINT
        PRINT:    INPUT "PRESS SPACE BAR AND RETURN KEY TO CONTINUE .. ";H$
        PRINT CLEAR$:    PRINT "GOING THROUGH SORT PROCEDURE .... BE PATIENT"
        DIM NA$(250),R%(250)
        FILL$ = "XXXXXXXXXXXXXXXXXXXX"
        FOR K% = 2 TO INDEX%
            READ #1, K%; NAME$
            NA$(K%-1) = LEFT$(NAME$ + FILL$,20)
            R%(K%-1) = K%
        NEXT K%
        J% = INDEX% - 1
71      J% = J% - 1
        FLAG% = 0:        M% = 0
72      M% = M% + 1
        IF NA$(M%) < NA$(M%+1) THEN 73
        SAV$ = NA$(M%):    NA$(M%) = NA$(M%+1):    NA$(M%+1) = SAV$
        SAV% = R%(M%):     R%(M%) = R%(M%+1):      R%(M%+1) = SAV%
        FLAG% = FLAG% + 1
73      IF J% > M% THEN 72
        IF J% > 1 AND FLAG% <> 0 THEN 71
        START% = R%(1):      PRINT
        FOR J% = 1 TO (INDEX%-2)
            READ #1, R%(J%);  NAME$, DISK$, KEY$, DESC$, PT%
            PT% = R%(J%+1)
            PRINT #1, R%(J%); NAME$, DISK$, KEY$, DESC$, PT%
        NEXT J%
        READ #1, R%(INDEX%-1); NAME$, DISK$, KEY$, DESC$, PT%
        PT% = 0
        PRINT #1, R%(INDEX%-1); NAME$, DISK$, KEY$, DESC$, PT%
        PRINT #1, 1; INDEX%, START%
        REM
        REM     PRINTER SET FOR 100 CHARACTERS; MODIFY FOR YOUR PRINTER
        REM
        PRINT CLEAR$: LPRINTER WIDTH 100
        PRINT "TODAY'S DATE IS ...... "; DATE$: PRINT
        PRINT "RECORD #"; TAB(12);"NAME"; TAB(23);"DISK #";\
             TAB(31);"KEYWORD"; TAB(52);"DESCRIPTION"
        PRINT:    K% = START%
74      READ #1, K%; NAME$,DISK$,KEY$,DESC$,PT%
             IF NAME$ = "ZZZ" THEN 76
        PRINT K%; TAB(7);NAME$; TAB(25);DISK$; TAB(31);KEY$;\
             TAB(45);DESC$
             IF PT% = 0 THEN 78
        K% = PT%: GOTO 74
76      PRINT:    PRINT
        PRINT "NOTE:  THE FOLLOWING RECORD NUMBERS ARE NOT USED AND"
        PRINT "CAN BE USED WITH CHANGE ROUTINE TO ADD A NEW RECORD:": PRINT
77      PRINT K%;
        IF PT% = 0 THEN 78
        K% = PT%
        READ #1, K%;NAME$,DISK$,KEY$,DESC$,PT%
             GOTO 77
78      CONSOLE
79      CLOSE 1:        GOTO 10
```

```
        REM
        REM  **********************************************************+·
        REM
        REM     ROUTINE TO SEARCH FILE BY NAME, DISK NUMBER OR KEYWORD
        REM
        REM  ***********************************************,*******,·,,
        REM
80      PRINT CLEAR$: PRINT "DO YOU WISH TO SEARCH BY:"
        PRINT " (1) NAME": PRINT " (2) DISK NUMBER": PRINT " (3) KEYWORD"
        PRINT: INPUT "ENTER YOUR CHOICE BY NUMBER ...";NO%
              IF NO% = Ø THEN 9Ø
        SNAME$ = " ":    SDISK$ = " ":    SKEY$ = " ":    J% = Ø
        ON NO% GOTO 81, 82, 83
              GOTO 8Ø
81      PRINT: INPUT "WHICH NAME........ "; SNAME$: PRINT: GOTO 84
82      PRINT: INPUT "WHICH DISK NUMBER.. "; SDISK$: PRINT: GOTO 84
83      PRINT: INPUT "WHICH KEYWORD...... "; SKEY$:  PRINT
84      INPUT "DO YOU WANT THE PRINTER ON? ... (Y/N) .... ";AN$
        PRINT CLEAR$
        IF UCASE$(AN$) <> "Y" THEN 85
        LPRINTER WIDTH 8Ø
85      FOR K% = 2 TO INDEX%
              READ #1, K%;NAME$,DISK$,KEY$,DESC$
              IF NAME$ = SNAME$ OR DISK$ = SDISK$ OR\
                   KEY$ = SKEY$ THEN 86
              GOTO 87
86            PRINT: PRINT NAME$, DISK$, KEY$, DESC$
              IF UCASE$(AN$) <> "Y" THEN \
                   INPUT "PRESS SPACE BAR AND RETURN KEY TO CONTINUE ";H$
              J% = J% + 1: PRINT
87      NEXT K%
              IF J% = Ø THEN 88
        INPUT "SEARCH COMPLETE - PRESS ANY LETTER TO CONTINUE"; H$: GOTO 89
88      PRINT:   PRINT "NAME, KEYWORD OR DISK NUMBER NOT FOUND."
        PRINT:   INPUT "PRESS SPACE BAR AND RETURN KEY TO CONTINUE "
89      CONSOLE
9Ø      CLOSE 1:   GOTO 1Ø
        REM
        REM  ****************************************************************
        REM
        REM                    STATEMENT TO END EXECUTION
        REM
        REM  ****************************************************************
        REM
95      PRINT: PRINT "NORMAL TERMINATION OF PROGRAM"
        END
```

CHAPTER 8

How to Create a
User-Protect Disk

Dividing a disk among several users who access a single microcomputer is the simplest way to provide limited security under CP/M and similar operating systems. This is done by utilizing the *user-area* feature of the operating system. Under CP/M, for example, it is possible to divide the disk's storage capacity among 16 different users, and each user must enter the individual user number to access the authorized portion of the disk.

When the microcomputer is IPLed, or started up, the operator is automatically "logged on" in the USER 0 area. The other areas require identification numbers ranging from 1 to 15. It is obvious, therefore, that anyone who IPLs the system can get to the USER 0 area, which is the common, or home, area and cannot be protected under this security system.

Anyone who is authorized to use the computer can easily *browse*; that is, by having legitimate access to part of the system, the individual can attempt to enter different user numbers to see if anything is available in the specific user areas. However, the individual runs the risk of being seen, and this search method takes time, which might deter someone from attempting such a breakin.

The use of the user-number feature is one of the most elementary and simple layers of security. It does not afford the degree of protection required in a business environment, but it can be used in conjunction with other security techniques. In this illustration we have included additional protective layers, which include

- use of the compiled versions of the operating programs, which are not readable by people, rather than the source programs, which are readable; and

- use of the R/O (read only) protect feature, which prevents anyone from making unauthorized changes in any of the files.

It is also possible, as is described in later chapters, to include password control in programs, special program-protect techniques, and other security measures in order to provide greater levels of protection.

Three methods of producing a user-protect disk are illustrated in this chapter. One involves the use of CP/M 2.2, and the other two require the use of special packaged programs: Digital Marketing Corporation's FILE-FIX and Kaia System's OKARA. A comparison of these three shows that:

1. When using CP/M 2.2 it is necessary to enter a total of 64 commands.
2. By using FILEFIX, the number of steps required to accomplish the same results is reduced to 29. Because of a special feature of this package, the storage space is greatly reduced, since only one copy of each program or data file need be stored to have each available to the designated users.
3. Use of OKARA reduces the number of steps required to 10, but storage requirements for the programs and data files are the same as with CP/M.

CREATING A USER-PROTECT SYSTEM UNDER CP/M

To illustrate this technique we have selected one phase of a business operation: the receipt of checks from customers. The USER 0 area has been left open to all; this could contain the product price list and ability to compute invoices. (Directions on how to do this are not included in the illustration.)

We have set up three user-protect areas, each of which would be available only to specific employees to perform their assigned tasks:

1. *USER 3* can check the master file (MASTER.FIL) to determine if a check had been received prior to today's date. USER 3 could read the file using the program named LOOKUP.BAS.
2. *USER 7* enters all the checks received today and creates a new file (DAILY.FIL) at the end of the business day. This employee also obtains a printout of all data entered, as well as an audit summary, which serves as a security verification check. To do this, the employee uses the program called CREATE.BAS.
3. *USER 13*, who would be a senior individual, has the task at the end of the day of updating the master file by joining the daily file and the previous master file using the program called JOIN.BAS.

NOTE: The three programs, LOOKUP.BAS, CREATE.BAS, and JOIN.BAS, which are written in CBASIC, are included on the disk only in the .INT or *compiled version* for use by the three users.

Phase 1—The Initial Setup

- Start by placing a disk in disk drive A, which contains:

  the PIP.COM routine, or program for copying,
  the STAT.COM routine, which will be needed later to protect the
    master file from user alteration,
  the DDT.COM routine, for determining the length of any program to
    be transferred,
  CBASIC's execution program, CRUN2,
  the latest master file, MASTER.FIL, and
  copies of the compiled version of the programs: LOOKUP.INT,
    CREATE.INT, and JOIN.INT.

- Place a newly formatted disk with a special operating system *without*
  the erase and rename programs in drive B. See Chapter 11.

Phase 2—Transferring the PIP, or Copy, Program

**NOTE: In the following copy, the <u>underlined</u> characters are those that are
typed by the operator and will appear on the screen; the system prompts
and any responses are not underlined. A "carriage return," a special key
on the keyboard, is shown as <CR>.**

- The following procedure transfers the PIP.COM routine from drive A
  to USER 7 and USER 13 areas on the disk in drive B. This is done by
  calling the DDT program.

```
A> DDT PIP.COM <CR>
```

- The computer responds with the following display on the CRT:

```
DDT VERS 2.2
NEXT  PC
IF00 0100
-
```

- As noted earlier, DDT prompts the operator with the character "_" and
  waits for an input command, which in this case is G0. This command
  saves the program in the computer's memory.

```
-G0 <CR>
```

- We are now ready to transfer PIP to both USER 7 and USER 13. The
  next step is shifting control to drive B:

```
A> B: <CR>
```

- With control on drive B, first indicate the user level, and then use the **SAVE** command to transfer the PIP program in four steps, two for each user level. The size of the PIP program was indicated under the DDT operation in the second step. The value 1F00 was printed under **NEXT**; this is the size in hexadecimal form. Convert the hexadecimal value 1F00 to 31 in decimal. (For assistance in converting hexadecimal to decimal value, see Chapter 6.)

```
B> USER 7 <CR>
B> SAVE 31 PIP.COM <CR>
B> USER 13 <CR>
B> SAVE 31 PIP.COM <CR>
```

- PIP has now been moved to USER 7 and USER 13 areas on the disk in drive B. We now return to USER 0 on drive B and transfer control to the disk in drive A by entering the following commands:

```
B> USER 0 <CR>
B> A: <CR>
```

Phase 3—Transferring the STAT Program

- Transferring this program will protect the master file from any changes after it is moved from the disk in drive A to the disk in drive B. This program will be needed in both the USER 3 and USER 13 areas in which the master file is located. The procedure is similar to the one just used to transfer the PIP.COM program. Start with the DDT program to find the size of the STAT.COM routine, and enter the **G0** after the prompt "_".

```
A> DDT STAT.COM <CR>
DDT VERS 2.2
NEXT    PC
1580   0100
-G0 <CR>
```

- Save this program for both USER 3 and USER 13 on the disk in drive B.

```
A> B: <CR>
B> USER 3 <CR>
B> SAVE 22 STAT.COM  <CR>
B> USER 13  <CR>
B> SAVE 22 STAT.COM  <CR>
```

- Return to USER 0 and transfer control to drive A:

```
B> USER 0 <CR>
B> A: <CR>
```

We have now completed the transfer of the STAT routine to both user areas.

Phase 4—Transferring the Execution Program of CBASIC

- To move CRUN2, the execution program of CBASIC, from the disk in drive A to the disk in drive B, use the DDT program and transfer control to drive B.

```
A> DDT CRUN2.COM <CR>
DDT VERS 2.2
NEXT   PC
4500 0100
-G0 <CR>
A> B: <CR>
```

- Move CRUN2 to USER 3, USER 7, and USER 13 by following the procedure used earlier to move the PIP program. Note that the size of CRUN2 is 4500 in hexadecimal; this is equivalent to 69 in decimal.

```
B> USER 3 <CR>
B> SAVE 69 CRUN2.COM <CR>
B> USER 7 <CR>
B> SAVE 69 CRUN2.COM <CR>
B> USER 13 <CR>
B> SAVE 69 CRUN2.COM <CR>
```

- CRUN2 has now been moved to all three areas. Return to USER 0 and transfer control back to drive A.

```
B> USER 0 <CR>
B> A: <CR>
```

Phase 5—Moving the LOOKUP Program to User 3

- Use DDT to obtain the size of the compiled program, LOOKUP.INT, and enter G0 after the DDT prompt.

```
A> DDT LOOKUP.INT <CR>
DDT VERS 2.2
NEXT   PC
0300 0100
-G0 <CR>
```

- Shift control to drive B and after entering the USER 3 area, SAVE the LOOKUP program in that area. Then return to USER 0 and again go back to drive A.

```
A> B: <CR>
B> USER 3 <CR>
B> SAVE 3 LOOKUP.INT <CR>
B> USER 0 <CR>
B> A: <CR>
```

Phase 6—Moving the CREATE Program to User 7

- DDT is used again to determine the size of this program; it is 5 in both hexadecimal and decimal form. Enter G0 after the DDT prompt "_".

```
A> DDT CREATE.INT <CR>
DDT VERS 2.2
NEXT   PC
0500 0100
-G0 <CR>
```

- Shift control to drive B, enter USER 7 area, and save the program. Once this is done, return to USER 0 and shift control to drive A.

```
A> B: <CR>
B> USER 7 <CR>
B> SAVE 5 CREATE.INT <CR>
B> USER 0 <CR>
B> A: <CR>
```

Phase 7—Moving the JOIN Program to User 13

- Use DDT to determine program size. Note that in order to obtain a hexadecimal value ending in 00, first change the 0980 to 0A00, which is equal to 10 in decimal value. Save JOIN.INT in memory, and shift control to drive B:

```
A> DDT JOIN.INT <CR>
DDT VERS 2.2
NEXT   PC
0980 0100
-G0 <CR>
A> B: <CR>
```

- Enter USER 13 area, and save the program. Then return to USER 0, and transfer control to disk A:

```
B> USER 13 <CR>
B> SAVE 10 JOIN.INT <CR>
B> USER 0 <CR>
B> A: <CR>
```

Phase 8—Writing the Master File for USER 3 and USER 13 and Adding DDT for USER 13

- Since USER 3 needs the master file to verify previously received checks and USER 13 needs the file to create a new master file at the day's end, it is necessary to transfer the file to both users. USER 13 will later need DDT to move the daily file (DAILY.FIL) from USER 7 to his or her area. Use DDT, save the file in the computer's memory, and then transfer control to drive B:

```
A> DDT MASTER.FIL <CR>
DDT VERS 2.2
NEXT   PC
0500 0100
-G0 <CR>
A> B: <CR>
```

- Save the master file under both user numbers, return to USER 0, and transfer control to drive A:

```
B> USER 3 <CR>
B> SAVE 5 MASTER.FIL <CR>
B> USER 13 <CR>
B> SAVE 5 MASTER.FIL <CR>
B> USER 0 <CR>
B> A: <CR>
```

- Move DDT.COM to USER 13:

```
A> DDT DDT.COM
 NEXT   PC
 1400   0100
 -GØ
A> B:
B> USER 13
B> SAVE 20 DDT.COM
```

Phase 9—A Final Verification

We have now completed the transfer of all necessary programs and files from drive A to the various users on drive B. There was no need to transfer the daily file (DAILY.FIL), since this is created under program control. At this point we can verify what is stored in each user area.

• To do this, first return control to drive B.

```
A> B:
```

• To check USER 3, request a directory using the DIR command. The computer responds by listing the programs for this user.

```
B> USER 3 <CR>
B> DIR <CR>
B: CRUN2 COM : LOOKUP INT : MASTER FIL: STAT COM
```

• Obtain the listing of programs stored for USER 7.

```
B> USER 7 <CR>
B> DIR <CR>
B: PIP     COM : CRUN2  COM : CREATE   INT
```

• Verify the directory of programs and files available to USER 13.

```
B> USER 13 <CR>
B> DIR <CR>
B: PIP   COM : CRUN2 COM : JOIN INT : MASTER20 FIL
B: STAT  COM
```

Phase 10—Setting the Master File to Read/Only Status

Finally, to ensure that no one makes any changes in the master file, use the operating system's READ/ONLY protection program. Since drive B is still the control disk, enter the user number, then call the STAT program to alter the status of the master file.

```
B> USER 13 <CR>
B> STAT MASTER20.FIL $R/O <CR>

MASTER.FIL set to R/O

B> USER 3 <CR>
B> STAT MASTER20.FIL $R/O <CR>

MASTER.FIL set to R/O
B>
```

We now have a complete, ready-to-use disk in drive B. The disk in drive A is removed and stored safely. The disk from drive B can now be entered in drive A and used safely with its added level of protection.

After we have completed preparing the user-protect disk:

- USER 3 has access to the STAT.COM utility, program LOOKUP. INT, which would be executed by CRUN2.COM using the file, MASTER.FIL.
- USER 7 not only has access to the PIP.COM utility, but also to the program CREATE.INT, which would be executed by CRUN2.COM

```
A>  USER 0  <CR>
A>  DIR  <CR>
A:  PIP      COM  :  STAT      COM  :  DDT      COM
A>  USER 3  <CR>
A>  DIR  <CR>
A:  CRUN2    COM  :  LOOKUP   INT  :  MASTER   FIL  :  STAT   COM
A>  USER 7  <CR>
A>  DIR  <CR>
A:  PIP      COM  :  CRUN2    COM  :  CREATE   INT
A>  USER 13  <CR>
A>  DIR  <CR>
A:  DDT      COM  :  PIP      COM  :  CRUN2    COM  :  JOIN   INT
A:  MASTER   FIL  :  STAT     COM
```

FIGURE 27

Program directory under CP/M of user-area disk showing program and data files available to users 0, 3, 7, and 13.

to create the new daily file (which is given the name DAILY. FIL when it is created).

• USER 13 has access to three utility programs, PIP.COM, STAT. COM, and DDT.COM; the JOIN.INT program, which would be executed by CRUN2.COM; and the master file (MASTER.FIL).

This list of programs and files can be obtained by using the DIR subprogram of the CCP module of CP/M. It would be necessary to request a separate directory for each user number. (See Figure 27.)

Using CP/M3 eliminates the added storage required under the earlier versions of CP/M; only a single copy of each program and data file need be copied on the disk for assignment to each user. When setting up user areas under the newer version of CP/M, the DDT is replaced with DUMP, and the STAT procedures are accomplished by using SHOW and DIR.

NOTE: For security purposes, the DDT.COM program (or DUMP.COM under CP/M 3.0) should be erased in the USER 0 area *before* using the disk.

A SECOND METHOD TO CREATE A USER-PROTECT DISK— FILEFIX

An interactive method of producing user-protect files that takes less time requires the special features of the FILEFIX program. Under the CP/M method just described, it was necessary for the computer to allocate storage on the disk for each user who needed the same program. The F command under FILEFIX forges a link from an existing file to another filename or to another user number. Using this command for user allocation, a separate directory entry is created for each user to the same file with no additional space required. Furthermore, it is not necessary to use either the DDT or SAVE commands as required under CP/M.

Phase 1—The Initial Setup

Start by creating a new disk with all the programs that will be required by the different users in the USER 0 area. These programs include, for this illustration,

```
PIP.COM       STAT.COM      DDT.COM
CRUN2.COM  LOOKUP.INT  CREATE.INT
JOIN.INT      MASTER.FIL
```

Place the disk containing the programs in drive A and a formatted disk with SYSGEN in drive B. Copy the eight required programs from the disk in drive A to the disk in drive B. Then remove the disk in drive A and replace it with a disk containing FILEFIX.

- IPL the system and "call" FILEFIX.

```
A> FILEFIX <CR>
```

- The program responds with a menu of 14 choices, ending with a request for you to enter your choice. Since you wish to create user-protect sectors on the disk in disk drive B, you indicate this as your response, B:, which notifies the program to use the disk in disk drive B. Remember to use the colon, :, or the program will fail to shift to disk drive B.

```
Enter command and <CR>: B:  <CR>
```

- The computer responds indicating it has shifted to disk drive B.

```
B is now current drive
```

Phase 2—Using the F Command

- Immediately after notifying you that it is using the disk in disk drive B, it prints another prompt to which you reply with F, since that routine will forge a link between different user areas.

```
Enter command and <CR>: F <CR>
```

- The program will now request the program name. We will shift PIP. COM to USER 7.

```
Source filename: PIP.COM <CR>
Destination filename or user number preceded by a
  comma: ,7  <CR>
1 extents created for user 7 on drive B
```

- The program will now repeat the command request and we can shift PIP.COM to USER 13 following the same procedure as above.

```
Enter command and <CR>: F <CR>
Source filename: PIP.COM <CR>
Destination filename or user number preceded by a
  comma: ,13 <CR>
1 extents created for user 13 on drive B
```

• The STAT.COM utility can likewise be shifted to USER 3 and USER 13, as follows:

```
Enter command and <CR>: F <CR>
Source filename: STAT.COM <CR>
Destination filename or user number preceded by a
  comma: ,3 <CR>
1 extents created for user 3 on drive B

Enter command and <CR>: F <CR>
Source filename: STAT.COM <CR>
Destination filename or user number preceded by a
  comma: ,13 <CR>
1 extents created for user 13 on drive B
```

• The DDT.COM utility is transferred to USER 13 as follows:

```
Enter command and <CR>: F <CR>
Source filename: DDT.COM <CR>
Destination filename or user number preceded by a
  comma: ,13 <CR>
1 extents created for user 13 on drive B
```

Phase 3—Shifting the Compiler

Since all three users will require the CBASIC compiler, CRUN2, we can use the same technique to permit this program to be used by USER 3, USER 7, and USER 13. The procedure requires our entering (1) the F command, (2) the name of the programs, and (3) the user number. The shifting of CRUN2 to all three users is shown below:

```
Enter command and <CR>: F <CR>
Source filename: CRUN2.COM <CR>
Destination filename or user number preceded by a
  comma: ,3 <CR>
2 extents created for user 3 on drive B

Enter command and <CR>: F <CR>
Source filename: CRUN2.COM <CR>
Destination filename or user number preceded by a
  comma: ,7 <CR>
2 extents created for user 7 on drive B
```

```
Enter command and <CR>: F <CR>
Source filename: CRUN2.COM <CR>
Destination filename or user number preceded by a
   comma: ,13 <CR>
2 extents created for user 13 on drive B
```

Phase 4—Shifting the Three Operating Programs

It is possible in the same way to shift the three programs, CREATE, LOOKUP, and JOIN, to their respective users as follows.

```
Enter command and <CR>: F <CR>
Source filename: LOOKUP.INT <CR>
Destination filename or user number preceded by a
   comma: ,3 <CR>
1 extents created for user 3 on drive B


Enter command and <CR>: F <CR>
Source filename: CREATE.INT <CR>
Destination filename or user number preceded by a
   comma: ,7 <CR>
1 extents created for user 7 on drive B


Enter command and <CR>: F <CR>
Source filename: JOIN.INT <CR>
Destination filename or user number preceded by a
   comma: ,13 <CR>
1 extents created for user 13 on drive B
```

Phase 5—Transferring the Master File

The master file, MASTER.FIL, is needed by USER 3 and USER 13. It is moved in the same manner with the F command:

```
Enter command and <CR>: F <CR>
Source filename: MASTER.FILE <CR>
Destination filename or user number preceded by a
   comma: ,3 <CR>
1 extents created for user 3 on drive B


Enter command and <CR>: F <CR>
Source filename: MASTER.FILE <CR>
Destination filename or user number preceded by a
   comma: ,13 <CR>
1 extents created for user 13 on drive B
```

Phase 6—The Final Protection Phase

When the FILEFIX program again requests an answer to its command prompt, you exit from the program by entering the letter E as noted:

```
Enter command and <CR>: E <CR>
```

Control has returned to the system. Now remove the disk from drive A and replace it with the user-protect disk that was in disk drive B. ReIPL the system.

- For security purposes it is necessary to erase the major programs and the master file from the USER Ø area so that they are not available for general use. Before doing so it is advisable to obtain a directory of programs in the USER Ø area.

```
A> DIR   <CR>


A: PIP    COM : STAT    COM : DDT   COM : CRUN2 COM
A: LOOKUP INT : CREATE INT : JOIN INT : MASTER FIL
```

- We now erase the programs in the USER Ø area by using the **ERA** command available under CP/M. It is also possible to do so under the D command of FILEFIX. The programs and the master file must definitely be erased from a security viewpoint. This is done by the following commands:

```
A> ERA LOOKUP.INT   <CR>
A> ERA CREATE.INT   <CR>
A> ERA JOIN.INT   <CR>
A> ERA MASTER.FIL   <CR>
```

Another request for a directory would find only four of the original programs still available under USER Ø. However, you might wish to remove some of the CP/M utilities for added safety.

We can use the disk directory (S program of FILEFIX) to obtain a printout of the programs and files by user number. (See Figure 28.)

```
B directory. Press space bar for next screen or <ESC> key to abort.

Ø PIP    COM   Ø DDT     COM   Ø STAT    COM    3 LOOKUP   INT
3 CRUN2  COM   3 STAT    COM   3 MASTER  FIL    7 PIP      COM
7 CRUN2  COM   7 CREATE  INT  13 PIP     COM   13 CRUN2    COM
13 JOIN   INT  13 MASTER  FIL  13 STAT    COM   13 DDT      COM

128 total directory entries, 16 in use, 112 remaining
```

FIGURE 28

Program directory of disk using FILEFIX. Number preceding program or data file is the user number.

A Note of Caution

When using the ERA command, the CP/M system will mark the corresponding sectors of the programs as unused. A subsequent SAVE command can overwrite these sectors, destroying the file. For this reason, multiple links created by the F command of FILEFIX are automatically set to read/only status.

If any element of a multiple link must be erased, it can be done with the D command of FILEFIX. This operation will not release the corresponding sectors. If the D command were used, the following interaction would occur:

```
Enter command and <CR>: D  <CR>
Enter filename: MASTER.FIL <CR>
   User number (0-15)?  3  <CR>
MASTER.FIL is READ ONLY. Delete?  Y  <CR>
1 extent deleted for user 3 on drive A
Enter command and <CR>: E <CR>
```

A THIRD METHOD TO CREATE A USER-PROTECT DISK—OKARA

An even faster method that can be used to create a user-protect disk requires the use of a package, OKARA. Only eight entries from the keyboard are needed to do the job. Although this technique is faster than the other two methods illustrated in this chapter, the amount of storage used on the disk is the same as that required under CP/M and therefore greater than that under the second method, FILEFIX. It is a matter of trade-offs: storage versus disk preparation time.

Phase 1—The Initial Setup: Calling OKARA

When using this method all the necessary programs and files may be stored in the common, public area, USER 0, on a disk in disk drive A. A formatted disk to which SYSGEN has been added is then placed in disk drive B.

After you have IPLed the system, you call this special program:

```
A> PAGE OKARA
```

and the system responds with the following on the screen:

```
OKARA 4.01 Copyright (c) 1982 by KIAI Systems
[+A0]
```

Note: The [+A0] is the prompt under the OKARA program similar to the CP/M system prompt, A>.

Phase 2—Setup for USER 3

- Only three input statements are required to transfer the three files required for USER 3, and these are entered after each prompt as it appears:

```
[+A0]  PATH  3  PIP  B:=A:CRUN2.COM[G0]   <CR>
[+A0]  PATH  3  PIP  B:=A:LOOKUP.INT[G0]  <CR>
[+A0]  PATH  3  PIP  B:=A:MASTER.FIL[G0]  <CR>
```

- Execution of these three input statements places the processor, CRUN2.COM, the program, LOOKUP.INT, and the data file, MASTER.FIL, in the USER 3 work area.

Phase 3—Setup for USER 7 and USER 13

- Two input statements after the prompt, [+A0], are required to place the processor, CRUN2.COM, and the program to create the daily file, CREATE.COM, in the USER 7 work area:

```
[+A0]  PATH  7  PIP  B:=A:CRUN2.COM[G0]   <CR>
[+A0]  PATH  7  PIP  B:=A:CREATE.INT[G0]  <CR>
```

- Only three input statements are needed under this special program to provide USER 13 with the three files required for the operation:

```
[+A0]  PATH  13  PIP  B:=A:CRUN2.COM[G0]   <CR>
[+A0]  PATH  13  PIP  B:=A:JOIN.INT[G0]    <CR>
[+A0]  PATH  13  PIP  B:=A:MASTER.FIL[GO]  <CR>
```

Phase 4—Termination of OKARA Program

To terminate this procedure for creating three user work areas, enter **OKARA EXIT** after the prompt appears on the screen. Once this is entered, the termination sign-off is noted, and a CP/M system's prompt, A>, will appear.

```
[+A0]  OKARA  EXIT  <CR>

OKARA  4.01  Copyright  (c)  1982  by  KIAI  Systems
OKARA  returning  control  to  CP/M
A>
```

CHAPTER 9

Passwords and Operating Systems

The most fundamental security level of any microcomputer system is determined by its operating system, a program or group of related programs of which the purpose is to act as an intermediary between the hardware and the user. It is generally supplied by the manufacturer of the computer. An operating system can provide security by

- allocating "work areas" by user number,
- requiring a user password to access the system,
- providing file protection so that a program and/or a data file is available only to authorized users,
- protecting data from corruption,
- providing separate "read" and "write" access controls, and
- permitting use of security "locks" to prevent the printing or copying of any file without authorization.

Aside from the user-protect feature previously described, most operating systems use password control to provide the first layer of security—the accessing of the system. The use of passwords is one form of *personal authentication*. Personal authentication procedures can be used in multiuser, single-computer systems under several operating systems, as well as in multiuser, multitasking systems.

There are three basic methods by which a person's identity may be authenticated

1. something the individual *knows*—user-number, password, and/or other personal information,
2. something the individual *has*—ID badge with raised numbers similar to a credit card, and

3. something the individual *is*—physical characteristics, such as voice, fingerprints, hand geometry, or signature.

All three methods are available for use with microcomputer systems. Passwords, however, cost less at present than the other techniques for personal authentication. With many microcomputer systems it is possible to use password control to prevent anyone who has entered the system via the terminal from reading or changing specific data and from printing and/or copying programs of data files.

PASSWORD SCHEMES

In order to be an effective deterrent to computer system penetration, a password should be

- difficult to guess,
- easy for the owner to remember,
- changed frequently, and
- well protected by the system.

Password schemes differ according to (1) the selection technique, (2) the physical characteristics of the passwords, (3) information content of the password, so that the machine can perform a double check on the authorization code, and (4) the password lifetime.

Password Selection

A password may be chosen by the user, or it may be assigned. User-selected passwords are far from secure, since most people tend to pick up words or numbers that have some personal meaning (e.g., birth date, a spouse's or child's name, street address, social security number, or telephone number) and consequently are easy to guess. The primary reason for a user-selected password is the ease of recall, eliminating the need for writing the password down, but passwords assigned by the security supervisor or even randomly generated by the computer system itself are more secure than user-selected passwords. Assigned passwords, however, are more difficult to remember and are often written down. Another disadvantage of assigned passwords is that the computer algorithm may be deducible.

When automatic bank teller windows were introduced and customers were required to select a four-digit password to access their bank accounts, it was found that they overwhelmingly favored the last four digits of their telephone numbers, the year of their birth, the first four digits of their automobile's license or social security number, or the year in which their first child was born. Knowing a little about any customer, it was possible in almost six of ten accounts to discover their passwords in fewer than five attempts.

Physical Characteristics of Passwords

The physical characteristics of any password are determined by its length in number of letters or characters and its makeup, that is, the 26 letters of the alphabet, the alphabet plus the 10 digits, or the entire set of characters the microcomputer can recognize. The number of passwords possible based on these two characteristics is called the *password space*.

The size of the password space often determines how easy it is to "break" the password code. For example, if the operating system of the microcomputer requires a three-character password and,

- If only numbers (numeric characters) can be used, it is possible to have 1000 different passwords.
- If only letters (alphabetic characters) can be used, it is possible to have 17,576 different passwords.
- If letters and numbers (alphameric characters) can be used, it is then possible to have 46,656 different passwords.
- If in addition to the 36 alphameric characters, 20 special characters (e.g., period, comma, or left or right bracket) can be used, it is possible to have 175,616 different passwords.

Still limiting our example to a maximum of three characters in the password, if we were to permit any single-letter, double-letter, or three-letter combination, we would have 18,278 possible passwords instead of the 17,576 when we were limited to only a three-letter combination. Similarly, with a 56-character set using one, two, or three for a password, we would have 178,808 possible passwords instead of 175,616. When using CP/M version 3.0, which permits eight-character passwords, it is possible to have more than 200,000,000,000 different passwords using only letters.

From these examples, it is obvious that the password space increases by permitting

- a larger number of usable characters in forming a password,
- a larger password size, and
- variable-length passwords.

Information Content

Some password systems incorporate a technique of obtaining additional information from a password in order to verify its validity. These are complex systems, and only a very simple type is illustrated here. For example, the system might require the entry of a number equal to the number of digits in the password as part of that word. PETERRABBIT11 would be read by the computer, which would separate the digits from the letters. The system would count the letters and match them against the number entered. If they did not match, the system would not accept the user.

Another example is similar to that used with credit cards and bank numbers and incorporates the use of what is known as an automatic check digit. Assume the user would like to use the number 562 as a password. Using a check digit, the security supervisor would then require the user to modify his number by adding a 9 as the last digit so that it becomes 5629. The 9 is a check digit obtained as follows:

Password number: 5   6   2
Multipliers: 3   2   1

$$
\begin{array}{rcl}
5 \times 3 & = & 15 \\
6 \times 2 & = & 12 \\
2 \times 1 & = & \underline{2} \\
\end{array}
$$

Total: 29

This sum would be divided by 10 to obtain 2.9; the 9 is the remainder and is attached as part of the password. This check-digit function is quickly calculated by the computer by a built-in function that is part of many programming languages and can be added to the password verification portion of the operating system.

Password Lifetime

Current password schemes allow password assignments to be used for an *indefinite period of time* (lifetime), for a *fixed period of time* (e.g., a month or a week), and for a *single use only* (one-time passwords). Passwords can even be made *time-dependent*, which means that they are valid only at a certain time of the day *or* during a specific interval of time.

Passwords that remain in effect indefinitely, often called *fixed passwords*, are the most susceptible to compromise. Due to the length of time available, these passwords are especially vulnerable to exhaustive searching and testing by an unauthorized user. Making the password appropriately long can slow up the process but cannot stop it.

One-time passwords, on the other hand, offer a high level of protection. At this stage in the development of microcomputer systems, this is not practical and, in most business environments, not necessary.

Fixed-period passwords are most commonly used. The frequency of change is determined by labor turnover, sensitivity of data, and common-sense practice. With most operating systems a user can easily change the password once the system is accessed. The effectiveness of these passwords is determined by the attitude of employees toward the security measures taken by a company to protect its data files and programs.

A summary of the advantages and disadvantages of password schemes is noted in the accompanying table.

SUMMARY OF PASSWORD SCHEMES

PASSWORD SCHEMES	SOME ADVANTAGES	SOME DISADVANTAGES
Selection process		
User-select	Easy to remember	Often easy to guess
Assigned	Difficult to guess	More difficult to remember, and often written down by user
Password space	The larger the password and alphabet, the more difficult to guess	The larger the word, the more difficult to remember and more storage needed
Content	Easier to detect any penetrators	May cause passwords to be too long and will result in their being written down
Lifetime		
Indefinite	Easy to remember	Most vulnerable to attack
Fixed-time	Easy to remember and more secure than the indefinite type	Vulnerability depends upon time interval
One-time	Most secure	Difficult to remember; often bothersome to user

RULES FOR PASSWORDS

Passwords are the most widely used means of controlling access to computer systems. They are effective if strict procedures are followed. Here are eight rules for creating, distributing, using, and storing passwords.

1. Only those users who have a legitimate need for passwords should be assigned unique passwords. Others in the organization can use the USER 0 area of the microcomputer system, which is easily available and impossible to secure.

2. Passwords should consist of a sufficient number of characters and generated to ensure a degree of protection commensurate with the value of the resources being protected. For most business uses either alphabetic (26 letters) or alphameric (letters plus ten digits) is adequate. Word size is determined by the operating system; the longer the word size, the greater the protection level. However, it is not necessary to use the maximum number of letters permitted.

3. Passwords should be composed of easily remembered combinations of letters and/or numbers. These words should also be hard to guess. It is good practice to permit users to select their own passwords subject to the approval of the security supervisor. This screening would help overcome some of the weaknesses discussed earlier in this chapter and would also prevent duplication of passwords.

4. Whenever possible, passwords should be issued orally without any written copy. The supervisor should maintain an encoded list of all passwords, including current and past ones, stored on a disk (see Chapter 12 for techniques of encryption). Neither a printed nor a handwritten unencoded list should be maintained.

5. Passwords stored in the computer or on disks should be carefully protected so that no one except the security supervisor has access to them. For example, limit the use of the disk with the operating system's utility program, DDT.COM, since with that program it is possible to penetrate the operating system and obtain the list of passwords with the programs to encipher and decipher if these are used. It is good practice to include DDT.COM *only* on disks used by employees who are writing complex programs or taking care of the operating system.

6. Whenever an employee leaves, it is essential to change all passwords to which the employee has had access. This includes not only the employee's own passwords, but also those used to access special programs and data files.

7. Passwords should be changed periodically. It is better not to make such changes on a regular basis but to vary the time interval between changes. In a typical small business it is best to change all passwords at least every 6 months.

8. Whenever possible, use an operating system that will permit nonechoing (no printing on the CRT) of passwords. A few operating systems currently available incorporate this feature. When this is not possible with an operating system, you can modify the operating

system to clear the screen immediately after a password has been entered to gain access to the system, a program, or a data file.

NOTE: Additional information about the construction and use of passwords is included in Chapter 12 in the analysis of both numeric keys and passwords. Also included in that chapter is a CBASIC program, **KEYPASS.BAS**, for simple generation of passwords by any user, negating the need to memorize or write and store complex passwords.

OPERATING SYSTEMS CONSIDERATIONS

Recognizing that the operating system not only affects the basic security of your microcomputer system, but also the ease of use and efficiency, you might consider the benefits of obtaining a different operating system than that normally supplied with the computer. How well the system handles files is a critical consideration since it affects the speed of operation. Unfortunately, there is no good way today for the unsophisticated user to evaluate an operating system, but the following definitions and discussion will aid in understanding the producer's literature and the dealer's recommendation.

Operating systems are usually designed to be used in one, and sometimes two, of the following categories:

- single-user, single-tasking system,
- single-user, multitasking system, and
- multiuser, multitasking microcomputer system.

Digital Research's CP/M in some form is most widely used by single-user, 8-bit microcomputers, and their MP/M II is most commonly used by multitasking, 8-bit microcomputer systems. In the 16-bit microcomputer field, Microsoft's MS/DOS has gained a marked lead because it has been accepted by IBM for its personal computer (PC). There are many other operating systems available on the market today, ranging in price from as low as $150 to almost $10,000. It is obvious that they are not the same.

Some Operating Systems and Their Properties

Since a comprehensive analysis of operating systems would require a book by itself, only a few systems are discussed here. The analysis is divided into two parts: systems available for 8-bit machines and those available for 16-bit microcomputer systems.

Five operating systems for the *8-bit microcomputers* are included.

1. Digital Research's CP/M, which was introduced in 1973, with the latest version 3.0 released in 1982, operates with 8-bit single machines. It is a general-purpose operating system and is often

A MATTER OF DEFINITION

The definition of a few terms will help clarify the brief discussion of operating systems and their impact on security.

The *single-user* operating system serves only one terminal or monitor. One or more people may use the system independently.

Task is primarily an applications program (to distinguish it from an operating system program), but it may also be in a routine that is part of the compiler or a subprogram used by the applications program.

A *multiuser* operating system is one that can serve more than one user at the same time.

Multitasking or *multiprogramming* permits more than one task or program to be run concurrently. It is available for single-user and multiuser systems and requires a much more sophisticated operating system.

A *background program* is not evident to the user and may be any program that does not require user assistance or prompting and generally runs a long time. This is available in multitasking operating systems, allowing a user to start a program, let it run, and place it into the background. A system's prompt will then permit the user to start on another program.

modified by the computer manufacturer to meet specific design requirements of the manufacturer's system. It does not have highly sophisticated file or memory management features. The latest version is available in two forms. The first requires at least 32K of memory and at least one disk drive. The other, a banked version, requires at least 96K of RAM. Security on earlier versions was limited to user area. Only the banked version of CP/M 3 provides for password protection.

2. TurboDOS by Software 2000, Inc., introduced in 1981, is more sophisticated and runs on a 64 K, 8-bit microcomputer. It provides a higher level of security than do the earlier versions of CP/M. It also performs pseudomultitasking by incorporating a print spooler utility, making it possible to use the computer while the printing of output is run in background.

3. UCSD p-system by SofTtech Microsystems, Inc., can be used on an 8-bit microcomputer with 48K to 128K. Although designed for a single-user system, it is highly efficient in its file management and, like TurboDOS, includes a print spooling program among its built-in utilities.

4. OASIS by Phase One Systems, Inc., can be used in both single-user and multiuser environments and is capable of supporting 16 users performing up to 16 multitasking operations concurrently. Furthermore, it provides good access and file security and can be used on machines with as much as 784K memory. It has very sophisticated (for a microcomputer system) file-handling abilities and includes a word processor as part of its built-in utilities.

5. MP/M II by Digital Research is designed for use in a multiuser, multitasking environment. It has several advantages beyond CP/M, with moderately good file-handling features. It may be used with systems with up to 336K memory.

In the *16-bit microcomputer* field, there is a growing number of operating systems available trying to capture this market. Five of these systems are described briefly.

1. MS-DOS by Microsoft, Inc., was introduced in 1981 and revised in 1982. It is essentially a single-user operating system. Its ability to handle files is very good, but its security features do not take advantage of the larger system design.

2. CPM/86 by Digital Research, usable with systems between 64K and 1M memory, is a single-user, single-task system that has moderately good file-handling ability.

3. MPM-86, also by Digital Research, is recommended for use on systems with 4 to 16 users and is reported capable of handling up to 255 tasks concurrently. Used on systems with 128K to 1M memory, the system is primarily a version of MP/M II altered to operate on a 16-bit system.

4. OASIS-16 by Phase One Systems, Inc., can be used on systems from 128K to 1M memory and features a good level of security. It is designed to be used with as many as 32 users and can perform up to 32 multitasking operations. It has exceedingly good capabilities for handling files and, similar to the 8-bit version, has powerful utilities, including a word processor.

5. PC-DOS was developed by Microsoft, Inc., for use on the IBM personal computer. It is a single-user operating system similar to MS-DOS and has similar attributes.

CHAPTER 10

Software Security:
Protecting Programs
and Data Files

In this chapter we cover some 20 different ways to protect programs and data files from illegal use and/or modification. Some of these techniques include several variations, and most are software-dependent; that is, they are incorporated into either the operating system or a program. Some topics, because of their detail, are noted in this chapter but explained in step-by-step form in other chapters. Each method is independent of the others and may be used in conjunction with one or more additional methods described in this chapter, as well as with the ten methods for security during operations covered in Chapter 13, "10 Simple Steps for Security during Operations."

USER-PROTECT FEATURE OF CP/M

The most elementary method of protecting programs and data files is through the use of the *user-protect* feature of CP/M. Under this and other operating systems, it is possible to divide a single disk among several users. The USER 0 area is common or public and is immediately available when the system is IPLed. Naturally, secure programs and data files would *not* be placed in this user area. There are, however, 15 additional user areas, and it is possible to assign individuals to any user areas.

Several techniques for setting up a user-protect disk were described earlier in Chapter 8. This method, however, has severe limitations, since any authorized user may easily, although illegally, access any user area. Yet, this technique can be used as the first layer of protection and can be supplemented by other techniques described in this chapter.

SETTING PROGRAMS AND FILES TO READ/ONLY STATUS

The STAT.COM utility program under CP/M 2.2 and earlier versions provides statistical information about the disk and the files and programs stored on the disk; it also controls the status of files and programs. Similar utility programs exist under other operating systems. Here we are concerned with only one of the many applications of this utility program: its ability to protect a file from alteration or erasure by any user, either intentionally or accidentally. (If you are using CP/M 3, see the later section on security measures using CP/M 3.)

When a program or data file is created, it has a read/write status; that is, it can be read and it can be modified by writing over any portion the user wishes. To protect the file, we invoke the STAT.COM utility as follows

```
A> STAT <filename> $R/O   <CR>
```

The response by the computer indicates that the file named in <filename> has been set to read only status.

```
<filename> set to R/O
```

If any attempt is made to alter the file, either by using the editor that is part of the operating system or any text editor used with the computer, the computer will respond to such an attempt by displaying the following on the CRT:

```
Bdos Err on A: <filename> R/O
```

Once this message appears on the screen, the system is "closed," and it is necessary to reIPL in order to use the computer.

Furthermore, there is telltale evidence that someone has attempted to tamper with the file. If you enter DIR after the system's prompt, A>, to call for a directory of the disk, the listing would contain the filename, for example, BATTLE.FIL, (the file with the R/O status) *and* also included in the directory list would be BATTLE.$$$. The .$$$ indicates a temporary file or an improperly saved file that is unusable; it was created when the user tried to alter or erase BATTLE.FIL. Therefore, setting a file or program to read/ only status not only prevents alteration, but provides you with information to show that someone has *attempted* to make a change.

The program or file is also protected from anyone intentionally or accidentally erasing it. An attempt to do so would result in a CRT display similar to that which appeared for illegal writing, namely,

```
Bdos Err on A: <filename> R/O
```

Naturally, the STAT.COM utility should *not* be included on the disk if one wishes to maintain this level of security. In order to erase the file or to make any change in it, someone authorized to use a disk with STAT.COM on it would be required to change its status as follows:

```
A> STAT <filename> $R/W <CR>
```

The computer would then acknowledge the requested change, and the following would appear on the screen:

```
<filename> set to R/W
```

PASSWORD CONTROL TO ACCESS THE SYSTEM AND/OR PROGRAMS

Several operating systems provide for the entry of user ID and/or password in order to access the system. If your operating system does not include user ID and/or password protection, it is possible to add this feature by using a version of the sample program, **PSWDPGM.BAS**, which is included at the end of the chapter. Or you may wish to use this sample program as a prototype to include at the beginning of those programs that you wish to secure. The security module included in a program would not only contain the names of authorized users of the data file or program, but also a series of individual questions and answers that only a particular authorized user would be able to answer correctly.

If you wish to use a version of PSWDPGM.BAS to limit access to the system, it is necessary to modify the operating system so that this program is called immediately after the system is IPLed. Once the user has entered his or her name and answered the questions, a system prompt will enable the program needed to be called. If you do this, it is also necessary to provide a routine linked to each program that would return to the password control program when any program is terminated. These are moderately simple procedures for anyone with a knowledge of assembly language.

Without assembly language, you can use this sample program as the first module in any program to which you want to limit access. It would then provide individual program security but would permit anyone to use the remaining programs of the system.

In this demonstration program, only a limited number of users and questions for each user is included. It is obvious that a longer list of users can be included and that the series of questions for each user can be much more complex. No attempt has been made here to encrypt this information; a more secure system would contain such information in encoded form. (Techniques and programs for encryption of data are covered in Chapter 12.)

In addition, this program illustrates the use of a *trap*, a technique used to provide evidence of attempted illegal use of the program. Upon entry of a name, the program searches for that name and the appropriate questions to ask the user. If an unauthorized name is used, or if the user is unable to answer any question correctly, the name that has been entered via the keyboard is immediately stored on the disk in a file called **SNOOPER.FIL**. Furthermore, the bell on the terminal is sounded for almost 5 seconds, and the following message appears on the CRT:

```
ACCESS TO FILE NOT AUTHORIZED

CALL SUPERVISOR TO RESUME PROCESSING
```

At this point the terminal is "locked" until the supervisor enters the password. If the user does IPL the system in an effort to circumvent the locked terminal, the disk will still have a telltale indicator that shows an illegal attempt has been made, since the name will have been entered into the snooper file, SNOOPER.FIL.

The snooper file can be checked periodically by the security supervisor to verify if any illegal attempts were made to enter the system. Even if an authorized name appears in that file, it would be obvious that a masquerading attempt has been made; that is, someone claimed the identity of an authorized user. If this is found, the supervisor would more closely observe individuals using the system. (A copy of the supervisor's program, **SNOOPCK.BAS**, is included at the end of this chapter.)

A Snooper Trap

PSWDPGM.BAS is designed for three authorized users: Tom Jones, Ted Brown, and Al Greene. Each user has a specific series of questions that must be answered in order to access the master file. After each question is answered by the user, the program clears the CRT so that any passerby would not be able to read what has just been entered. Screen echoing should be inhibited in systems where this is possible. This is possible by using the CBASIC compiler and modifying the program using the INKEY function.

The following is the procedure used by Tom Jones, an authorized user:

```
ENTER YOUR NAME     TOM JONES   <CR>

PASSWORD ...        WOW  <CR>

YOUR FATHER's MIDDLE NAME?
ENTER ANSWER        PATRICK  <CR>
```

```
YOUR MOTHER's MAIDEN NAME?
ENTER ANSWER          MARY SMITH   <CR>


NAME OF THE FILE IS ...          MASTER.FIL   <CR>
```

Only after entering his password, answering the two questions, and entering the name of the file properly would Tom Jones be able to use the program to access the master file.

ALERT AND ANALYZE TECHNIQUE FOR SECURITY

A variation of the program password technique can be used for software security, particularly for a small, select number of files for which added security is necessary. Using this method extensively would undoubtedly reduce and possibly even eliminate its effectiveness; it would be a case of "crying wolf" too often.

There are two elements in this procedure that can be prepared as a separate program module and added to the few files for which you wish to provide extra security.

1. The first element is the alert, or the ringing of the microcomputer's bell. This is a disturbing sound and attracts attention; an unauthorized user would hesitate to call this program unless there were no one else in the office.
2. The second element is a *protocol verification,* or procedure checking, module. The response to the questions by the computer to set up the program would be verified for entry style.

These two elements are incorporated in the program **FILEPRO.BAS**, included at the end of the chapter. The following two entry lines displayed on the CRT illustrate this concept:

```
NAME...              H. HIGHLAND   <CR>
ENTER TODAY'S DATE   1983/08/13   <CR>
```

In the first line, where the name is requested, the program would verify that (1) a period was used as the second character in the entry and (2) a single blank space was left after the period. Unless the individual running the program entered the first initial followed by a period and then skipped at least one space before starting the second name, the program would indicate that the user made an illegal attempt to access the file.

In the second line, the date, the program would verify whether the first four characters were the current year and the fifth character was a slash, /. Failure to enter the date or any user-selected key in this prescribed sequence would again indicate an illegal attempt to access the file.

Other similar protocols could be included in this security module. It is essential, however, that only a very limited number of individuals within the office be authorized to use such programs and that they do not reveal the special protocols required.

SECURITY USING CP/M PLUS

CP/M Plus or CP/M 3 offers several special security provisions. It should be noted, however, that password protection discussed in this section is available only in the banked version of CP/M 3, which requires at least 96K of RAM. The SET *command* is used for the various protection options.

Drive Protection: Using CP/M 3 drive, protection is obtained by the command:

```
A> SET B: [RO]   <CR>
```

This sets drive B to Read/Only, and it is not possible to

- copy any file onto the disk in the drive using the PIP command,
- delete a file from the disk with the ERASE command, or
- rename any file on the disk with the RENAME command.

To release the drive, it is necessary to enter the same command with RW in place of the RO, making the drive Read/Write instead of Read/Only.

Using a Label and Password to Protect a Disk: It is also possible to secure a disk by assigning a label to it and then assigning a password to the label. To do this it is first necessary to enter the "protect mode," assign the label, and then the password. The following procedure shows how to set up the protection mode, enter the label, PAYROLL.FIL, for the disk in drive B, and provide for the use of the password, PAYDAY, in order to access the disk.

```
A> SET B: [PROTECT=ON]        <CR>
A> SET B: [NAME=PAYROLL.FIL] <CR>
A> SET B: [PASSWORD=PAYDAY]   <CR>
```

Assigning Passwords to Files: An eight-character password can be used to protect any program or data file on a disk. This, too, requires the use of the SET command, as follows

```
A> SET FUNDS.FIL [PASSWORD=OURMONEY]   <CR>
```

This command would require the user to enter the password, OURMONEY, in order to gain access to the file, FUNDS.FIL.

Protection Mode for Secured Files: Under CP/M 3 there are three modes of protection for a program and/or a data file that provide for protection by password. They are somewhat similar to the R/O option under earlier versions of CP/M. The table summarizes the level of protection of each of the modes.

		Password is Required to:			
PROTECTION MODE	READ	COPY	WRITE	DELETE	RENAME
READ	X	X	X	X	X
WRITE			X	X	X
DELETE				X	X

In the READ mode, a password is required to read, copy, write, delete, or rename the file. In the WRITE mode, no password is required to either read or copy but is needed for everything else. In the DELETE mode, the password is required to delete or rename the file. The protection mode is created by:

```
A> SET TAX.FIL [PASSWORD=MPC1600, PROTECT=WRITE]   <CR>
```

This instruction would require anyone interested in writing, deleting, or renaming the file, TAX.FIL, to enter the password, MPC1600. It is not necessary to enter a password to read or copy the file. Note that PROTECT is used for the READ, WRITE, and DELETE modes.

Time Stamping for Security: Another security measure that is available under CP/M 3 is time and date stamping. Time and date can be automatically set by the computer for each program and/or data file for:

- *create*, which indicates when the file was created,
- *access*, indicating the time and date the file was last accessed, and
- *update*, indicating the time and date of the last modification.

Only two sets of terms and dates can be stored in the disk directory, *either* the create or access and the update. From a security viewpoint, it is best to maintain the access and update times and date. This would permit the supervisor to use the DIR command to obtain a report on the last time the file was used and whether any changes were made.

   Again, the SET command is used to obtain this security function; for example:

```
A> SET [ACCESS=ON,UPDATE=ON]   <CR>
```

would have the system automatically enter the date and time any file on the disk was accessed and/or modified.

USING PASSWORDS TO PREVENT FILE ACCESS AND/OR PRINTING

It is possible to provide even greater security to protect data files from being accessed illegally, to avoid illegal transfer of data files from disk storage to other computers over transmission lines, and even to prevent hard-copy printing of programs and data files. Sufficiently advanced technology exists today to provide such protection for microcomputer systems, and the means of protection can be cost effective for sensitive data.

Two devices, both peripheral units, are available to provide this extra layer of security. Although they are available as standard peripherals, they are easily modified by the manufacturer for a small fee to require passwords in order to access the units. This control is achieved through the use of specially prepared EPROMs, which are substituted for ROMs within the device.

One, DataMate II, is a versatile store, edit, and transmit device. It can be used to collect data from several key-to-disk workstations and to store, edit, and transmit data rapidly in order to save telephone and computer time and storage charges. The unit stores up to 328,000 characters, provides fast random access to files, and has a built-in text editor.

A four-letter password may be required with a special option built into the system. Unless the proper password is entered, it would be impossible to obtain any data from the system.

Another device that provides an added layer of security is a spooler, SooperSpooler, which is available in modified form to require the use of a password in order to obtain hard-copy printouts. With this unit in series

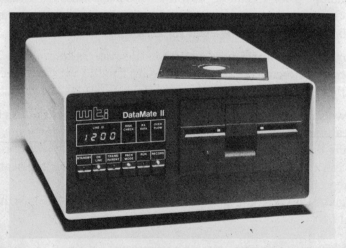

FIGURE 29

Access to DataMate II's disk requires a special password in addition to that required by the microcomputer's operating system and/or the program. (Courtesy of Western Telematic, Inc.)

between the CPU and printer, it would be necessary for a user to enter a password in order to obtain a printed copy. Although the main function of spooling programs and spooler hardware is to free the computer for use during the printing of large amounts of copy, this one can also be modified to provide one more level of protection.

The final hardware unit is a special board that can be added to the 16-bit IBM Personal Computer (PC) and look-alike units, such as the MPC by Columbia Data Products. **The PC Lock** by MPPi, Ltd., is equipped with reprogrammable EPROM and interacts with the operating system to require a sign-on password before anyone can access the system. In addition, the board provides the microcomputer with a serial ID, making it possible to identify the interface unit if the microcomputer is used in a network.

USE OF INTERMEDIATE/COMPILED PROGRAMS

Storing a copy of a sensitive source program on a disk or system available to several users is not recommended from a security viewpoint. Even if the source program has been placed under Read/Only protect status, it is still available to anyone on the system to see, read, and even copy by hand. With some operating systems or specially designed programs it is necessary to use a password to gain access to a specific program. Yet even this does not provide total security.

An extra layer of protection is available with a number of the computer language compilers that can be run on microcomputer systems. These compilers produce intermediate code or direct machine-executable code. The two examined here are Digital Research's CBASIC family and Microsoft's BASIC.

The CBASIC family is available for both 8-bit and 16-bit microcomputers and comes in two "forms." The first form, **CBASIC**, has two main components: a compiler and a run-time interpreter. The compiler translates

FIGURE 30

In addition to providing a buffer to release the microcomputer during the printing task, SooperSpooler can also require password entry to control printing output. (Courtesy of Consolink Corporation.)

SOURCE PROGRAMS AND OBJECT PROGRAMS

A brief explanation of program terminology may be required for some readers at this point.

> A *source program* is one written in a computer language, such as BASIC, COBOL, PL/I, FORTRAN, or FORTH.
>
> An *object program* is one that has been translated into a code readable by the computer's microprocessor.

There are three ways in which BASIC programs are translated and executed by a microcomputer:

1. There are compilers that require that the source program be present on a disk, and these programs are translated each time the user wishes to execute the program.
2. There are compilers that translate the source program into intermediate code, .INT files. It is necessary for both the .INT file and a run-time interpreter to be on the disk(s), but *not* the source program. The run-time interpreter executes the .INT file.
3. There are compilers that translate source programs into an intermediate file, which is then linked with the compiler's library to produce object files that can be executed directly by entering the filename, just as one does with system's .COM or .CMD files. No run-time interpreter or source program need be on the disk.

the source program, which must be in a .BAS file, into intermediate code, an .INT file. The intermediate file can be stored on a disk without the source program. In this form it is not readable by the user. The run-time interpreter is used to execute the .INT file the compiler has generated. Storing only the .INT file and the run-time interpreter, CRUN2 or CRUN238, on a disk prevents anyone from gaining access to the source program. The .INT program cannot be modified.

The second form of the CBASIC family is the **CBASIC Compiler**, CB-80 for 8-bit microcomputers and CB-86 for 16-bit microcomputers. The compiler translates the BASIC source program into machine-executable instructions. That is, the compiler takes as input a .BAS, or user-written program, and produces an .OBJ, or machine-level object program. Some compilers do this directly, but the CBASIC Compiler uses a link editor and a library in the translation of the original user program. This not only enables the user to utilize the computer's memory more efficiently, but also to produce an executable program that can be stored in nonreadable form for a human being.

Microsoft's BASIC Compiler affords a similar level of user program protection. Its **BASIC-80** compiler is also a two-pass operation. In the first pass, a .REL, or relocatable object file, is created by the compiler. This relocatable file is then linked with the library module to form a .COM, or command file, which is directly executable by the computer. Storing the .COM file on a disk without the source listing provides the user with top security, since the .COM file cannot be read or altered by the user.

To secure the source program and the .COM file it is necessary to use BASIC-80's SAVE command with a *protection* option, which saves the file in an encoded binary form. An attempt to read the source program under any edit routine would only find the symbol, >, in the file. Using any debugging utility to obtain a hexadecimal and ASCII output of the object program would reveal that this section had been *encrypted*.

> **Note:** Most quality compilers incorporate some special utility programs to provide for the security of an object program. As a fundamental security measure, do *not* store any source program on a disk in use unless it has been secured by one or more of the methods recommended. An unsecured copy of the source program may be stored in a secure location. Those BASIC interpreters/compilers that do not enable you to produce and store the object program leave your system exceedingly vulnerable.

USING A DATABASE PACKAGE TO PROVIDE ADDED SECURITY

An additional layer of protection in any microcomputer system is the use of a database package to integrate related programs and data files. These can be obtained from many commercial sources, as well as written in-house by an experienced programmer. Dynamic Microprocessor Associates' package, **The Formula**, is used as an example of what is available from a security viewpoint. It should be noted that this is an interactive package; that is, the user has the ability to embed various security elements when selecting the different components of the package to be used.

With this database package, the CBS (configurable business system) password security system can be used to restrict access to an application system and/or any menu options (list of programs) therein. The user of any program is required to enter a password that may be different from that used to access the system in order to reach the program. The characters of the password with this package are not echoed during their entry.

After checking that the password is valid and the user has also entered a valid user number, the user will be "logged on"; a complete record of user name, date, and entry and exit times is maintained by the package. Not only will the user go through this procedure to access the menu of available programs, but the CBS security module can also be used with each of the programs listed on the menu.

It is possible, therefore, to verify password and user number to (1) gain access to the system, (2) call the program and display the menu or list of options available in the program, (3) execute any of the options, and (4) permit the use of any data file.

Unlike many more abbreviated versions, **The Formula**, permits the use of a password of up to six alphameric characters, including

- the 26 letters of the alphabet, A through Z,
- all 10 digits, 0 through 9, and
- 4 special characters (period, comma, hyphen, and space).

Using any of the 40 characters in passwords of up to six characters permits the system to employ any of over 250 million unique possible passwords. When one considers that four levels of password control can be activated when creating the database, it is obvious that the several layers of password control can definitely impede illegal penetration, provided that password rules, as noted in Chapter 9, are followed.

A LIBRARY PACKAGE FOR ADDED SECURITY

A disk file library package is designed primarily to reduce the amount of space required to hold individual files on a disk through the use of special compacting algorithms. Although these packages are designed to provide the user with greater control over file handling and to make more efficient use of storage space on the disk, they also provide one or more levels of security. **MicroLIB** by Advanced Micro Techniques, for example, provides three levels of security:

1. password protection of any user-selected program or data file, or the entire library package that has been given a user-defined name,
2. encryption of any program or data file, and
3. date stamping, indicating the last time the program or data file was processed.

These security measures are fringe benefits, since a disk file librarian performs many additional functions that are not attainable by using an operating system itself. This package uses ten menu-driven routines that are easy to use because of the prompt questions. For example, when creating a library, a collection of individual files, the user is given several security options.

The user may elect to enter a description and/or related value (keyword) for each file when it is entered into the library. The entire library may be protected by a password, which must be an alphabetic string up to eight characters. Another option is the use of different passwords for each file. It is also possible to encrypt a file, but only if password protection is used.

Afterwards, as each program or data file is added to the particular library, the user includes, in addition to the filename, its description, the

```
MicroLIB.      Version: 1.20        Series No: GAMMA13
-------------------------------------------------------------------
Function = DISP         Library = C:DAYFUNDS.LIB    Select = ????????.???
Options  = LIBRARY
-------------------------------------------------------------------

  FILENAME    RELATED  ATR        DESCRIPTION      LAST ACC   ACC   SIZE
------------  -------  ---  -------------------------  ---------  ---  ----
CBAS2         Compiler  I   Digital Research 2.8      Dec  5,82   1     24
CRUNS         Compiler  I   Digital Research 2.8      Dec  5,82   1     20
DEDICATE/32   Encypt    E   Version 2.0 PKS          Dec  5,82   2      8
FILEFIX       Verify    S   Diagnostic analysis      Dec  5,82   1      6
DISK DOCTOR   Salvage   S   Damage control           Dec  5,82   1     14
OKARA         Copy      S   PHOTO.COM                Dec  5,82   3      4
EDIT.COM      Text:ed   I   Peachtree Text Editor:1  Dec  5,82   1     16
PRINT.COM     Printer   I   Peachtree Text Editor:2  Dec  5,82   1     20
H007.INT      Encrypt   E   Highland + Highland 1.3  Dec  5,82   2      4
E007.INT      Decrypt   E   Highland + Highland 1.7  Dec  5,82   1      4
CREATE.INT    ISFile    S   Funds file starter       Dec  5,82   1      4
LOOKUP.INT    Seek      S   Search procedures        Dec  5,82   2     12
JOIN.INT      Merge     E   Merge/Update procedure   Dec  5,82   1      8
FUNDS.FIL     Info      E   Financial data           Dec  5,82   1     36
```

FIGURE 31

Printout of a program library created under MicroLIB program. A special library provides for password control to access the library as well as passwords to control individual programs and data files.

file password, and other related data. The directory command of the menu is used to produce a display of any library. An illustration of such an output is DAYFUNDS.LIB, shown in Figure 31. The output contains a listing by filename and the following additional information about each file:

- *Related:* This field has been used for file classification for quick identification.
- *Attribute:* The file's attribute can be any of the following:
  I notes that the file is in use for updating or other use.
  S indicates that the file is password protected.
  E denotes that the file has been encrypted, as well as being password secured.
- *Description:* Only the first 25 characters of the description, which may be as long as 50 characters, are displayed in the directory printout.
- *Latest access:* This diplays the last date that the program in the library was accessed or placed in the library.
- *Accesses:* Indicates the number of times the individual file has been used and replaced in the library.
- *Size:* Numeric value indicates the size of the file in the number of 128-byte blocks.

DATA COMPRESSION TECHNIQUES FOR FILE SECURITY

Data compression techniques can be used not only for security purposes but also to reduce the storage requirements of programs and data files. *Data compression,* or *file packing,* is the process of removing blank spaces and/or zeros without losing any information. Because of the way in which the machine manipulates data, there are additional zeros and/or blanks in normally stored numeric and/or alphabetic data. The direct cost of storing files is the cost for the storage media; compacted files require less space, and more programs and the data files can be placed on either a floppy disk or hard disk. The indirect cost, measured in time, is that of transferring data when making backup copies.

There are various data compression methods in use. The simplest is *null suppression.* This technique encompasses those methods that suppress zeros, blanks, or both. This type of compression could be called the de facto standard method. It takes advantage of the prevalence of blanks and zeros in data files and programs and is easy and economical to implement. Null suppression may not, however, achieve as high a degree-of-compression ratio as some other techniques. An example of null suppression with zeros and blanks (b) is shown below:

DATA	SYMBOLS STORED
Original	A1000000XB250000000Nbbbbbbbbbbbb COST
Compressed	A1#6XB25#7N%9COST

A pound sign (#) is used to indicate zeros; for example, #6 indicates that six zeros have been deleted. A percentage sign (%) is used to indicate blanks; for example, %9 indicates that there were nine blanks in the original data.

This null suppression, or run length, technique is a primitive form of a class of techniques known as pattern substitution, in which codes are substituted for specific character patterns. When data files contain repeating patterns, such as illustrated below, a more sophisticated data compression method, *pattern substitution,* may be used.

Original data:

```
AW10004MFQ00000F320006BCX4
AW20000DBF00000F300000BCX1
AW30002RBA00000F301214BCX7
```

Pattern table:

```
AW       = #
000      = $
00000F3  = %
BCX      = *
```

Compressed data:

```
#1$4MFQ%2$6*4
#2$0DBF%$00*1
#3$2RBA%01214*7
```

There are numerous other methods of data compression, such as *Huffman codes, Ling and Palermo,* or *Schuegraf and Heaps*. These are much more complex but highly efficient.

Two programs suitable for 8-bit microcomputers, **SQ.COM** and **USQ.COM**, developed by Richard Greenlaw, are available to any user as part of a wealth of programs in the public domain, operating under CP/M, at a slight cost from the CP/M Users Group. Using this compression program, it is possible to squeeze any program, but the efficiency rate varies depending upon the type of file. For example,

- With source programs, <filename>.**BAS**, the compression rate may vary between 40% and 45%.
- With assembly language files, <filename>.**ASM**, the typical compression rate is about 33%.
- With intermediate files, <filename>.**INT**, I have found the compression rate to be about 15%.
- With <filename>.**COM**, the compression rate is only about 6%. For storage savings it is probably not worth the time needed to compress and decompress the file, but the security factor is still valuable.

Below is an example of how to compress a source program using **SQ.COM**:

```
A> SQ <filename>.BAS  <CR>
File squeezer version 1.3  06/15/81 by
        Richard Greenlaw
        251 Colony Ct.
        Gahanna, Ohio 43230
Accepts redirection and pipes.

 <filename>.BAS  ->
        <filename>.BQS analyzing, squeezing, done.
A>
```

Note that a new version of the original program has been created with the identifier of .**BQS**, showing that the program has been squeezed. Any attempt to read the file under an editor, and I tried eight that I possess, results in a message that the file contains nontext characters and cannot be printed or read. To complete the security procedure, the original

<filename>.BAS file would be erased. The source file is now secure *unless* a user has the unsqueeze program, which should not be stored on the same disk as the .BQS program.

To use a squeezed or compressed program, it is necessary to use an unsqueeze program, as shown below:

```
A> USQ   <filename>.BQS   <CR>
File unsqueezer version 1.4  07/03/81 by
          Richard Greenlaw
          251 Colony Ct.
          Gahanna, Ohio 43230
Accepts redirection and pipes.

<filename>.BQS  ->  <filename>.BAS
A>
```

It is possible to have the unsqueezed version of a program on a disk in disk drive A and obtain a squeezed version on the disk in disk drive B by entering the command:

```
A> SQ B: A:<filename>.BAS   <CR>
```

which would result in filename>.BQS being placed on the disk in drive B. Similarly, when you are ready to use the program on drive B, you can enter a disk in drive A with the unsqueeze program and write the unsqueezed version on the disk in drive B, as follows

```
A> USQ B:   B:<filename>.BQS   <CR>
```

which would produce <filename>.BAS on the disk in drive B. After execution of the program, the .BAS file can be erased, or "clobbered," as shown in Chapter 13.

For 16-bit microcomputers Starside Engineering's **COMPRESS** by Jeff Duntemann provides the same utility functions as the squeeze and unsqueeze programs described for the 8-bit units. Using Huffman encoding techniques, this assembly language program reduces the typical file by about 40%. The program operates under PC-DOS as well as MS-DOS and requires at least 48K of memory.

Assuming we have a file, SAMPLE.TXT, we can compress that file using the COMPRESS package as follows:

```
A:COMPRESS SAMPLE.TXT  <CR>

File Compression Utility Version 2.5  08/4/82
PC Version Copyright 1982 MSZachmann
```

```
Compressing SAMPLE.TXT
                    .analysis. .compression. finished.
Compressed file is: SAMPLE.TQT
```

After the program signs on the CRT it notifies you that (1) it is analyzing the text using the Huffman algorithm, (2) performing the compression, and (3) indicates when it has completed the compression. It then prints the name of the compressed file.

To restore the file, SAMPLE.TQT, to readable form, you can unsqueeze the file as shown below:

```
A:DCOMPRES SAMPLE.TQT  <CR>
```

```
File de-compressor Version 2.5  08/4/82
PC Version Copyright 1982 MSZachmann
```

```
DeCOMPRESSing SAMPLE.TQT.
Target filename is SAMPLE.TXT.
```

Like the SQ.COM and USQ.COM programs for the 8-bit machines, the COMPRESS package permits the user to assign the files to different disks. Therefore, if SAMPLE.TXT is on disk A and you wish to place the compressed file on disk B, the following command would be entered:

```
A: COMPRESS  B:  A:SAMPLE.TXT  <CR>
```

Note that the output drive is given before the source drive and filename. Also it is possible to direct the computer to print the compressed file without writing the decompressed file on the disk by entering:

```
A: DCOMPRES > PRN: SAMPLE.TQT <CR>
```

SELF-DESTRUCTION OF PROGRAM IF ALTERED

It is possible for an experienced programmer to incorporate special modules in a program that would destroy the program if an attempt is made to modify any part of it. Both **SECURITY.ASM** by Keith Peterson and Bob Mathias, and Kelly Smith's **BANZAI.ASM** are examples of such modules.

These are assembly language programs that are linked with a program in another language. These are only two of several such programs available and are in the public domain. Any attempt to modify a protected program will scramble the file on the disk so that it is unreadable and unusable. Also, any portion of the program in the microcomputer's memory is made useless.

REMOVAL OF SUBPROGRAMS SUCH AS ERASE OR RENAME FROM THE DISK

As noted earlier in Chapter 6 under the discussion of "Elements of the Operating System," there are powerful subprograms in the Console Command Processor—**COPYSYS** under CP/M 3 or **SYSGEN** under earlier versions of CP/M. **ERA** permits a user to erase any program or data file on a disk; **REN** enables a user to rename a file. The **DIR** subprogram permits the listing of all programs on the disk. These are "dangerous to the security" of any system.

A disgruntled employee can destroy programs and data files, or someone can playfully change the names of the programs and files. It is strongly recommended that these subprograms *not* be included on the disk used in a multiuser environment. Any erasing or renaming of programs should be done only by an authorized supervisor. Similarly, to keep individuals from browsing through the directory, even this function might be excluded.

It is possible to remove these subprograms or modify their names so that they are different from those normally used under CP/M and would not be recognized by unauthorized personnel. (How to do this is explained in Chapter 11.)

ENCRYPTION AS A SECURITY TOOL

Encryption is a technique to protect valuable programs and data files by making them unintelligible to anyone who is not authorized to decrypt the data. *Cryptography* embraces the entire field of secret writing, including both *cipher* and *code*. The term *cipher* implies a method of secret writing whereby any message or readable material, called *plaintext*, is altered by any given method into a *ciphertext*, which is not normally readable. An explanation of cipher techniques and examples of several programs are included in Chapter 12.

```
REM     ***********************************************************************
REM
REM     PROGRAM:   PSWDPGM.BAS            FILE: MASTER.FIL
REM
REM     PURPOSE:   PASSWORD CONTROL TO USE PROGRAM
REM
REM                NAME OF ANY UNAUTHORIZED USER PLACED IN A SPECIAL
REM                FILE, "SNOOPER.FIL," WHICH MAY BE EXAMINED BY THE
REM                SUPERVISOR USING PROGRAM - "SNOOPCK.BAS"
REM
REM     PROGRAMMED IN CBASIC BY ESTHER H. HIGHLAND
REM                PROGRAMMED:        SEPTEMBER 15, 1982
REM                LATEST UPDATE:     SEPTEMBER 25, 1982
REM             *  COPYRIGHT 1982, HIGHLAND + HIGHLAND   *
REM
REM     ***********************************************************************
```

```
        REM
        REM                         HOUSEKEEPING SECTION
        REM
        REM ****************************************************************
        REM
        CLEAR$ = CHR$(126) + CHR$(28)
        BELL$  = CHR$(7)
        PRINT CLEAR$
        REM
        REM ****************************************************************
        REM
        REM      INPUT NAME / VERIFICATION AGAINST CONTROL LIST IN PROGRAM;
        REM      LOOP GOES TO NUMBER OF NAMES GIVEN ACCESS; INDEX FOR J%
        REM      MUST BE CHANGED TO CONFORM WITH NUMBER OF NAMES IN LIST.
        REM      IF NAME IS NOT AUTHORIZED, SNOOPER PROCEDURE IS INITIATED
        REM
        REM ****************************************************************
        REM
        INPUT "ENTER YOUR NAME  "; YNAME$
        FOR J% = 1 TO 3
                READ ACLN$, PW$, Q1$, A1$, Q2$, A2$
                IF UCASE$ (YNAME$) = ACLN$ THEN 10
        NEXT J%: GOTO 70
        REM
        REM ****************************************************************
        REM
        REM      PASS THROUGH AUTHENTICATION PROCEDURE FOR EACH AUTHORIZED
        REM      PERSON PERMITTED TO USE THE PROGRAM.   FAILURE TO ANSWER
        REM      ANY QUESTION CORRECTLY INITIATES SNOOPER PROCEDURE.
        REM
        REM ****************************************************************
        REM
10      PRINT:   INPUT "PASSWORD ... "; YPW$:     PRINT CLEAR$
        IF UCASE$ (YPW$) <> PW$ THEN 70
        PRINT Q1$: PRINT: INPUT "ENTER ANSWER "; YA1$: PRINT CLEAR$
        IF UCASE$ (YA1$) <> A1$ THEN 70
        PRINT Q2$: PRINT: INPUT "ENTER ANSWER "; YA2$: PRINT CLEAR$
        IF UCASE$ (YA2$) <> A2$ THEN 70
        REM
        REM ****************************************************************
        REM
        REM      OPENING OF FILE AND PERMISSION TO SEARCH IF AUTHORIZED.
        REM      CONTROL STATEMENTS TO READ A FILE.   NOTE CHANGE FILE
        REM      NAME AND CODING TO MEET YOUR OWN NEEDS.
        REM
        REM ****************************************************************
        REM
        PRINT:   INPUT "NAME OF FILE IS ...........";NOF$
        IF NOF$ <> "B:MASTER.FIL" THEN 70
        OPEN NOF$ RECL 128 AS 1
        READ #1, 1; INDEX%
20      PRINT CLEAR$
        INPUT "CUSTOMER NAME IS .......... ";CNAME$:     J% = 0
        FOR K% = 2 TO INDEX%
            READ #1, K%; NAME$,AMT,CHEK$,INV$,DATE$,CLN$
                IF NAME$ <> CNAME$ THEN 30
            PRINT NAME$; TAB(25);AMT; TAB(37);CHEK$; TAB(50);INV$;\
                TAB(60);DATE$; TAB(70);CLN$

                PRINT: INPUT "CONTINUE SEARCH? ...(Y/N) .... ";ÀN$
                IF AN$ = "N" THEN 50
                PRINT: J%= J% + 1
30      NEXT K%
        IF J% <> 0 THEN 40
        PRINT
        INPUT "NAME NOT FOUND / PRESS ANY LETTER TO CONTINUE  ";H$
        GOTO 50
40      PRINT
        INPUT "SEARCH COMPLETE / PRESS ANY LETTER TO CONTINUE ";H$
50      PRINT: INPUT "ANOTHER SEARCH? ... (Y/N) .... ";AN$
        IF AN$ = "Y" THEN 20
        CLOSE 1: GOTO 100
```

```
         REM
         REM  *******************************************************************
         REM
         REM       END OF DEMENSTRATION PROGRAM FOR READING SAMPLE FILE
         REM
         REM       PROCEDURE TO OPEN OR ADD TO "SNOOPER.FIL" IF UNAUTHORIZED
         REM       NAME IS ENTERED AT BEGINNING OF THIS SCREENING PROGRAM.
         REM
         REM  *******************************************************************
         REM
70       IF END # 2 THEN 72
         OPEN "SNOOPER.FIL" AS 2:   GOTO 74
72       CREATE "SNOOPER.FIL" AS 2:   GOTO 90
74       IF END # 2 THEN 90
80       READ # 2;  ZNAME$:   GOTO 80
90       PRINT # 2; YNAME$:   CLOSE 2
         REM
         REM  *******************************************************************
         REM
         REM       ALARM BELL IS SOUNDED AND PROGRAM IS "LOCKED" UNTIL IT IS
         REM       RELEASED BY SUPERVISOR ENTERING AUTHORIZED CODE.   ANY
         REM       ATTEMPT TO ENTER ILLEGAL CLEAR CODE WILL CAUSE ALARM BELL
         REM       TO BE SOUNDED AGAIN AND PROGRAM WILL NOT CONTINUE.
         REM
         REM  *******************************************************************
         REM
95       PRINT: FOR K = 1 TO 500
                 PRINT BELL$
         NEXT K
         PRINT "ACESS TO FILE NOT AUTHORIZED": PRINT
         INPUT "CALL SUPERVISOR TO RESUME PROCESSING "; H$
         REM
         REM       SUPERVISOR'S PASSWORD FOR DEMO = ALLEN O'BRIEN LARKIN
         REM
         IF UCASE$ (H$) = "ALLEN O'BRIEN LARKIN" THEN 100
         GOTO 95
         REM
         REM  *******************************************************************
         REM
         REM       IT IS NECESSARY TO ENTER THREE DATA LINES EACH WITH TWO
         REM       FIELDS FOR EACH EMPLOYEE AUTHORIZED TO USE THE PROGRAM:
         REM       DATA LINE #1: EMPLOYEE NAME, PASSWORD
         REM       DATA LINE #2: QUESTION ONE AND ANSWER TO QUESTION ONE
         REM       DATA LINE #3: QUESTION TWO AND ANSWER TO QUESTION TWO
         REM
         REM  *******************************************************************
         REM
         DATA "TOM JONES", "WOW"
         DATA "YOUR FATHER'S MIDDLE NAME?  ", "PATRICK"
         DATA "YOUR MOTHER'S MAIDEN NAME?  ", "MARY SMITH"
         DATA "TED BROWN", "NYET"
         DATA "HOW TALL ARE YOU  ", "5-11"
         DATA "WHAT FOREIGN LANGUAGE DO YOU SPEAK?  ", "RUSSIAN"
         DATA "AL GREENE", "IAM007"
         DATA "NAME YOUR ALMA MATER  ", "DROPOUT U"
         DATA "WHAT WAS YOUR LAST ARMY RANK?  ", "PRIVATE"
         REM
         REM  *******************************************************************
         REM
         REM       TERMINATION OF PROGRAM
         REM
         REM  *******************************************************************
         REM
100      PRINT:  PRINT "NORMAL TERMINATION OF PROGRAM"
         END
```

```
REM
REM
REM      PROGRAM: SNOOPCK.BAS                    FILE: SNOOPER.FIL
REM
REM      PURPOSE: TO SEARCH FOR POSSIBLE UNAUTHORIZED USERS WHO
REM               HAVE ATTEMPTED TO USE THE PSWDPGM.BAS PROGRAM
REM
REM      PROGRAMMED IN CBASIC BY ESTHER HARRIS HIGHLAND
REM               PROGRAMMED:        SEPTEMBER 16, 1982
REM               LATEST UPDATE:     SEPTEMBER 25, 1982
REM           *  COPYRIGHT 1982,  HIGHLAND + HIGHLAND   *
REM
REM      ****************************************************************
REM
REM
REM                       HOUSEKEEPING SECTION
REM
REM      ****************************************************************
REM

         CLEAR$ = CHR$(126) + CHR$(28)
         PRINT CLEAR$
REM
REM      ****************************************************************
REM
REM               INPUT OF SUPERVISOR'S PASSWORD
REM        "ALLEN O'BRIEN LARKIN" USED ONLY FOR DEMONSTRATION
REM
REM      ****************************************************************
REM
         INPUT "ENTER YOUR PASSWORD ";PW$
         PRINT CLEAR$
         IF UCASE$ (PW$) <> "ALLEN O'BRIEN LARKIN" THEN 200
REM
REM      ****************************************************************
REM
REM         OPEN SNOOPER.FIL / PRINT ITS CONTENTS.   IF NO ILLEGAL
REM        ATTEMPT HAS BEEN MADE "NO FILE FOUND" WILL BE PRINTED.
REM
REM      ****************************************************************
REM
         IF END # 1 THEN 210
         OPEN "SNOOPER.FIL" AS 1
         IF END # 1 THEN 220
100      READ # 1; NAME$
         PRINT NAME$
         GOTO 100
200      PRINT:   PRINT "ACCESS NOT AUTHORIZED"
         GOTO 230
210      PRINT:   PRINT "FILE NOT FOUND"
         GOTO 230
220      PRINT:   PRINT "END OF FILE"
REM
REM      ****************************************************************
REM
REM        PROCEDURE TO HOLD OUTPUT ON SCREEN UNTIL TERMINATION
REM
REM      ****************************************************************
REM
230      PRINT:   INPUT "PRESS ANY LETTER TO CONTINUE "; H$
         PRINT:   PRINT "NORMAL TERMINATION OF PROGRAM"
         END
```

```
REM      ****************************************************************
REM
REM      PROGRAM:   FILEPRO.BAS
REM
REM      PURPOSE:   TO ILLUSTRATE PROTECTION BY SPECIAL ENTRY OF
REM                 USER NAME AND FILE NAME ID
REM
REM      PROGRAMMED IN CBASIC BY DR. HAROLD JOSEPH HIGHLAND
REM                 PROGRAMMED:       SEPTEMBER 12,1982
REM                 LATEST UPDATE:    SEPTEMBER 19,1982
REM                * COPYRIGHT 1982  HIGHLAND + HIGHLAND *
REM
REM      ****************************************************************
REM
REM                   HOUSEKEEPING AND ENTRY OF NAME
REM
REM      ****************************************************************
REM
10       CLEAR$ = CHR$(126) + CHR$(28)
         BELL$  = CHR$(7)
         PRINT CLEAR$
         INPUT "ENTER YOUR NAME ......... "; YN$
REM
REM      ****************************************************************
REM
REM        CHECK TO SEE IF PERIOD [.] IS USED AS SECOND CHARACTER
REM
REM      ****************************************************************
REM
         CHK1$ = MID$ (YN$, 2, 1)
         IF CHK1$ <> "." THEN 99
         CHK2$ = MID$ (YN$, 3, 1)
         IF CHK2$ <> " " THEN 99
         PRINT: INPUT "FILE NAME ID IS .... "; FIN$
REM
REM      ****************************************************************
REM
REM          CHECK TO SEE THAT FILE ID BEGINS WITH "1983/"
REM
REM      ****************************************************************
REM
         CHK3$ = MID$ (FIN$, 1, 5)
         IF CHK3$ <> "1983/" THEN 99
REM
REM      ****************************************************************
REM
REM                    TERMINATION OF PROGRAM
REM
REM      ****************************************************************
REM
         PRINT: PRINT
         PRINT "LEGAL ENTRANCE GAINED TO FILE":      PRINT
         GOTO 100
99       PRINT BELL$: PRINT BELL$: PRINT BELL$: PRINT BELL$
         PRINT CLEAR$
         PRINT: PRINT BELL$: PRINT: PRINT BELL$: PRINT
         PRINT "   ILLEGAL ATTEMPT TO ENTER THE FILE"
         PRINT BELL$: PRINT BELL$: PRINT BELL$: PRINT BELL$
         PRINT
100      INPUT "WISH TO TRY AGAIN? .... (Y/N) ...  "; A$
         IF A$ = "Y" THEN 10
         PRINT:   PRINT "PROGRAM FILEPRO HAS BEEN TERMINATED"
         END
```

CHAPTER 11

How to Create a Special CP/M Operating Disk for Security

One way to provide security in a multiuser environment is to prepare disks that prevent any user from

- erasing any file from the prepared disk accidentally or intentionally,
- renaming any file on that disk, and
- obtaining a directory of the programs on the disk.

This can be accomplished by creating a *special disk operating system* and modifying the existing operating system used in your microcomputer. In order to demonstrate the procedural technique, we have used CP/M 2.2, which is widely used in business systems. An alternative method of achieving the same results using **OKARA**, a commercial package, is also explained.

When I first considered this phase of microcomputer security, I asked dealers who specialize in microcomputers to prepare such a disk for my use. In one case the dealer indicated that it would require a whole day to prepare the special disk and that the cost would be about $300. In another case I was told that this preparation would require the writing of several special assembly language programs that might not really do the job, or that it might be impossible to do. Another dealer told me to read the manual since it is there in "black and white," and that anyone with some sense could do the job. When pressed, he indicated that it might cost about $50.

Even if you have little experience with computing, you can follow these directions to produce the appropriate operating system for this level of security. As long as you have a backup copy of your CP/M disk, the damage you may do is *only* to the program in memory and possibly to the program on the disk. There is only a remote possibility that you will damage the disk itself, and you won't be able to damage the computer hardware. As long as you have a backup disk, you have not damaged or destroyed the original CP/M. If you have any doubts or hesitancy, you can have either your dealer or any person who has programmed a microcomputer follow this procedure or *algorithm*, but before you do, try it yourself. A similar technique can be used with PC-DOS, MS-DOS, and CP/M-86.

USING CP/M TO CREATE A SPECIAL SUBPROGRAM DISK

Phase One: Making a Backup Disk

- Take a blank disk that has been formatted and to which SYSGEN (as noted earlier in Chapter 6) has been added, and place it in disk drive B.
- Place the single-density CP/M disk, which was part of the package you received with your microcomputer system, in disk drive A.

NOTE: Be sure that you use the *single-density* disk since in some systems the double-density disk will cause an operating error later in this procedure.

- Copy the entire disk in drive A to drive B by using the PIP command:

```
PIP B:=A:*.* [V]   <CR>
```

NOTE: We will use <CR> throughout this section to indicate a carriage return; all type that is underlined is entered via the terminal. All other printing (not underlined) is produced by the microcomputer itself and appears on the screen.

- Once you have made a duplicate copy of the disk, remove the disk from drive B and store it with your source disks. Keep the other disk with the original CP/M in drive A.

Phase Two: Saving the Operating System in Memory

- At this point, obtain a directory or listing of all the programs on this disk by:

```
A> DIR   <CR>
```

This will produce a complete listing of the CP/M disk. One of the programs in the list will be called **MOVCPM.COM**.

NOTE: If at any stage you find that you have made an error, it is best to restart the procedure from the second step. It is possible to recover from certain errors, but that would involve too technical an explanation.

- Now, move that program into the computer's memory by entering from the console the following command after the prompt A> appears on the screen:

```
A>MOVCPM * * <CR>
```

The MOVCPM command, were it not followed by operands, such as the asterisks, would construct a maximum-size operating system and would execute it immediately. By following the command with space * space *, the computer is notified to prepare a maximum-size CP/M, store it in its memory, and wait for further instructions.
- In a short time the microcomputer will respond with the following on the CRT screen:

```
CONSTRUCTING 64k CP/M vers 2.2
READY FOR "SYSGEN" OR
"SAVE 34 CPM64.COM"
```

- Since our objective is to modify the CP/M to remove certain built-in program modules, we want the computer to save the CP/M, and we respond with

```
A>SAVE 34 CPM64.COM <CR>
```

- The program is now stored in the computer's memory under the name "CPM64.COM" and occupies 34 "pages" within the memory.

Phase Three: Locating the Modules to Be Modified

- We are now ready to remove those program modules that we do not wish to have on the new disk. These may include ERA (Erase), REN (Rename), and DIR (directory), or any combination of these functions. It is also possible to delete the program modules, SAVE (save copy) and TYPE (output to a printer), but the elimination of these modules is not recommended.
- The DDT program, which is part of CP/M, permits dynamic interactive testing and debugging of programs generated in the CP/M environment. We use this program to locate within the MOVCPM program those program modules we wish to delete. To "call" DDT, enter:

```
A>DDT CPM64.COM <CR>
```

- The computer responds with the following printout on the CRT:

```
DDT VERS 2.2
NEXT   PC
2300 0100

-
```

- DDT prompts the operator with the character "_" and waits for an input command from the console. The operator can type any of several single-character commands, terminated by a carriage return to execute the command. If the letter D is used, the microcomputer will display the hexadecimal code and ASCII code of a section of memory. Figure 32 shows the screen display produced by my microcomputer in response to entering D <CR> on the terminal. The only parts that need concern you in following this procedure in this phase are the memory locations in hexadecimal form (first four characters) and the names of the program modules at those locations. The locations of the modules may be different in your CP/M, but you can start with D0C40 <CR>, as indicated below. Note that the prompt (-) appears at the end of the 12 lines of copy. This permits you to enter D <CR> again, and the next section of memory will be displayed. Repeating this short command, if necessary, will permit you to locate the modules you wish to erase. After the prompt, enter

```
-D0C40 <CR>
```

Note in Figure 32 that starting at the address "0C90" we have the program "pointers" or "call commands" for six of the modules that are part of the basic SYSGEN.COM procedure of CP/M:

DIR *(location 0C90)* prints a directory of all programs on the disk.
ERA *(location 0C94)* deletes programs from the disk.
TYPE *(location 0C98)* displays the copy on the CRT.
SAVE *(location 0C9C)* saves a program or a file that has been entered.
REN *(location 0CA0)*, the rename module, renames a program or file.
USER *(location 0CA4)* permits access under various user numbers.

Phase Four: Modifying the Modules

- We are now ready to modify the basic operating system by removing the program modules DIR, ERA, and REN. Note in Figure 32 that there are 16 pairs of numbers following each memory location, which correspond to the 16 characters in the ASCII section. They indicate what is in each location beginning with 0C90 through 0C9F.

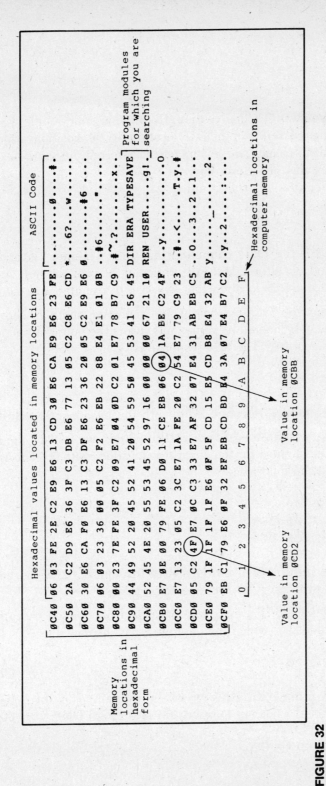

FIGURE 32

Dump of the console command processor portion of the operating system showing the "locations" of the DIR, ERA, and REN modules.

Location	0C90	0C91	0C92	. . .
0C90	44	49	52	. . .
Corresponds				
to	D	I	R	. . .

If you want to remove the DIR function, for example, you replace the values currently in the DIR locations by 00. Positions which you do not wish to change are left intact by entering the same hexadecimal numbers that are there now.

After the "_" prompt enter

```
-S0C90 <CR>
```

where S is the DDT command that allows memory locations to be examined and altered at the discretion of the programmer, and 0C90 is the first memory location that we wish to examine and modify.

- The computer responds with one line after another, showing one memory position and its value, and awaits the operator's action at the end of each line. The first response is

```
0C90 44
```

which is memory location 0C90 with the hexadecimal value of 44.

- Since we wish to remove the DIR function, we replace the values in computer memory for the next three locations with 00. This is done by entering the following:

```
0C90 44 00 <CR>
0C91 49 00 <CR>
0C92 52 00 <CR>
```

Thus, by putting 00 in locations 0C90 through 0C92, we have removed the call procedure for the directory, DIR.

- The next location is a space which we leave unchanged, by entering the same value, 20, which the computer has displayed.

```
0C93 20 20 <CR>
```

- We now remove the ERA module in the same way, by replacing the hexadecimal values in locations 0C94 through 0C96 with 00:

```
0C94 45 00 <CR>
0C95 52 00 <CR>
0C96 41 00 <CR>
```

- Since we do not wish to alter either the TYPE or SAVE modules, we echo or repeat the hexadecimal values as they are displayed for each memory location.

```
0C97 20 20 <CR>
0C98 54 54 <CR>
0C99 59 59 <CR>
0C9A 59 50 <CR>
0C9B 45 45 <CR>
0C9C 53 53 <CR>
0C9D 41 41 <CR>
0C9E 56 56 <CR>
0C9F 45 45 <CR>
```

- Now we are ready to erase the rename module, REN, which is located in memory at 0CA0 through 0CA2, by replacing the values with 00. The computer will automatically display the next line.

```
0CA0 52 00 <CR>
0CA1 45 00 <CR>
0CA2 4E 00 <CR>
```

- To terminate the substitution procedure, we enter a period after the machine has displayed the memory location and its value.

```
0CA3 20 . <CR>
```

Phase Five: Verifying the Changes and Saving the New Program

- When a period is entered, the machine again issues a prompt, "-". To verify the modification, we again enter D0C40, so that the computer will display the hexadecimal values and the ASCII code for the section containing the changes.

```
-D0C40 <CR>
```

- The computer will again display the memory between 0C40 and 0CF0, which now appears as shown in Figure 33.

   Compare this output with that shown in the fourth step 4 of Phase Three and you will see that the three modules—DIR, ERA, and REN—no longer appear on the right-hand side of the page at lines 0C90 and 0CA0. We have, therefore, been successful in removing these three program modules.

```
                    Hexadecimal values located in memory locations        ASCII Code

               0C40  06 03 FE 2E C2 E9 E6 13 CD 30 E6 CA E9 E6 23 FE   .........0.....#
               0C50  2A C2 D9 E6 36 3F C3 DB E6 77 13 05 C2 C8 E6 CD   *...6?...w.....
               0C60  30 E6 CA F0 E6 13 C3 DF E6 23 36 20 05 C2 E9 E6   0.......#6 ....
               0C70  06 03 23 36 00 05 C2 F2 E6 EB 22 88 E4 E1 01 0B   ..#6....."......
               0C80  00 23 7E FE 3F C2 09 E7 04 0D C2 01 E7 78 B7 C9   .#..?........x..
Memory         0C90  00 00 00 20 00 00 00 20 54 59 50 45 53 41 56 45   ... ... TYPESAVE
locations in   0CA0  00 00 00 20 55 53 45 52 97 16 00 00 67 21 10      ... USER....g!.
hexadecimal    0CB0  E7 0E 00 79 FE 06 D0 11 CE EB 06(04)1A BE C2 4F   ...y...........O
form           0CC0  E7 13 23 05 C2 3C E7 1A FE 20 C2 54 E7 79 C9 23   ..#..<.... .T.y.#
               0CD0  05 C2(4F)E7 0C C3 33 E7 AF 32 07 E4 31 AB EB C5   ..O...3..2..1...
               0CE0  79 1F 1F 1F E6 0F 5F CD 15 E5 CD B8 E4 32 AB Y    y......_......2.
               0CF0  EB C1 79 E6 0F 32 EF EB CD BD E4 3A 07 E4 B7 C2   ..y..2.....:...
```

Program modules for which you are searching

Value in memory location 0CD2

Value in memory location 0CBB

FIGURE 33

Dump of the console command processor portion of the operating system showing the removal of the DIR, ERA, and REN modules.

- We are now ready to terminate the CP/M modification and prepare a new modified operating system. To do this, "exit" from DDT by entering G0.

```
-G0 <CR>
```

- The system will go back into "command mode" and display "A>". It is now necessary to save the modified program under a *new* name on the disk. We have decided to call the modified program **CMPX64.COM**, and we enter

```
A>SAVE 34 CPMX64.COM <CR>
```

Phase Six: Producing the New Operating System on a Disk

- To produce a new disk with this operating system, start by placing a blank formatted disk, single- or double-density, into drive B.
- The machine has already returned a new prompt, A>. To place the new operating system on the disk in drive B enter

```
A>SYSGEN CPMX64.COM <CR>
```

- The microcomputer now displays the following on the screen:

```
SYSGEN VER 2.0
DESTINATION DRIVE NAME (OR RETURN TO REBOOT)
```

Enter B and a carriage return.

```
DESTINATION DRIVE NAME (OR RETURN TO REBOOT)  B  <CR>
```

- The screen display will now be:

```
DESTINATION ON B, THEN TYPE RETURN
```

Press the carriage return to complete the process.

```
DESTINATION ON B, THEN TYPE RETURN <CR>
```

- The screen now shows:

```
FUNCTION COMPLETE
DESTINATION DRIVE NAME (OR RETURN TO REBOOT)
```

Press carriage return to restart the system.

```
DESTINATION DRIVE NAME (OR RETURN TO REBOOT) <CR>
```

We now have the modified program **CPMX64.COM** on disk A and the new operating system on disk B.

Phase Seven: Checking the New Operating System

- To test the new disk's operating system, transfer a program or part of the CP/M to the new disk by using the PIP routine, as follows

```
A> PIP B:=A:PIP.COM [V]   <CR>
```

This will transfer the PIP command onto the new disk.

- Remove the disk from drive A, and store it. It contains the new, modified operating system for future use on other disks.
- Take the disk from drive B and place it in drive A. IPL the system in accordance with the procedure used with your microcomputer. If all is well, the CRT screen display should appear as

```
64k CP/M vers xx.xx
A>
```

- To verify that the directory (DIR), erase (ERA), and rename (REN) program modules have really been erased, type **DIR** immediately after the prompt A>.

```
A>  DIR <CR>
```

The microcomputer should respond with **DIR?**. This indicates that the DIR program module does not operate; the machine cannot understand the command.

- The following shows the test for both the erase and rename modules of the operating system:

```
A>  ERA PIP.COM <CR>
    ERA?
A>  REN PIPX.COM=PIP.COM <CR>
    REN?
```

The appearance of the module name followed by a question mark indicates that the command is not known to the operating system. Thus, we have verified that we have a new operating system on a disk without the DIR, ERA, and REN program modules.

USING OKARA TO CREATE A SPECIAL SYSTEMS DISK

A shorter and simpler method of creating an operating disk with certain of the subprograms of the **CCP** (Console Command Processor) either removed or renamed, can be done by using a packaged program, Kiai System's **OKARA**. This, however, requires either a more experienced individual or the direct assistance of your microcomputer dealer, since it is necessary to know some of the physical characteristics of the terminal and how to compile an assembly language program.

Under this package, there is a special customizing routine, **CUSTO KAR.ASM**. Using an editor or text-editor to scan the program, you can find within this routine a special portion that appears on the screen as follows:

```
org       cus$biltins
DB        'DIR '
DB        'ERA '
DB        'TYPE'
DB        'SAVE'
DB        'REN '
DB        'USER'
```

When customizing the CP/M, it is possible to change as many of the names of the CCP's subprograms as one wishes. It is not possible to change their order or to delete one of the program's lines. Every name is four characters long, and blanks are used only to the right of the name, such as ERA, if it is shorter than four characters.

To make any name (command) unusable, it is only necessary to type the name, or any four letters, in lower case. For example, to delete the DIR, ERA, and REN subprograms, all one would do is rewrite those lines as follows.

```
DB        'dir '
DB        'era '
DB        'TYPE'
DB        'SAVE'
DB        'ren '
DB        'USER'
```

To change the name of any of the subprograms, replace it with a new name four characters long entered in all capital letters. For example, in place of **DIR** you may wish to use **LIST**; in place of the **ERA** command use **XXXX**; and use **NAME** for the **REN** command. In that case, you would edit the OKARA program as follows:

```
DB          'LIST'      <CR>
DB          'XXXX'      <CR>
DB          'TYPE'      <CR>
DB          'SAVE'      <CR>
DB          'NAME'      <CR>
DB          'USER'      <CR>
```

You still have each of the subprograms available for use on the system, but any one trying to use them would have to know the *new names* selected for calling these routines.

CHAPTER 12

Encryption Techniques for Data Security

In this chapter we discuss the ultimate in data file and program security: *encryption,* which comes from the Greek word meaning "to hide." Codes and ciphers have a fascination for many people, who instantly think of spies and secret agents. We have put off a discussion of this topic until now, since this technique is not recommended for use with *all* of a company's files, because then too many employees are involved and it loses its effectiveness. It does have a place in protecting the most critical files and should also be used when transmitting information from one location to another.

Encryption was used almost 4000 years ago. The ancient Egyptians were known to encipher their hieroglyphic writing on monuments. Some believe that this was done to entice passersby to stop and try to solve for the hidden message. Was this a form of modern advertising in the Valley of the Kings? Similarly, the ancient Hebrews enciphered certain words in the Holy Scriptures. At some period long ago, hidden messages began to be used for military and political secrecy. We know of the torch code used by the ancient Greeks and the simple cipher, used almost 2000 years ago, which is still known as the *Caesar cipher*.

The use of coded messages has not grown steadily throughout history. The invention of the telegraph had a great influence on the development of various coding systems. The American Civil War produced great progress. The teletypewriter opened the way for the next big jump—the introducton of automatic coding.

It should be noted that not all the major contributors in this field were specialists in the development and use of ciphers and codes. Some time between 1790 and 1800 an amateur invented a remarkable coding machine.

The inventor was a well-known writer, agriculturalist, bibliophile, architect, diplomat, statesman, and gadgeteer. His "cypher wheel" was 2 inches in diameter and made of white wood. It was not until 1922, the year in which the U.S. Army adopted a similar device, that the "cypher wheel" was rediscovered in the Library of Congress among the papers of President Thomas Jefferson. A replica of a cipher wheel used during World War II is shown in Figure 34.

With the development and wide use of the computer, rapid strides were made in encipherment. In the business world today, encryption is used as security against accidental or deliberate disclosure of highly important information. Consider the following two incidents.

One user of a microcomputer system found that his system was being used to near-capacity levels when he wanted to expand. He decided to interconnect his system with a large communications network service. One day, when the company's product development plans and budgets were being transmitted for storage onto the network service's files, a system malfunction caused the entire data to be printed on a remote terminal in the advertising agency for one of his competitors.

Another microcomputer user updated his customer files at the end of each workweek. An employee managed to conceal a backup copy of this disk in his briefcase and "lent" the disk to a competitor for the weekend. Early on Monday the employee carefully replaced the disk in its proper storage file.

Had the data in each of these instances been enciphered (gibberish instead of intelligible data), it would have been impossible for the receiver to have used that data without knowledge of the enciphering technique.

To understand this topic of secret or hidden messages, it is necessary first to define several elementary terms.

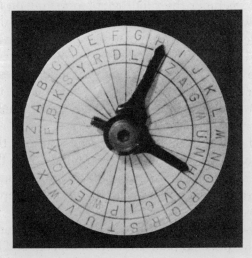

FIGURE 34

Replica of a World War II cipher wheel made for the author by a former student.

BASIC CONCEPTS AND APPLICATIONS

A plaintext is changed into a ciphertext by one or a combination of two or three basic methods or algorithms. Each of the three has many variations, but for the sake of simplicity we use a very elementary form of each and illustrate their use with the plaintext message: *Buy gold*.

BASIC ENCRYPTION DEFINITIONS

Cryptography is an art or science of transforming a clearly written message or text into one that is unintelligible and for retransforming that unintelligible message into one that can be read.

Plaintext is the clearly written, easily understood message rendered unintelligible, or the unintelligible text transformed into a readable message.

Ciphertext, or *cryptogram*, is the unintelligible message or text.

Data Encryption Standard (DES) was issued in 1977 by the National Bureau of Standards. Using a single key and a special algorithm, DEA (Data Encryption Algorithm), this encryption method is available in program form and is also incorporated in special hardware.

Encipher, or *encode*, is the technique used to convert a plaintext into a ciphertext. (Encryption is often given the same meaning, although there is a difference to a cryptography specialist.)

Decipher, or *decode*, is the method used to change a ciphertext into a plaintext.

Cryptanalysis is the deciphering of a ciphertext or cryptogram not intended for you and for which you do not know the key. In popular terms this is *codebreaking*.

Cryptology includes both cryptography and cryptanalysis.

Key specifies the sequence of symbols or letters of the cipher alphabet, and/or the pattern of shuffling or mixing letters in a transposition cipher system.

Public Key Cryptosystem uses two keys, one for encrypting the message and the other to decrypt the message. The PKA (Public Key Algorithm) employs special mathematical functions known as trapdoor one-way functions.

NOTE: Technically, there is a difference between a *cipher* and a *code*. A code is the aristocrat of the cipher family. In a cipher system the plaintext is translated into a ciphertext by concealment, transposition, and/or substitution methods. A code system requires a codebook or dictionary that relates specific words, phrases, and even sentences of the plaintext to its equivalent ciphertext. For example, "home" may be used in place of the word "company"; "set up" may replace the sentence, "produce 10,000 spindles, model #1326-H." The versatility and usefulness of code systems are limited, especially in encipherment with computers. Therefore, the techniques used in this chapter are cipher systems, not codes.

---

1. In a *concealment cipher*, the true letters of the plaintext are hidden or disguised by a device or algorithm. For example, we might agree to divide the message, use one word at a time, and have it appear as every fifth word in a sentence. Thus, our message "buy gold" could appear as:

   Product is a good buy. It has ten percent gold content.

2. In the *transposition cipher*, the letters of the original message are taken out of their regular order by some previously agreed upon method. In this case we have agreed to use (a) the first letter of the first word, (b) the first letter of the second word, (c) the second letter of the first word, (d) the second letter of the second word, (e) the third letter of the first word, and so on, and then to break the message into blocks of five letters. Our message "buy gold" could appear as

   B G U O Y L D

3. In the *substitution cipher*, each letter of the original message is replaced by a substitute according to some prearranged key. The simplest is the Caesar cipher, in which we shift the letters of the alphabet by some given number; for example:

Plaintext: A B C D E F G H I J K L M N O P Q R S T U V W X Y Z
Ciphertext: D E F G H I J K L M N O P Q R S T U V W X Y Z A B C

The letter A in the message would be replaced with a D, the letter H with a K. Our message "buy gold" would then appear as

   E X B J R O G

COMPUTER-AIDED CRYPTOGRAPHY

The computer has made it possible to develop complex methods of encipherment that would have been virtually impossible to do by hand. Many cryptography algorithms have been used for years, and a number of new ones have been developed for use with computers. No attempt will be made in this book to present the differences between classic cryptography in the precomputer era and modern cryptography, with its stream and block ciphers. In the development of the special algorithms for use with the computer, the effectiveness of the algorithm is more important than the cost of its creation.

The Data Encryption Standard

Some specialists in this field believe that it is better to use a common key-controlled algorithm of known strength than to risk a privately developed algorithm that might have unknown weaknesses. Such a single-standard algorithm could facilitate the exchange of enciphered data among many users and even separate computer systems requiring only an exchange of keys rather than algorithms.

This premise is the basis for the development of the *Data Encryption Standard* (**DES**) by the U.S. National Bureau of Standards, which was issued in 1977. It is a modification of *Lucifer*, developed earlier by IBM. The NBS/DES uses a 64-bit block and a 56-bit key selected by the user. To bring the key up to block size, it is artificially expanded to obtain a 64-bit "key" that is 8 bytes long. It is this key that enables the program to turn plaintext into ciphertext and later to restore the ciphertext into plaintext. As there are

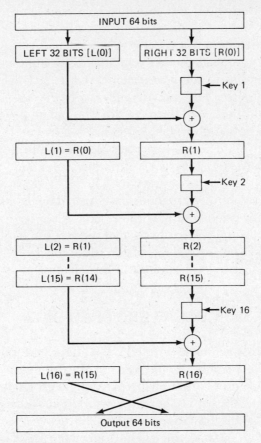

FIGURE 35

With the Data Encryption Algorithm there are 16 successive encryptions in which the key is used to make substitutions and permutations in a string of 32 bits. After each such operation the right output of 32 bits then becomes the left input for the next round.

over 70,000,000,000,000,000 (seventy quadrillion) possible keys of 56 bits and the keys can be changed frequently, the threat of someone finding your key is, for the present at least, *almost* eliminated.

Public-Key Cryptosystems

Late in 1976, Martin E. Hellman and Whitfield Diffie, both of Stanford University, introduced the concept of a public-key system for encipherment of data that would be transmitted over communications lines. When Ronald L. Rivert, Adi Shamir, and Len Adleman, all from MIT, offered to any reader of a popular science magazine, copies of their implementation of the Diffie-Hellman system, *A Method for Obtaining Digital Signatures and Public-Key Cryptosystems*, there was an attempt to keep the report from the public. It should be noted that, under Operation Shamrock, the U.S. government intercepted and computer analyzed all international TELEX messages into and out of the country for years.

This cryptosystem works with two keys, a *public key* and a *private key*. Your public key is analogous to your telephone number. It is available to anyone who wishes to send you enciphered data. It locks or encodes the information intended for you. Anyone who has it can encipher data to be sent to you, but that is all they can do. The public key cannot be used to decode data. The secret private key is needed by you to decipher the data you have received. The mathematical algorithm of the public-key system uses your public key, together with your secret key, to return the enciphered data.

Several enciphering programs have been developed for microcomputer systems. They can be used to protect data stored on disks or for transmission. There is also special hardware that can be used in place of software for this purpose. The use of some of the different enciphering programs is shown in the next several sections of this chapter.

THE USE OF CRYPT.COM TO ENCIPHER DATA

One program that will be illustrated is **CRYPT.COM**, by Arthur R. Miller. It is, as a record fancier would say, on the "flip side" of the **FILEFIX** program discussed in earlier chapters. Along with Digital Marketing Corporation's FILEFIX are 11 short utility programs, among which is one for encipherment. This program enciphers by using a single uppercase or lowercase letter, or a single digit. The original file is restored by running the CRYPT program a second time, giving the same single letter, or digit key.

We use the same text in all the illustrations of enciphering programs. Those interested in attempting to decrypt the outputs will have plenty of material with which to work. The text, called **TEXTNAME**, is shown in Figure 36.

To use the cipher program CRYPT.COM, call it in the usual way by entering its name after the system prompt, A>. Then, enter the name of the file to be encoded after the program requests it, as shown.

```
A> CRYPT <CR>

Enter filename: TEXTNAME <CR>
```

The program then requests the encoding key, after which it notes how it has renamed the original program and assigned a name to the encoded data.

```
Input one letter for encoding key: H <CR>

TEXTNAME        ===>    TEXTNAME.BAK
TEXTNAME.$$$  ===>    TEXTNAME
Delete original file?  Y  <CR>
```

The program asks whether the user wishes to erase the original file. From a security viewpoint, the user would answer "Y", since there would be no point in encoding if the original text were readily available on the disk. At this point the program returns to the system prompt, A>.

Note that the original file has been renamed as a backup with **.BAK** and the encoded file given the name of the original file. If anyone attempts to read the encoded file with any text editor, all one would see is a set of meaningless symbols, as shown in Figure 37. To restore the encoded file to readable form, the same procedure would be used as to encode the file.

It is possible to avoid having the cipher program rename the enciphered file by designating the text to be encoded (TEXTNAME) followed

---

```
                    TEXTNAME


    Since there has been language there has been cryptography.    For
example, a cuneiform tablet from the Mesopotamian civilization dating
back to 1500 B.C. contains an encipherment of a formula for making
pottery glaze.    Transposition ciphers (ones in which letters of a
message are exchanged) were developed by the Spartans about 475 B.C.
The Romans as well as the Greeks toyed with simple letter substitution
ciphers.
```

FIGURE 36

Plaintext message used for various examples of encryption in this chapter.

```
A !&+-h< -:-h );h*--&h$)&/=)/-h< -:-h );h*--&h+:18<'/:)8 1fhhh
':h-0)%8$-dh)h+=&!.':%h<)*$-<h.:'%h< -h
-;'8'<)%!)&h+!>!$!2)<!'&h,)<!&/h*)+#h<'hy}xxhffh+'&<)!&;h)&h-&+!8
-:%-&<h'.h)h.':%=$)h.':h%)#!&/h8'-<<:1h/$)2-fhhh :)&;8';!<!'&h+!8
-:;hq'&-;h!&h? !+ h< -h$-<<-:;h'.h)h%-;-;;)/-h):-h-0+
)&/-/,ah?-:-h,->-$'8-,h*1h< -h 8):<)&/h)*')'1h*'=<h| }hffhhh -h
```

FIGURE 37

Dump of encrypted text of message in Figure 36 using the CRYPT program.

by the name you choose for the encoded file (CODENAME) when calling the program:

A> <u>CRYPT TEXTNAME CODENAME</u> <CR>

If you examine the directory of the disk you will find that **TEXTNAME** has been erased and that **CODENAME** has been added.

One note of interest to those who have played with cryptography: It is possible with this program to do successive encodings, that is, to reencode the coded message a second, third, or more times to provide for additional security. To restore the multiple-encoded file, it is necessary to enter the same letters used in the various single-letter encodings, but *not* necessarily in the same sequence.

A HOMEMADE ENCIPHERING PROGRAM: H007.BAS

Preparing a program to encipher data does not require much programming effort if you are familiar with cryptological techniques. Such a program, **H007.BAS**, included at the end of this chapter, is an example of a coding method called transposition. It is somewhat more complex than a simple transposition, since it "packs" the data with meaningless characters so that each encoded entry is 30 characters long. Furthermore, it also includes a *signature key*, a set of numeric values, which would reveal any tampering with the data when the key is decoded. The decoding program, **E007.BAS**, is also included at the end of the chapter.

For example, the name, HAROLD JOSEPH HIGHLAND, when encoded by this program, would appear as:

724INZJGHEPLDXQLAH JHAROOSHINDKV 1700 2316 758

The first three digits, 724, are the encoded length of the original name. The string of letters starting with I and ending with V is the transposed name packed with extra letters. The final three sets of digits are the signature key.

For readers interested in solving cryptograms or other puzzles and who would like to decrypt the algorithm without looking at the program at the end of the chapter, let me include another name, REBECCA FRANCIS

HIGHLAND. This is a three-segment name with the last segment the same as in the previous illustration. Encoded, this would appear as

```
742KVNDHIANCCZJGHCEA REBEFRS LAXQ   1875 2298 714
```

This program has been developed for demonstration purposes and has been designed for use with names that are 30 characters or less in length. It can be modified to accept as many as 256 characters, the usual maximum size of any single-line entry on the microcomputer system. There are several other features that can be modified, so this program provides a high level of security.

- There are three numeric keys, KEY1%, KEY2%, and KEY3%, which are now part of the program. It takes little programming effort to change this portion of the program to enable the user to enter any three numeric keys. These keys are used to transform the signature key.
- Within the program is a line of code which appears as

```
LONA$ = STR$ (LON$ + 50) + STR$ (INT% (RND * 10))
```

For added security, the 50 can be replaced with a number to be entered by the user, and even the 10 at the end can be a user-entered key.

Thus, it is possible to reinforce **H007.BAS** with five user keys. It is also possible to have the line that defines FILL$ to be user entered. The number of possibilities for modification is limited only by the imagination and experience of the programmer.

USING ENCODE/DECODE FOR DATA SECURITY

Herbert Schildt's **Encode/Decode**, distributed by SuperSoft, is a more sophisticated coding/decoding system that utilizes standard coding techniques of transposition, substitution, and inversion, as well as the Schildt surge-transversal algorithm. The user is required to enter a five-character password and also a ten-digit key. There are 10,000,000,000 possible "keys" when using this package. Also, separate files can have different passwords and numeric keys. Finally, it should be noted that these two programs for encoding and decoding can be used with **.COM** files as well as any data files and programs.

To Encode a File

To use the Schildt program, there is a module, **PASS2.COM**, that permits the user to modify the password to be accepted by the encoding and decoding programs. Once the user has set the password desired, it is important that this module not be left on any disk in the system, since any user would then be able to access the coding/decoding programs by altering the password. Once the user has established a password for use with the programs, the encoding program would be called after the system prompt, and the following would appear on the screen:

```
A> ENCOD2 <CR>

ENCOD2 vers 1.0
Copyright (c) 1980 - SuperSoft & Herbert Schildt
Enter password: ...
```

The user would be required to enter the proper password to use the program. If an improper password is entered, the program is aborted and a system prompt reappears. When the correct password is entered, the program responds by overwriting the password with Xs, so that anyone passing by would be unable to read the password from the screen. With the proper password, the program calls for the name of the file to be encoded.

```
Enter password: SVFBM  <CR>

Enter the file to be coded: TEXTNAME  <CR>
```

Once the filename has been entered, the program overwrites that name and issues its next prompt, requesting the name of the output file that has been encoded:

```
Enter the output file - if same type <return>: ...
```

This time the user is given a choice. It is possible to save the original file under its name, which is not a good security practice, and the output file can be given a new name. For this illustration we have decided to save the original file and give the encoded file a new name:

```
Enter the output file --
            if same type <return>: TEXT.CPT  <CR>
```

If a new filename has been designated, the program will display the following on the screen. If the same filename is used, the computer will not create a new file.

```
specified output file does not exist: creating it now
```

The program now requests the numeric key:

```
Enter combination (exactly 10 digits): ..........
```

It is necessary to enter all ten digits of the numeric key; after they are entered they are overwritten with Xs by the program.

```
Enter combination (exactly 10 digits): 2033538613  <CR>
```

Once the encoding has been completed, the program responds with a request for another filename. If no other files are to be encoded, the user signs off by entering ,DONE, and the program is terminated.

```
Enter the file to be coded: ,DONE <CR>

Program terminated...returning to operating system
```

After the program is terminated, the encoded file, if examined by a text editor, would appear as a set of meaningless symbols somewhat similar to those that appeared in Figure 37. If one were to use DDT.COM, as explained in earlier chapters, one would find all the hexadecimal and ASCII values of the program altered. A dump under DDT.COM of the original text and a dump of the encoded text are shown in Figure 38.

```
            DDT DUMP OF ORIGINAL COPY OF TEXTNAME


0100 20 53 69 6E 63 65 20 74 68 65 72 65 20 68 61 73  Since there has
0110 20 62 65 65 6E 20 6C 61 6E 67 75 61 67 65 20 74   been language t
0120 68 65 72 65 20 68 61 73 20 62 65 65 6E 20 63 72  here has been cr
0130 79 70 74 6F 67 72 61 70 68 79 2E 20 20 20 46 6F  yptography.   Fo
0140 72 20 65 78 61 6D 70 6C 65 2C 20 61 20 63 75 6E  r example, a cun
0150 65 69 66 6F 72 6D 20 74 61 62 6C 65 74 20 66 72  eiform tablet fr
0160 6F 6D 20 74 68 65 20 4D 65 73 6F 70 6F 74 61 6D  om the Mesopotam
0170 69 61 6E 20 63 69 76 69 6C 69 7A 61 74 69 6F 6E  ian civilization
0180 20 64 61 74 69 6E 67 20 62 61 63 6B 20 74 6F 20   dating back to
0190 31 35 30 30 20 42 2E 43 2E 20 63 6F 6E 74 61 69  1500 B.C. contai
01A0 6E 73 20 61 6E 20 65 6E 63 69 70 68 65 72 6D 65  ns an encipherme
01B0 6E 74 20 6F 66 20 61 20 66 6F 72 6D 75 6C 61 20  nt of a formula
```

```
            PRINTOUT OF ENCODED TEXTNAME

] c m % _0Vf`  |  ?Z<Q6 1 ~ egh $V8 *Hk cz6R<W> t p } j s" / eV
```

```
    DDT DUMP OF ENCODED PROGRAM USING ENCODE/DECODE PROGRAM


0100 DD 86 E3 88 ED 8E A5 DF B0 D6 E6 C0 E0 8E FC 91  ................
0110 BF DA BC D1 B6 96 EC 9B FE 97 E5 E7 E8 84 A4 D6  ................
0120 B8 87 AA C8 EB 8B E3 FA B6 D2 BC D7 BE 90 F6 8D  ................
0130 F4 82 F0 94 FD 92 EA 88 F3 8A A2 84 AF 81 C0 E5  ................
0140 D6 FF 9A E4 83 AC 9B F0 96 B2 9B 9D C5 B9 C7 A7  ................
0150 DC AF C1 A7 D5 BE 98 D6 88 ED 82 EF 92 B2 D2 A6  ................
0160 C2 9B 86 F1 91 FD DD 96 F5 8D E9 A1 F7 8B AC C3  ................
0170 E1 86 E3 CD A9 8E BD DD B1 DE A2 C8 B2 DC B0 D6  ................
0180 DD B1 AC AD C2 AA C6 E8 8D EF D9 E6 C6 B4 B3 F6  ................
0190 C9 FB C8 F0 D9 9B BD F6 D3 FD 99 BD 93 EE 8F E0  ................
01A0 88 F5 DE B8 D5 FD 91 E2 9A F5 8E E8 8A FF 9E F2  ................
01B0 9C EE C8 AC C4 A9 81 E3 C6 A9 DD B6 C8 AA CC B2  ................
```

FIGURE 38

Dump of part of the plaintext in hexadecimal and ASCII form (top), printout of encoded text (center), and corresponding dump of same material after it has been encrypted using the ENCOD2 program (bottom).

To Decode a File

The procedure to decode a file using the encode/decode package would be similar to that used to encode the original file. After the proper password has been entered, it is necessary to enter the name of the file to be decoded:

```
A> DECOD2  <CR>

Decode II  v1.0
Copyright (c) 1980 - SuperSoft & Herbert Schildt
Enter password: SVFBM   <CR>


Enter the file to be decoded: TEXT.CPT   <CR>
```

The program overwrites the user's responses with Xs after each response is made. Again, the program requests the name of the output file as well as the ten-digit numeric key. Failure to enter the proper key aborts the decoding of the file.

```
Enter the output file --
                if same type <return>: REALTEXT   <CR>

specified output file does not exist: creating it now

Enter combination (exactly 10 digits): 2033538613
```

If no other files are to be decoded, then the user again enters ,DONE and the program terminates printing its normal exit and a system prompt, A>, appears.

```
Enter the file to be decoded: ,DONE   <CR>

Program terminated...returning to operating system
```

PUBLIC-KEY SYSTEMS FOR MICROCOMPUTERS

Several public-key cryptography systems have been developed by the Public Key Systems Corporation to work on any microcomputer system that has (1) a Z-80 microprocessor operating under CP/M, (2) at least 38K bytes of memory, and (3) a minimum of two disk drives. It has been designed primarily for security of communications within a microcomputer network or between a microcomputer and mainframe computer. It may also be used with a stand-alone microcomputer for securing data files and programs stored on disks.

In public-key systems, large random numbers are used to generate both the *public key* and the *secret key*. In programs developed by PKS (Public Key Systems Corporation), a special module, *disc random*, is the source of the random numbers used to develop the two keys. The *cipherseed*, or large random number, is obtained by the timing of "disk latency," an irreducible and unpredictable variation in the time it takes the read/write head of the disk drive of your machine to perform the specific operations requested by the disk random program, multiplied by a random factor.

Disk latency depends upon the physical characteristics of the specific microcomputer disk drive, the microprocessor, the ambient temperature, and the relative humidity of the room. The timing is somewhat similar to timing a marathon race, using only the second hand of a watch and disregarding the number of times it goes around during the race. The time for the race depends simply on the location of the second hand when the first runner crosses the finish line.

Two of the PKS public-key cryptosystems are described. Both are designed so that any error in one or more letters of the public-key encoded message during data transmission will only affect those letters and the rest of the message will remain intact so that it can be deciphered. An error in the key portion of the message will destroy the entire message. The first program is **The Protector** and second is **DEDICATE/32**.

THE PROTECTOR

"**The Protector**," one of the cryptosystems developed by Public Key Systems Corporation and distributed by Standard Software Corporation of America, is based on the **RSA** (Rivert, Shamir, and Adelman) algorithm. There are three programs in the package:

1. **KEYGEN** is used to generate your public key and your secret key.
2. **ENCODE** encodes the text or data file. If you are encoding a file to store on your own system, you would use your own public key generated by the Keygen program. If you are transmitting the file, you would encode the file using the recipient's public key. It is possible to maintain several different public keys and use them to encode messages to their different owners.
3. **DECODE** decodes the message using the secret key produced by the Keygen program. It will work only if the user has the secret key on the same disk as the Decode program; otherwise it will not decode the message that was encoded with its matching public key.

Creating Public and Secret Keys with The Protector

Using the "disk latency" technique just described, the Keygen program produces a 512-bit key, which is split into two parts: one the public key and the other the private key that matches it. Each of the two keys is 256 bits (32 bytes) long, as compared with the 64-bit (8-byte) key used with the National Bureau of Standard's DES. The chance that the actual keys you generate are the same as any other keys produced for anyone else is one chance in 10^{50}, or 1 followed by 50 zeros.

The program creates both keys in as little as 3 minutes or as long as 6 hours; the usual running time is reported to be about 45 minutes. If for any reason you need the computer during this time, it is possible to interrupt the program, which will store its current values for later use. These are kept in a file, KEYGEN.TMP, which is created by the program. When you recall the KEYGEN program later, the key generation will pick up from where it stopped in the KEYGEN.TMP file.

Probably I was fortunate, since my key generation took only 19 minutes. Once the program signed on the CRT screen noting the copyright, type, and serial number of my disk, it also printed Status 1.

- Five minutes later, Status 2 appeared on the screen, letting me know that the computer was busy working and had not forgotten me or gotten locked in a loop.
- Three minutes later, some eight minutes after the start, Status 3 appeared, and two minutes after that came the report, Status 4.
- Fourteen minutes after my calling the program, Key Imminent appeared on the screen, followed by Testing Key Pair.
- About 30 seconds later, Almost done, about 2 more minutes appeared, and in somewhat less than 100 seconds, the following two lines appeared:

```
KEY   GENERATION   SUCCESSFUL !
DONE
```

and a system prompt, A>, appeared on the screen. Two new files had been added to my disk, *PUBLIC.KEY* and *SECRET.KEY*. A copy of both appears in Figure 39.

Encoding a File with The Protector

The encoding program of this package requires that you enter (1) the name of the file to be encoded (we have selected the file TEXTNAME, which appears earlier in this chapter) and (2) the public key you wish to use with the message.

```
┌─────────────────────────────────────────────────────────────────┐
│      PUBLIC  KEY                         SECRET  KEY              │
│                                                                   │
│  PKSKEY(tm)                           PKSKEY(tm)                  │
│  032                                  032                         │
│  AA PP GA HN HD DM PE CB BB           AA AA FB JP LH PF BN FL AK  │
│  GC EA OD MM PF AE LG FJ BO           HD LB FB JP DP HN BN FL AI  │
│  DF BG AJ JB DO IM DH KE AJ           LH PF NJ BH LH PF JF ND AI  │
│  IC LJ DG MG IN ID II PF BJ           HD LB FB JP DP HN BN FN AK  │
│  AC DI PB FM AD BN CA AF BK           AC DI PB FM AD BN CA AF BK  │
│  IF CA PK AE LO EG EB OC BI           IF CA PK AE LO EG EB OC BI  │
│  FM KF AE IC BP DD AH GP AE           FM KF AE IC BP DD AH GP AE  │
│  HH BA CE PC JB JE JF JJ BN           HH BA CE PC JB JE JF JJ BN  │
└─────────────────────────────────────────────────────────────────┘
```

FIGURE 39

Public and secret keys generated by *The Protector* program. A different key can be produced at user's option since disk latency is used by program as a random input.

```
A> ENCODE   TEXTNAME  PUBLIC.KEY  <CR>
```

In practice, if you have several public keys you would rename the files with names appropriate to those with whom you are communicating. For example, SUNYF.PUB might be the name given to one, PRINCE.PUB to another, and ENVIRON.PUB to a third. Note that the suffix .PUB is used with each to make it easier to identify these as public keys.

When the request to encode TEXTNAME has been entered, the computer responds with:

```
                "THE PROTECTOR" (tm)
          ** PUBLIC KEY ENCODER MODULE **
                  COPYRIGHT 1982
                        by
        STANDARD SOFTWARE CORPORATION OF AMERICA


    USE OF THIS MODULE IS DESIGNED FOR USE ON ONE
    SYSTEM ONLY. USE ON ANOTHER SYSTEM CONSTITUTES A
    COPYRIGHT VIOLATION AND COULD JEOPORDIZE THE
    INTEGRITY OF YOUR DATA. PLEASE BE CAREFUL!!!
    Thirty two byte key.
    Public key encoder type: PKS032AXPAND00001
    Serial # 00000


    KEY FILE NAME    A:PUBLIC.KEY
    INPUT FILE NAME  A:TEXTNAME
    OUTPUT FILE NAME A:TEXTNAME.CTX


    CHECKING FOR ENOUGH ROOM TO WRITE ENCODED FILE
    ...Confirmed.
```

After a short time, the program continues with:

```
GENERATING HARDWARE RANDOM NUMBER Done.

EXECUTING PUBLIC KEY ALGORITHM (about a minute).
Done.
```

After notifying me that it is executing the public key algorithm, the program notifies me that it requires about a minute to execute this operation. Once it is completed, "Done" is added to the line. The program then prints:

```
WRITING ENCRYPTED FILE TO DISK...
Done.
```

The encoded file is stored on the disk as TEXTNAME.CTX (see Figure 40), along with the original file. From a security viewpoint, it would be best to erase the original file and rename the encoded file using the original name. It should be noted that when using *The Protector*, the encoded file will appear on the same disk as the original file.

How to Decode a File with The Protector

Once the encoded file has been transmitted and the receiver wishes to decode it, or if you have encoded a file to store on a disk that you now wish to use, it is necessary to use the DECODE program with two modifiers. After

```
                        Encoded Message

THIS IS AN ENCODED FILE
FORMAT            PKS032AXPAND00001
ORIGINAL FILE NAME    MESSAGE.

ABDLFPFHHGCCAJPJDIDLGDGCGBCHFPAPGJHIIBEFFMKBBOPIMNIGEMAOMHKFKMLH
AAAAAAAAAAAAAAAAAAAAAAAAAAAAAAAAAAAAAAAAAAAAAAAAAAAAAAAAAAAAAAAA
OKDFBLHNNNDENKCADCEHFALBELKFPFBIBCEHENLDJBCDAACFPHHKOJPMOCFHFHIJ
JHOMEBIPDANLHMOMKOAPNAKHJBAIMDFCEANJENMMCLEFKJBFDKIHHEIDKMELEGCG
FHAPGJPALMCJDCIHDJDNIHPHOPNAENFCIHDKIHOHCAHLIODFEKCOPHINFBFPIGJI
CGGMBPEELFOCAKJJIDFOJHOFGHEKONPJGJFOHOJPAAEDLGGHHMNFGINNLIKKFMNG
EFEFDKLFEOOHHJFGODAIKPAALAKHMNAGIOKHBJEMDPJJJCINHCOOLHNFMDLMEKDE
LIFIGOGHABFOJAGPEDDCDNABPNHBBJEKFMLBGHHIILDJEDKIGDIFAJFOGHEPGPJK
MFOGBJGFBGAMFBAEDNLCKNBNBCGLHEFFNBHFAJNHPABNMOHNEJLFFMGABMJGIOEH
EIELKKDMFFKGNAGNEFJFBEMIJODLENNFMMABCOEPEIEBLCGGNKOOBKMODACFLKMB
HLDPJAAOGKPFDKEMKGLPPNMPKFPLMCJPCKENNJEKDEPILHMNPAGEDEPFFBHCOHOF
OPHFNGOIDDMHDKOBBKBNHGNBHNCJFJJAHJIINFBNBMKEKLCKKCAMGDLPHDADAJMJ
OGDNGFEPAHMCEMDFBPEAKDECMPFABNFFCCINJEENFLKFPOPJCDHFLCFPIPMMPKBK
CJPODPCBMBJIENBJPEFMOFFPLPPNGKLENHPOOGBLIPBHJJAOGNLLGHPICIBLOKJA
CGCGIGFNEHOJCOHOBOAPCAJPHBENMAPAKAELBKGAMPMBIBEJDNFLOGPFDHHKABKC
ENJFINEOKCMCBIADALMCCBEKKGJPGMEKDJBCJJIFHNGFHJBOPBJCANLIKCDANMLB
KAJPCIIMHOMJBBBFAPMHHHDNFIPKOLLNAMHOCHHBDGBKPBPMEBCBHOLNGCEIKDMJ
JBMGKCANODADHFPCFJOJAPELKICGOMFOHPPMGPPJGDBILPJFFHBKFENHCNJHJNEC
```

FIGURE 40

Printout of encoded form of message in Figure 36 using the Rivest, Shamir, and Adleman algorithm incorporated in the program by Public Key Systems Corp.

entering the name of the file to be decoded, it is essential to indicate its matching PRIVATE.KEY for the program to work. We start this by entering:

```
A> DECODE TEXTNAME.CTX SECRET.KEY <CR>
```

Again the program responds with its name, the Decoder module, and serial number of the disk and then verifies whether the file to be decoded exists and the secret key is stored on the same disk.

```
CHECKING KEY FILE FOR FORMAT., Confirmed.
```

The program now verifies that there is sufficient space on the disk to write the decoded message. If there is, it executes the secret key and when completed, writes the decoded file on the disk.

```
CHECKING FOR ROOM TO WRITE DECODED FILE, Confirmed.
EXECUTING SECRET KEY ALGORITHM.(ABOUT A MINUTE).Done.
WRITING DECODED FILE TO DISK.Done.

NAME OF FILE JUST DECODED          "A:TEXTNAME.CTX"
ORIGINAL FILE NAME BEFORE ENCODING "A:TEXTNAME"
KEY FILE USED IN DECODING          "A:SECRET.KEY"
THE DECODED FILE NOW EXISTS AS     "A:TEXTNAME"

DONE
```

This package has been developed primarily for use in data transmission and requires that both the user and sender have different copies of *The Protector* program package with different serial numbers. If only one computer is used, then a warning message will appear on the screen.

DEDICATE/32

DEDICATE/32, developed by Public Key Systems Corporation, is a powerful public-key program using PKSC's **CHAOS ENGINE**, which develops an **RSA** (Rivest, Shamir, and Adleman) key, 32 bytes (32 characters) long. It can be used on any Z-80 microcomputer system with at least 32K memory. It is faster than *The Protector* in both generating the public and secret keys and also in encoding/decoding. It can be used on a single system for data storage protection without warning of a possible copyright violation.

Creating the Public and Secret Keys

The **KEYGEN** module uses four prime numbers instead of two for added security. It is invoked by typing

```
A> KEYGEN <CR>
```

The program responds with the following sign-on message on the screen and begins to generate the four prime numbers:

```
Keygen 32 byte Rev 2.0
(C) Copyright 1982, Public Key Systems Corp.
Public key generator type PKS032AXPAND00001
Serial # 09006
```

It searches for the four primes, two of which are called subprimes by the program. In my first attempt at the program, these four primes were generated in somewhat less than 8 minutes. Two additional messages were noted, *Key Imminent* and *Testing Key Pair*, after the primes were found:

```
SEARCHING FOR SUB PRIME 1
SEARCHING FOR PRIME 1
SEARCHING FOR SUB PRIME 2
SEARCHING FOR PRIME 2
KEY IMMINENT
TESTING KEY PAIR, ALMOST DONE, A FEW MORE MINUTES.
```

Less than 2 minutes later the two keys were tested and stored on the disk and the program signed-off with the following:

```
KEYGEN SUCCESSFUL!
DONE.
```

Encoding a Message

The same message, TEXTNAME, as shown on page 000, has been used as in earlier examples of enciphering programs to test DEDICATE/32. The ENCODE program is called by entering:

```
A> ENCODE TEXTNAME PUBLIC.KEY  <CR>
```

The program responded with the following on the CRT:

```
                    DEDICATE/32
                      Rev 2.0
         ENCODE MODULE Type: PKS032AXPAND00001
      Copyright 1981,82 by Public Key Systems Corp.
```

In a few seconds, the program had found the files and started processing; it reported the name of the message, the key used, and the name of the coded message:

```
KEY FILE NAME    A:PUBLIC.KEY
INPUT FILE NAME  A:TEXTNAME
OUTPUT FILE NAME A:TEXTNAME.CTX
Now encoding, please stand by.
```

In less than 25 seconds the encoding was completed, and the following appeared on the CRT:

```
Done.
```

In normal practice the original plaintext message, **TEXTNAME**, would be erased from the disk. The encoded message, **TEXTNAME.CTX**, was renamed using the CP/M utility to **MESSAGE.CTX**.

Decoding the Message

Decoding the message enciphered by the Public Key required calling the DECODE program and using the Secret Key, which matched the Public Key used during the encoding process:

```
A> DECODE MESSAGE SECRET.KEY  <CR>
```

Again the program signed-on with the following message on the CRT:

```
                DEDICATE/32
                 Rev 2.0
     DECODE MODULE Type: PKS032AXPAND00001
Copyright 1981,82 by Public Key Systems Corp.
Serial # 09006
DECODING FILE, PLEASE WAIT.
```

In about 25 seconds the message was decoded, and the program displayed the following information on the screen:

```
NAME OF FILE JUST DECODED           "A:MESSAGE.CTX"
ORIGINAL FILE NAME BEFORE ENCODING "A:TEXTNAME."
KEY FILE USED IN DECODING           "A:SECRET.KEY"
THE DECODED FILE NOW EXISTS AS      "A:MESSAGE."
DONE
```

DATA SECURITY AND SOURCE AUTHENTICATION

The public key system can be used in several ways in business data communications. Not only does it enable the user to send enciphered text from one computer user to another, but it also can be used to help the receiver of a message verify its source.

For example, you might wish to use your microcomputer system to notify your bank to transfer funds in payment for a specific invoice. How would the bank be certain that the request came from you? Or, you might receive an order via microcomputer transmission over telephone lines. How certain would you be that the order was actually made by the indicated sender?

There are several ways to use the public key system to verify the source of the sender. Here are two ways in which this can be done.

An "Open Message"

The simplest procedure is one in which the sender is more interested in confirming his or her identity as sender than in keeping the message secret. This is an example of a *signed* but insecure file.

- The sender encodes the message in a Private Key, transmits the message over telephone lines, and notifies the recipient that the message is sent.
- Upon receipt of the message, the receiver uses the sender's Public Key, which is readily available, to decode the message.

A "Secure and Signed Message"

In this example, the sender wishes to assure the receiver that the sender is the source of the message, but also wishes to keep the contents of the message secure from anyone else:

- The sender first encodes the message in his or her own Secret Key.
- The encoded message is then reencoded in the receiver's Public Key and transmitted to the receiver.
- Upon receipt of the message, the receiver decodes the message in his or her Secret Key.
- Finally, the receiver decodes the message, again using the sender's Public Key.

OTHER ENCRYPTION METHODS

Some encryption programs use algorithms other than the DES and PKA techniques. Several programs, such as those found in Bruce Bosworth's

Codes, Ciphers and Computers or Caxton C. Foster's *Cryptanalysis for Microcomputers*, have already appeared in books. Other encryption programs have appeared from time to time in various magazines. These programs may be used directly or may be modified for individual needs.

In addition to the encryption packages noted earlier in this chapter, there is Cybersoft's **DSS**, a data security system, which uses a proprietary algorithm. This package is designed for use on 16-bit microcomputers operating under IBM/DOS. It is fully interactive and menu-driven. The key length for this system may be up to 64 characters, which makes the system highly secure from attack.

HARDWARE ENCRYPTION TECHNIQUES

Hardware encryption is considerably faster than software encryption. Some hardware devices are available for use with several of the microcomputers on the market. In fact there is one microcomputer, the **OUTBOARD** by Cryptext Corporation, that already includes the necessary encryption hardware as part of the basic computer, and uses a complex, nondeterministic cryptographic system developed by Carl Nicolai.

One hardware device designed for use with PC-DOS on the IBM personal computer is MPPi's **PC LOCK II**, a half card printed circuit board that inserts on the mother board or in an expansion slot. Some 42 different passwords or softlock numbers can be used with encryption. If the lock is removed from the microcomputer, the data may be copied but they will be encrypted. If anyone attempts to use a different lock to decipher the data, it will not work. Each lock and superuser disk are matched at the factory.

Another hardware device that can be used with the IBM PC, Columbia Data Products' MPC or any other 16-bit microcomputer as well as with non-Z80 systems, is the **HERMES-4.** It is a "black box" version of DEDI-CATE/32, produced by Merritt Software, Inc., and is used in conjunction with a Z80 plug-in card and interfaced with the microcomputer through the RS-232 serial port.

Some hardware devices use the National Bureau of Standard's Data Encryption Algorithm. The Bureau has a testing and certification program for such hardware and feels that the implementation of the DES algorithm in special-purpose electronic devices provides greater cost effectiveness and increased security.

One NBS-approved device is the *Sherlock Bubble*, found in the Computer Transceiver Systems' **EXECUPORT 4000**. It is a portable terminal with keyboard and printer, as well as its own acoustic coupler modem for communications. These terminals provide a high level of security with very little burden put upon the user. The Sherlock Bubble is effectively "double-locked." The terminal has its own master key, which is part of the hardware encryption device. A second key, known as a session key, is randomly generated when the terminal is used and encrypted by the master key. It is possible to use the terminal without its encoding/decoding key.

Other DES encryption hardware units are available as plug-in devices. One is a microprocessor board, which plugs into any microcomputer system that uses an S-100 communications bus to interface the elements of the CPU. Another is the **CX-2** by Cryptext Corporation, which is designed for use with the TRS-80, Apple, and the IBM personal computers. The last named uses a ten-character key to initialize the code generator.

In evaluating any hardware devices it is necessary to consider trade-offs. It is important to compare the security offered by a longer key used with some of the software encryption packages with short keys used by the hardware devices that operate at higher speeds.

THE CLASSIFICATION OF DATA FOR SECURITY

It should be obvious that not all of a company's data needs to be classified "Top Secret" and encoded. Even if one uses hardware instead of software for the encoding/decoding of data, there is an overhead cost—the time required to encode and/or decode the data. Whether the time is measured in fractions of a second or minutes, the time does add up during a day. A rational approach to the classification of data is needed.

Various schemes of classification resembling the government's Top Secret, Classified, and so on, have been proposed for use in business. From a security viewpoint, it is necessary to review all the programs and data files used by the company in order to establish a rational policy for the classification of data. A four-tier system would serve most business firms, with the possible exception of those engaged in defense work. This system would include:

1. *Company Secret* or *Highly Restricted:* These are data files and programs that are highly confidential and should be available to only the highest level of personnel in any office. These disks should be kept separate from all others, preferably in a highly secure, locked file, to be accessed by one responsible individual within the company. A record of who has taken a disk and the date and time taken and returned should be kept in a log. The only files that belong in this classification are those that would have a serious adverse impact on the company's financial position, possibly affecting 5 to 10% of its profits. For example, projected product development, estimated company financial statements, and similar files would fall into this category.

2. *Company Confidential* or *Very Restricted:* These are data files that in unauthorized hands might be detrimental to the company, an

account, or an individual. These files could affect about 1 to 5% of the company's annual profits, and would include such files as payroll information, product sales, and active customer accounts.

3. *Internal Use Only* or *Restricted:* These are data files and programs containing information that a company prefers not to make public, but which would not seriously affect the company's financial position. Items such as company manuals, names and addresses of employees, and product literature before the product is released are examples of such data.

4. *Unclassified* or *For General Release:* All remaining data files would fall into this category.

A graphic technique can help you establish a data classification system for security and provide you with a visual summary of the protection you have set up. Figure 41 is an illustration of a *restriction to access chart,* showing at a glance each major program and data file and its specific security level.

HOW MUCH SHOULD YOU ENCODE?

Even after you have decided which data should be encoded, there is a question about how much of a specific file actually requires protection. Remember that encoding and decoding do take time, more when you use software than when you use hardware. As a rule, encryption is applied in two environments:

1. data in motion—data requiring security in communications, and
2. data in storage—data kept on file in your office.

Under communications security, the duration of the required protection of the data is usually only for the time of transmission. Under file storage security, the duration is usually longer while the data are in storage awaiting future processing.

In communications security you may decide to encipher

- all messages being transmitted over communications lines,
- selected messages because of their content, or
- specific fields within a message being transmitted.

Similarly, in file storage security, you may decide to encipher

- the entire file,
- selected data records within the file, or
- specific fields within all or some of the data records in the file.

Security Classification of
Programs and Data Files

File Name	Description	Secret	Company confidential	Internal use only	Unclassified
CB-86	Compiler for programs			■	
CUSTLST.FIL	Customer list	■			
DISPAY.COM	Print/display for products and prices			■	
INV.COM	Inventory control program		■		
INV/TOT.FIL	Inventory – complete		■		
INV/PRO.FIL	Inventory – in process		■		
IRS.COM	Program for tax data [TAX.FIL]	■			
PAYABLE.FIL	Accounts payable			■	
PAYROLL.COM	Payroll program [PAYROLL.FIL]			■	
PAYROLL.FIL	Payroll file	■			
PRICELST.FIL	Price lists				■
PRODDESC.FIL	Product descriptions				■
PROMITEM.FIL	Promotion item listings				■
PURCHASE.FIL	Purchase orders for components		■		
RECEIVE.FIL	Accounts receivable	■			
SALES.COM	Analysis program: product and staff		■		
SALESPRO.FIL	Sales analysis file – by product			■	
SALESSTF.FIL	Sales analysis file – by salesperson		■		
TAX.FIL	Tax data for corporation	■			

FIGURE 41

Graphic charts, such as restriction to access, provide a quick and positive reference to indicate the security level of major programs and data files.

HOW TO CREATE NUMERIC KEYS AND PASSWORDS BY COMPUTER

Some cryptographic programs require the user to input a numeric key. For example, in the ENCODE/DECODE program described earlier in this chapter, the user must input a ten-digit key and password. Would you remember these without writing them down if you were using the program? They were generated by a special program that will soon be described.

Many individuals, if asked to provide a ten-digit key, might respond with their telephone number, including the area code, or their social security number, a nine-digit value with some favorite digit added. Obviously, the use of such numeric keys would present a weakness in the security of the system. Writing the ten-digit key and storing it somewhere "safely" may also cause a breach of system security. The same applies to passwords that are not pronounceable and have no meaning.

Attempting to memorize a ten-digit key, or an even longer one with some of the special encoding programs, is difficult and almost impossible if one were asked for a 32-digit key for the DES. One way to make this easier for the user is to provide several mathematical transformation programs on the system that can be called to generate a series of digits. As long as the same simple digits or letters are used as inputs, the output will be the same.

For example, one might use a Fibonacci series. Leonardo of Pisa, or Fibonacci as he was called, was a twelfth century Italian mathematician who developed an algorithm in which every succeeding number was the sum of the previous two numbers. If we start with 1 and 1, the next number would be 2. The number after is the sum of 1 and 2, or 3; the number after that is the sum of 2 and 3, or 5, and so on:

$$1, 1, 2, 3, 5, 8, 13, 21, 34, 55, 89, 144$$

This series actually appears in nature, e.g., as the spaces between leaves on a vine.

It is possible to start with any two numbers and build a Fibonacci series. **KEYPASS.BAS**, at the end of this chapter, is a sample of a CBASIC program that will generate this type of series. To use this program the user would call it as follows:

```
A> CRUNZ KEYPASS   <CR>
```

and the program would respond with its first request, asking if you wish a numeric key or a password:

```
DO YOU WISH [1] NUMERIC KEY OR [2] PASSWORD
```

To obtain a numeric key enter 1, and the program then responds with its next prompt:

```
ENTER INITIAL VALUE ... 7 <CR>
```

The user can select any one-digit or multidigit value, except a zero or negative number. If the user enters an excluded value, the program responds with a warning note and again requests the entry of the value.

Once the computer has accepted the first value, it then requests a second value. We have entered 13:

```
ENTER SECOND VALUE ... 13  <CR>
```

The program then produces a series of Fibonacci values that appear as groups of five digits each:

20335 38613 92253 64589 95315 42249 54037 65321 05691 71012 76701 75523 99521 54725

Once the series appears on the screen, the program asks if the user wishes to produce another series. If the response is Y, the program restarts, but if the answer is N, the program indicates that it has been terminated normally.

```
RESTART? ... (Y/N) ... N  <CR>

NORMAL EXIT
```

Note that the original two values may be any two the user finds easy to remember. From the series that appears on the screen, the user may select any number of digits required as a key for the encryption program being used. The sequence can start at any point and go in either direction. If it is necessary to copy the key because of its length, make certain that the paper is destroyed.

From a security viewpoint, more than one transformation program should be kept on the system for a user to create a numeric key. Some simple programs of this type would be

- logarithms of a series given only the initial starting number,
- cube root of a series with only a single starting number, or
- product of each of the two preceding numbers.

Anyone with some mathematical background can create programs using such transformations, and these programs can be stored on the system.

It is also possible to use this program to obtain passwords that are meaningless and unpronounceable. After the program is called, the answer to the first question is 2.

```
DO YOU WISH [1] NUMERIC KEY OR [2] PASSWORD  2  <CR>
```

Again the program would request two numeric values that it will use to obtain the alphabetic password:

```
ENTER INITIAL VALUE ........   13   <CR>
ENTER SECOND VALUE .........   26   <CR>
```

This time, instead of the numeric values, the program would produce an alphabetic string, again printed in groups of five.

```
SVFBM JGGDF OOHFD BWKUL
```

The password can consist of as many letters as the user wishes. The sequence can be read from left to right or right to left; the first few letters can be skipped and the following ones used for the password. The program signs off in the same way as the numeric key illustration noted earlier.

If the user had entered a 4 for the initial value and a 26 for the second value, the password returned would be:

```
SUXJH MYVAK GBFCN TBFWA
```

Any number of discrete, individual numeric keys and/or passwords can be generated by this program simply by changing the input values. With several different numeric key and password-generating programs on the system, anyone attempting to crack the system would not only have to determine which numeric key/password generator was used, but also the numeric values that were entered.

```
REM     *************************************************************
REM
REM     PROGRAM:    H007.BAS
REM
REM     PURPOSE:    SAMPLE PROGRAM TO ILLUSTRATE ENCIPHERING --
REM                 INCLUDES ASCII CODE VERIFICATION TO DETECT
REM                 POSSIBLE ALTERATION DURING TRANSMISSION.
REM                 PROGRAM AS WRITTEN CURRENTLY IS LIMITED FOR
REM                 USE WITH NAMES OF A MAXIMUM OF 30 CHARACTERS
REM
REM     PROGRAMMED IN CBASIC BY DR. HAROLD JOSEPH HIGHLAND
REM                 PROGRAMMED:        SEPTEMBER 16, 1982
REM                 LATEST UPDATE:     SEPTEMBER 25, 1982
REM             *  COPYRIGHT 1982,  HIGHLAND + HIGHLAND  *
REM
REM     *************************************************************
REM
REM         INITIALIZATION OF VARIABLES AND BASIC HOUSEKEEPING
REM
REM     *************************************************************
REM
        DIM N$(15), NA%(15)
        CLEAR$ = CHR$(126) + CHR$(28)
10      J%      =  1
        OUT1$  = "": OUT2$ = "": OUT3$ = ""
        SUM1%  =  0: SUM2% = 0 : SUM3% = 0
REM
REM     *************************************************************
REM
REM     KEYS [KEY1%, KEY2% AND KEY3%] CAN BE MODIFIED IN TWO WAYS:
REM     [1] DIFFERENT NUMERIC VALUES CAN BE ASSIGNED WITHIN PROGRAM,
REM     OR [2] NUMERIC VALUES CAN BE USED WITH INPUT STATEMENT.
REM
REM     *************************************************************
REM
        KEY1%  =   5:        REM FACTOR FOR SUM1%
        KEY2%  =   6:        REM FACTOR FOR SUM2%
        KEY3%  =   2:        REM FACTOR FOR SUM3%
REM
REM     *************************************************************
REM
REM         START OF INPUT AND PRINTOUT OF NAME IN CLEARTEXT
REM
REM     *************************************************************
REM
        PRINT CLEAR$
        INPUT "ENTER NAME ....... "; NAME$: PRINT
REM
REM     *************************************************************
REM
REM     FILLOUT OF NAME AND TRUNCATION TO 30 CHARACTERS:
REM         LON%   IS USED TO DETERMINE LENGTH OF ORIGINAL NAME
REM         LONA$  IS THE ENCIPHERED LENGTH OF ORIGINAL NAME
REM         FILL$  SET BY USING CRYPTOGRAPHIC LETTER-FREQUENCY CODE
REM
REM     *************************************************************
REM
        FILL$ = "ZJXQKVINOATEZEJTXAQOKNVIEXOCPMQUAY"
        LON%  = LEN (NAME$)
        LONA$ = STR$ (LON% + 50) + STR$ (INT% (RND * 10))
        NAM$  = UCASE$ (NAME$) + FILL$
REM
REM     *************************************************************
REM
REM     SEGMENTATION OF NAME INTO 15 PARTS OF 2 CHARACTERS EACH;
REM     ASCII CODE FOR EACH LEAD CHARACTER OF N$(I%): 1 THROUGH 15
REM     IS USED FOR LINE TRANSMISSION VERIFICATION.
REM
REM     *************************************************************
REM
```

```
        FOR I% = 1 TO 15
                N$(I%)  = MID$ (NAM$,J%,2)
                NA%(I%) = ASC (N$(I%))
                J% = J% + 2
REM     NEXT I%
REM     ****************************************************************
REM
REM     JOINING OF 3 STRINGS [OUT1$, OUT2$ AND OUT3$] USING THE 15
REM     ELEMENTS [N$(I)] USING SEQUENCE-DIRECTED ALGORITHMS:
REM         OUT1$ = N$(1, 4, 7, 10, 13) IN REVERSE SEQUENCE
REM         OUT2$ = N$(2, 5, 8, 11, 14) IN SEQUENCE, AND
REM         OUT3$ = N$(3, 6, 9, 12, 15) IN REVERSE SEQUENCE
REM     SUM1% THROUGH SUM3% ACCUMULATED USING NA%(I) ARRAY
REM
REM     ****************************************************************
REM
        FOR I% = 1 TO 15 STEP 3
                K% = 14 - I%
                L% = I% + 1
                M% = 16 - I%
                OUT1$ = OUT1$ + N$(K%)
                OUT2$ = OUT2$ + N$(L%)
                OUT3$ = OUT3$ + N$(M%)
                SUM1% = SUM1% + NA%(K%)
                SUM2% = SUM2% + NA%(L%)
                SUM3% = SUM3% + NA%(M%)
        NEXT I%
REM
REM     ****************************************************************
REM
REM              CONCATENATION OF ENCIPHERED NAME, "CODENM$"
REM
REM     ****************************************************************
REM
        CODENM$ = LONA$ + OUT3$ + OUT1$ + OUT2$
REM
REM     ****************************************************************
REM
REM     SCRAMBLE OF ASCII CODE OF SEGMENTS FOR TRANSMISSION CONTROL
REM
REM     ****************************************************************
REM
        SUM1% = SUM1% * KEY1%
        SUM2% = SUM2% * KEY2%
        SUM3% = SUM3% * KEY3%
REM
REM     ****************************************************************
REM
REM         PRINTOUT OF ENCIPHERED NAME$ AND ASCII TRAILER
REM
REM     ****************************************************************
REM
        PRINT: PRINT CODENM$; SUM3%; SUM1%; SUM2%: PRINT: CONSOLE
REM
REM     ****************************************************************
REM
REM         RESTART PROCEDURE FOR DEMONSTRATION PURPOSES
REM
REM     ****************************************************************
REM
        INPUT "TRY AGAIN ?   (Y/N) ... ";AN$
        IF AN$ = "Y" THEN 10
REM
REM     ****************************************************************
REM
REM                TERMINATION OF THE PROGRAM
REM
REM     ****************************************************************
REM
        PRINT:  PRINT "NORMAL END OF PROGRAM"
        END
```

```
REM
      ****************************************************************
REM
REM   PROGRAM:   E007.BAS
REM
REM   PURPOSE:   DECIPHERING PROGRAM TO BE USED WITH OUTPUT FROM
REM              H007.BAS PROGRAM WHICH ENCIPHERS DATA
REM
REM   PROGRAMMED IN CBASIC BY ESTHER H. HIGHLAND
REM          PROGRAMMED:        OCTOBER 13, 1982
REM          LATEST UPDATE:     NOVEMBER 7, 1982
REM          *  COPYRIGHT 1982,  HIGHLAND + HIGHLAND  *
REM
REM   ****************************************************************
REM
REM                   INITIALIZATION OF VARIABLES
REM
REM   ****************************************************************
REM
      DIM N$(15), NA%(15)
      CLEAR$ = CHR$(126) + CHR$(28)
10    J% = 4: SUMD1%=0: SUMD2% = 0: SUMD3% = 0: NAM$=""
      KEY1% = 5: KEY2% = 6: KEY3% = 2
REM
REM   ****************************************************************
REM
REM                   INPUT OF ENCIPHERED TEXT
REM
REM   ****************************************************************
REM
      PRINT CLEAR$
      PRINT "Enter the enciphered name -- "
      PRINT "Start with the initial digits followed by"
      PRINT "ALL the letters to the last letter, and"
      PRINT "remember to enter any BLANKS that appear."
      PRINT:    PRINT:   INPUT "Data: "; CODENM$: PRINT
      INPUT "Enter first number:  "; SUM3%:   PRINT
      INPUT "Enter second number: "; SUM1%:   PRINT
      INPUT "Enter third number:  "; SUM2%:   PRINT
REM
REM   ****************************************************************
REM
REM                   ROUTINE FOR DECIPHERING OF INPUT TEXT
REM
REM   ****************************************************************
REM
      CODENM$ = UCASE$ (CODENM$)
      LGTH$ = LEFT$ (CODENM$,2):    LGTH% = VAL (LGTH$) - 50
      FOR I%= 1 TO 15
            N$(I%) = MID$ (CODENM$,J%,2)
            NA%(I%) = ASC (N$ (I%)):    J% = J% + 2
      NEXT I%
      FOR I% = 1 TO 5
            K% = 11 - I%:    L% = 10 + I%:    M% = 6 - I%
            NAM1$ = N$(K%) + N$(L%) + N$(M%)
            NAM$ = NAM$ + NAM1$
            SUMD1% = SUMD1% + NA%(K%)
            SUMD2% = SUMD2% + NA%(L%)
            SUMD3% = SUMD3% + NA%(M%)
      NEXT I%
      SUMD1% = SUMD1% * KEY1%:    SUMD2% = SUMD2% * KEY2%
      SUMD3% = SUMD3% * KEY3%:    NAME$ = LEFT$ (NAM$,LGTH%)
REM
REM   ****************************************************************
REM
REM        ERROR CONTROL IF TEXT HAS BEEN TAMPERED WITH --
REM        OUTPUT OF TEXT AND CONTROL VALUES
REM
REM   ****************************************************************
REM
      IF SUMD1% = SUM1% AND SUMD2% = SUM2% AND SUMD3% = SUM3% THEN 20
      PRINT "      ******************"
      PRINT "      SUMS DO NOT MATCH"
      PRINT "      ******************"
```

```
20        PRINT:    PRINT NAME$:     PRINT:     PRINT SUM1%, SUMD1%
          PRINT SUM2%, SUMD2%:       PRINT SUM3%, SUMD3%
REM
REM       ************************************************************
REM
REM                  RESTART AND / OR TERMINATION PROCEDURE
REM
REM       ************************************************************
REM
          PRINT:  INPUT "Wish another decipher? ... (Y/N) .... "; ANS
          IF UCASE$ (AN$) = "Y" THEN 10
          PRINT:     PRINT "Decipher program terminated normally"
          END


REM       ************************************************************
REM
REM       PROGRAM:  KEYPASS.BAS
REM
REM       PURPOSE:  PROGRAM TO GENERATE NUMERIC KEYS OR PASSWORDS
REM
REM                 PROGRAM USES FIBONACCI TRANSFORMATION PLUS A
REM                 RANDOM VARIABLE PROCEDURE TO CREATE EITHER
REM                 [1] NUMERIC KEY OR [2] PASSWORD
REM
REM       PROGRAMMED IN CBASIC BY DR. HAROLD JOSEPH HIGHLAND
REM                 PROGRAMMED:        NOVEMBER 15,1982
REM                 LATEST UPDATE:     NOVEMBER 20,1982
REM             * COPYRIGHT 1982,  HIGHLAND + HIGHLAND *
REM
REM       ************************************************************
REM
REM                       HOUSEKEEPING SECTION
REM
REM       ************************************************************
REM
          DIM K%(20), V%(20), C$(20), NC$(25), XA$(25)
          CLEAR$ = CHR$(126) + CHR$(28)
10        A% = 0:     N$ = "":    X$ = "":     S$ = " "
REM
REM       INPUT OF TWO NUMBERIC VALUES:   RANGE FROM 1 TO 32,767
REM
          PRINT CLEAR$
15        INPUT "DO YOU WISH  [1] NUMERIC KEY OR   [2] PASSWORD  ";A%
          IF A% < 1 OR A% > 2 THEN PRINT "ENTER 1 OR 2 - TRY AGAIN":\
          PRINT:     GOTO 15
          PRINT:     PRINT "VALUE MUST BE BETWEEN 1 AND 32,767"
18        PRINT:     INPUT "ENTER INITIAL VALUE ....... "; I%
          IF I% < 1 OR I% > 32767 THEN PRINT "VALUE OUT OF RANGE" :\
          PRINT:     GOTO 18
20        PRINT:     INPUT "ENTER SECOND VALUE ........ "; J%
          IF J% < 1 OR I% > 32767 THEN PRINT "VALUE OUT OF RANGE" :\
          PRINT:     GOTO 20
REM
REM       ************************************************************
REM
REM          FIBONACCI TRANSFORMATION AND RANDOM MODIFICATION
REM
REM       ************************************************************
REM
          FOR M% = 1 TO 20
                K%(M%) = I% + J%
30              IF K%(M%) < 0 THEN K%(M%) = ABS (K%(M%)) * RND * 2
                IF K%(M%) > 32767 THEN K%(M%) = K%(M%)/ 2 * RND * 2
                IF K%(M%) < 0 THEN 30
                I% = J%: J% = K%(M%)
          NEXT M%
```

```
          FOR M% = 1 TO 20
                  K$ = STR$(K%(M%)):  L% = LEN (K$):  E% = L% - 2
                  IF E% < 1 THEN E% = 1
                  V%(M%) = K%(M%) / 10 ^ E%
   50         IF V%(M%) > 65 AND V%(M%) < 91 THEN 100
                  IF V%(M%) < 30 THEN V%(M%) = V%(M%) + 50: GOTO 50
                  IF V%(M%) < 40 THEN V%(M%) = V%(M%) + 40: GOTO 50
                  IF V%(M%) < 60 THEN V%(M%) = V%(M%) + 30: GOTO 50
                  IF V%(M%) < 65 THEN V%(M%) = V%(M%) + 10: GOTO 50
                  IF V%(M%) > 90 THEN V%(M%) = V%(M%) - 10: GOTO 50
  100     NEXT M%
  REM
  REM     ****************************************************************
  REM
  REM           ALPHABETICAL TRANSFORMATION OF MATHEMATICAL DATA
  REM
  REM     ****************************************************************
  REM
          FOR M% = 1 TO 20
                  C$(M%) = CHR$(V%(M%))
          NEXT M%
          PRINT:    PRINT:    ON A% GOTO 200, 300
  REM
  REM     ****************************************************************
  REM
  REM           FURTHER TRANSFORMATION AND PRINTOUT OF NUMERIC KEY
  REM
  REM     ****************************************************************
  REM
  200     FOR M% = 1 TO 20
                  K$ = STR$(K%(M%)):    N$ = N$ + K$
          NEXT M%
          PRINT:    PRINT:    TOTAL% = LEN (N$)
          KEYS% = TOTAL% / 5:    I% = 1
          FOR M% = 1 TO KEYS%
                  NC$(M%) = MID$ (N$, I%, 5):    I% = I% + 5
          NEXT M%
          FOR M% = 1 TO KEYS%
                  PRINT NC$(M%); S$;
          NEXT M%
          GOTO 400
  REM
  REM     ****************************************************************
  REM
  REM           FURTHER TRANSFORMATION AND PRINTOUT OF PASSWORD
  REM
  REM     ****************************************************************
  REM
  300     FOR M% = 1 TO 20
                  X$ = X$ + C$(M%)
          NEXT M%
          TOTAL% = LEN (X$): KEYS% = TOTAL% / 5:    I% = 1
          FOR M% = 1 TO KEYS%
                  XA$(M%) = MID$ (X$, I%, 5):    I% = I% + 5
          NEXT M%
          FOR M% = 1 TO KEYS%
                  PRINT XA$(M%); S$;
          NEXT M%
  REM
  REM     ****************************************************************
  REM
  REM           RESTART PROCEDURE AND TERMINATION
  REM
  REM     ****************************************************************
  REM
  400     PRINT: PRINT: INPUT "RESTART? ... (Y/N) .... "; ANS
          IF ANS = "Y" THEN 10
          PRINT:    PRINT "NORMAL TERMINATION OF PROGRAM"
          END
```

CHAPTER 13

Ten Simple Steps for Security during Operations

In this chapter we discuss ten procedures and/or operating policies that can be easily implemented to enhance the security of any microcomputer system. These apply to both multiuser, single-computer systems, as well as multitasking, multiuser microcomputer systems. It should be noted that, to many professionals today, systems reliability is part of computer security. The ten procedures and/or policies discussed in this chapter are

1. Test the entire system quickly *before* you run programs.
2. Check disks for defects *before* you use them.
3. Recover from a "crashed" disk.
4. Fully erase a program or file when it is no longer needed.
5. Set up common-sense personnel policies and office work procedures.
6. Restrict the use of several CP/M utilities.
7. Maintain a computer utilization log.
8. Find out what is on the *whole* disk.
9. Respond to accidental erasure of programs and/or files.
10. Maintain proper documentation.

HOW TO CHECK THE PHYSICAL HEALTH OF YOUR SYSTEM

Since the earliest days of major business computers, programs have been written to test whether the various components of a computer system were functioning properly. With mainframe and even minicomputer systems, manufacturers have assumed the responsibility for providing such programs to the user. Some manufacturers of terminals and printers build such test programs into their units, but most microcomputer manufacturers have failed to do this.

From a security viewpoint, the entire system should be given a fast test, at least at the start of the day before any work is run. Before a special program is run, for example, one that involves large data files or generates extensive computations, it is advisable to do the same. It is too costly to find out later in the day or week that an error in writing on a disk has occurred because of an equipment glitch. Verifying the CPU output to a disk every time you write copy on a disk takes too much time.

A quick test, the *QRUN* program of **Diagnostics II**, is a good way to detect major malfunctions in a short time. Actually, it chains three of the programs that are part of the package to perform

1. a quick test of the entire user memory of the CPU,
2. a nondestructive, rapid test of the disk drive currently in use, and
3. a test of the CPU by testing its timing and each instruction that the CPU is able to execute, the results, and any errors are reported.

The other portions of the Diagnostics II package contain programs to test all parts of memory, the alignment of the read/write heads, and the printer. They take more time, but are recommended as part of a security mainte-nance program to be run periodically, the frequency depending upon the system's use. Once a month is a minimum.

One of my 8-bit systems takes only 2 minutes to test, and this test is performed at the start of each day, or more frequently if sensitive data are being processed. All that is necessary is to call the program; output from the run is shown in Figure 42. A more comprehensive test of the system is possible, and one example of this output is shown in Figure 43.

```
A>  QRUN
Supersoft Associates Diagnostics II
Quick test   Copyright (c) 1981

Memory test
Memory test complete

Disk test
Read/Write test
Random seek test
0 read/write errors detected
0 seek errors detected

Diagnostics II V1.2 - CPU Test
Copyright (c) 1981 - Supersoft Associates

ABCDEFGHIJKLMNOPQRSTUVWXYZ
CPU is Z80
Begin timing test
End timing test
CPU tests OK
```

FIGURE 42

CRT display of output of a quick diagnostic run under *Diagnostics II*.

```
DIAGNOSTICS II - MEMORY TEST

COPYRIGHT (C) 1981  SUPERSOFT INC.

ANY MEMORY FROM 1500H TO FFFFH MAY BE TESTED.
TEST WILL BE REPEATED UNTIL SPECIFIED NUMBER
OF ITERATIONS HAVE BEEN COMPLETED.  STRIKING
ANY KEY WILL ABORT THE TEST.


STRIKING SPACE BAR OR RETURN KEY CAUSES START
AND END ADDRESSES TO DEFAULT TO 1500H AND TOP
OF TPA RESPECTIVELY.

STRIKING ANY KEY WILL CAUSE ERROR TOTALS
UP TO THAT POINT TO BE DISPLAYED BY BIT
POSITION FOR 1K REGIONS.

ALL NUMBERS INPUT AND OUTPUT ARE IN HEX.


TYPE L TO LOG OUTPUT TO DISK IN DRIVE A: L
OUTPUT WILL BE LOGGED TO A:DIAG.LOG


ENTER START ADDRESS (IIEX): 2000
ENTER  END  ADDRESS (HEX): A000

PLEASE SELECT:

Q - QUICK TEST
W - WALKING BIT TEST
B - BURN TEST
S - SPEED TEST
Q
ENTER B FOR BANK SELECT:
ENTER NUMBER OF ITERATIONS (DEFAULT = 1): 1

                 MAP OF TESTED MEMORY

0K      8K      16K     24K     32K     40K     48K     56K     64K
0000H   2000H   4000H   6000H   8000H   A000H   C000H   E000H   FFFFH
+.......+.......+.......+.......+.......+.......+.......+.......+
          111111111111111111111111111111111
PASSES COMPLETE = 0001 ; COUNT OF ERROR BYTES = 0000 .

   TOTAL ERROR COUNT -
PASSES COMPLETE = 0001 ; COUNT OF ERROR BYTES = 0000 .

ENTER START ADDRESS (HEX):
```

FIGURE 43

CRT display of a more exhaustive hardware test under *Diagnostics II*.

PRIOR TO FORMATTING A DISK . . .

There are few things more disconcerting, even to an experienced programmer or microcomputer operator, than the appearance on the screen of

```
    Bdos Err on B: Bad Sector
```

This is the computer's way of informing you that the disk has "crashed." (What to do in that event is covered later in this chapter.)

Even if you use quality disks, there is always the possibility that at some stage you will encounter some type of disk read/write error. If the computer, while reading or writing a program or file on a disk, finds a bad sector, the CP/M operating system will not permit the system to read any portion of the disk beyond that sector. The entire file, or even the disk, may be useless.

In the section on formatting a disk in Chapter 6, "Microcomputer Systems Terminology," it was noted that if you encounter a formatting error, you should try to reformat the disk once or twice more. However, you can forestall many of these problems if you use a special program to inspect the disk *before* you format it. If you have purchased a disk with a bad sector from a reputable dealer, you should be able to exchange it. However, even if you cannot, all is not lost.

Prior to formatting, I run a special program, **BADLIM**, that checks all sectors of the disk. It links defective sectors in a shadow file that becomes part of the disk directory. The operating system considers those bad sectors as allocated and prevents data from being written in any bad sector. The program can be run on single-density or double-density disks, and even on hard disks. It is, however, necessary to have two disk drives in order to run the program.

My basic systems security disk, which contains this program, is

```
A> BADLIM   <CR>

BADLIM   ver 1.3
(c) 1981 Blat, Research+Development Corp.

ENTER DRIVE (OR RETURN TO REBOOT): B

BADLIM NEEDS A DISKETTE IN DRIVE 'A', PLEASE LEAVE ONE INSERTED
ENTER TIMES (1-9) TO CHECK FOR SOFT ERRORS (<CR>=1):
INSERT DISKETTE TO TEST ON DRIVE B AND PRESS RETURN

Checking Directory
...............
Directory area ckecks  O.K.

Checking data area... Please wait

+++++++++++++++++++++++++++++++++
++++++++++++++++++++++++++++++++++
++++++++++++++++++++++++++++++++++
++++++++++++++++++++++++++++++++++
++++++++++++++++++++++++++++++++++
++++++++++++++++++++++++++++++++++
++++++++++++++++++++++++++++++++++
++++++++++++++++++
    THERE ARE 0 BAD BLOCKS

              BADLIM FINISHED
ENTER DRIVE (OR RETURN TO REBOOT):

NORMAL EXIT
```

FIGURE 44

Visual display of a test of a new floppy disk using the BADLIM program, which checks the directory as well as the disk's blocks. No defects have been found.

mounted on disk drive A and is kept there throughout the test. The new disk is placed in disk drive B. The program is interactive; once it is called there are only two questions the user must answer. The first response a user must make is to indicate the disk drive on which the new blank disk is placed. Using a two-drive system, I respond with B. The other question is the number of times the program should check for sector errors. The user has a choice from 1 to 9, but remember that the more often searches are repeated, the longer it takes to verify the disk. Some repetition is recommended because minor disk faults may not be detected on the first run. I have found three repeated searches a suitable arbitrary number for my use; there are other things I can do at the terminal while waiting for the test to be finished.

After the program has completed its search for bad sectors, it will report the results on the CRT. Figure 44 shows the interactive program for a new disk that has no bad sectors. Figure 45 shows the output of a disk with a bad directory sector.

This program can also be used with a disk that has already been formatted and used. No data on the disk are touched or modified by the program; only directory blocks are changed if a bad sector is found. Furthermore, the program will list the filenames of any files now residing in bad sectors. The remaining files on the disk can still be used.

HOW TO RECOVER A "CRASHED" DISK

A "crashed" disk, like a power blackout, starts the flow of adrenaline. Whether the cause of the crash is a lightning storm, static electricity, a

```
A> BADLIM   <CR>

BADLIM   ver 1.3
(c) 1981 Blat, Research+Development Corp.

ENTER DRIVE (OR RETURN TO REBOOT): B

BADLIM NEEDS A DISKETTE IN DRIVE 'A', PLEASE LEAVE ONE INSERTED
ENTER TIMES (1-9) TO CHECK FOR SOFT ERRORS (<CR>=1):   <CR>
INSERT DISKETTE TO TEST ON DRIVE B AND PRESS RETURN

Checking Directory

Bad directory sector, cannot be de-allocated


ENTER DRIVE (OR RETURN TO REBOOT):

NORMAL EXIT
```

FIGURE 45

CRT display of a disk check showing that a bad sector exists in the directory and that the disk cannot be used as its exists. If this occurs, use a bulk eraser to clean the disk and restart by formatting the disk again. This generally works unless the disk has been severely damaged.

power surge, equipment failure, or an operator error, there is usually a loss of valuable programs and/or data. If a backup is available or the amount of material that must be reentered is small, the problem is not acute. However, there are times when it is too costly in time and money to recover material newly entered on the disk by starting over again.

Before discussing recovery techniques, it is prudent to mention one other disk error that sometimes appears, but that is not so serious. That is

```
Bdos Err on B: Select
```

This message on the screen indicates an operations error; it does not mean that there is a disk error due to an equipment or disk problem. The program being run, or perhaps even the operator, has called for the use of a disk on disk drive B when no disk has been mounted. A similar error message would appear if a disk drive has been called for that does not exist on the system.

Three types of bad sector conditions can plague the microcomputer user:

1. As noted earlier, if a program or file contains a single bad sector, CP/M will not read beyond that sector and the file is useless.
2. If a bad sector appears on the disk in an unassigned group (sectors that have not yet been used), CP/M will not use any portion of the disk beyond this sector to write data.
3. If there is a bad sector in the disk's directory, CP/M will not read the directory past that sector. Therefore, although some files may still be read by the computer, nothing additional can be written on the disk.

The *bad sector* error can be attacked by using a special package called **DISK DOCTOR**, which does not require the user to have any knowledge of the CP/M file structure. The package consists of five parts, or *wards* as they are called, and is interactive, so that the user need only respond to the questions that appear on the CRT.

- *Ward A* is used mainly to restore the usefulness of a disk, rather than recover data from it. It verifies the disk and locks out the bad sectors without touching the good files that exist. All the groups (a fixed number of sectors, usually 8 or 16) containing a bad sector are assigned to a special morgue file. This file is retained on the disk so that groups containing a bad sector are not used in the future running of the disk. This portion of the package is used for quick recovery of a disk you need to use. The ward, incidentally, can serve the same function as the BADLIM program described earlier.
- *Ward B* permits the user to designate specific groups or sectors of data on a disk and rewrite them on another disk. In this way it is possible to

transfer the material you wish to recover and discard whatever is of no value to you or material on the disk that has been destroyed. A sample of this procedure is shown in Figure 46.

- *Ward C* is probably the best resource for dealing with disks with bad sectors. Containing a very tolerant copying routine, it permits the user to make another copy of the crashed disk and places blank spaces within the bad sector. It is slow but very useful, especially if you have a considerable amount of new data for which you have not yet made backups.

```
A> DOCTOR [CR]

DISK DOCTOR VER  1.41  COPYRIGHT (C) 1981
SUPERSOFT,INC. AND J.M. HOLLAND.

Console Display Options:
S = by sector    T = by track    N = no display
select option (CR = N):  T  [CR]

Select drive for recovery disk   (CR = drive A): A [CR]
Select drive for patient disk    (CR = drive B): B [CR]

You are in Admitting.

Ward A: Assign bad groups to MORGUE.
Ward B: Transplant sectors or groups to recovery disk.
Ward C: Recover damaged disk by copying to another.
Ward D: Recover erased files.
Ward E: Directory of recoverable erased files.
Exit  X: Exit to system

Select Ward: B [CR]

Ward B

Transplants sectors or groups of data from patient
disk to specified file on receovery disk.

Place recovery disk in drive A
Place patient  disk in drive B
and hit RETURN to continue  [CR]

Specify file name:  CPU.COM [CR]

Recovery options :
S = by sector    G = by group
Select option  : G [CR]

Specify groups to be recovered in hex
as found in directory.  Enter a period "."
to close file.
Groups are numbered 0 thru 95
Directory is in group 0 to 0
Group 10 [CR]

------ detailed searches printed out at
    this stage of the program ---------

Found file extent - 00
```

FIGURE 46

Output obtained when using Disk Doctor. In this case, sectors from damaged disk in drive B have been transferred to a recovery disk in drive A.

The other two wards of this package are covered later in this chapter in the section on the recovery of erased files.

ERA DOES NOT MEAN ERASE

One of the first warnings anyone using a microcomputer receives is caution in the use of the ERA subprogram under CP/M or **DEL** under PC-DOS or MS-DOS. According to the operating system manual, the built-in command is used to erase files from the disk's directory and from the disk. Therefore, it would seem logical that if you wished to destroy confidential data on a disk, all that would be necessary is to enter

```
A>  ERA   <filename>      <CR>
```

where <filename> is the name of the file you wish destroyed by erasing it from the disk.

This does *not* produce the same results as if you had taken a written report and run it through a paper shredder. The ERA or DEL does remove the filename from the directory, *but* the material in the file remains *unaltered*. It is possible, using special utility programs discussed later in this chapter, to restore these files.

It is true that if you enter a new file or expand an existing file on the disk, the computer *will* use that area of the disk to write over the erased file, but you are taking a risk if there is no additional data entry. Therefore, from a security viewpoint, you should "clobber" the actual file to make it completely unreadable by anyone who may illegally restore it later.

The CLOBBER.BAS Program

To prevent anyone from gaining access to confidential information on the disk after you no longer need it, you should first write over the file before you erase its name from the disk's directory using the ERA command. This can be done with a special program, **CLOBBER.BAS**, which appears at the end of this chapter. The program is designed to replace each record in the existing file with * DO NOT SNOOP *, which will remain in that file until it is overwritten sometime later when additional data are entered.

From a security viewpoint the recommended procedure to remove any program or file from a disk is

- execute the program, CLOBBER.BAS, to totally delete the information in the file, and
- use the ERA command to remove the filename from the directory.

This technique will ensure your having removed vital information rather than relying on having the file overwritten by the computer at some later date.

Using an Electromagnetic Eraser

If you wish to erase an entire disk, not selected programs, you may consider the electromagnetic bulk eraser that is used with tape reels and the hard disks that are used with mainframe computers (see Figure 47). It works the same way as the bulk eraser used with magnetic recording tapes. One limitation on the use of these electromagnetic erasers, however, is that they can be used only for removing all data on an *entire* disk; you cannot remove individual programs and files selectively. Furthermore, once you have exposed a floppy disk to the magnetic fields of these erasers, it is necessary to format the disk again and to add the SYSGEN portion of the operating system, plus any of the utility programs you wish to use. If you have an entire disk with confidential data, this technique is more complete and often faster than using the CLOBBER program, even if you have to reformat the disk and add operating systems programs.

MAKING MICROCOMPUTER OPERATIONS SECURE

Company policy and work rules should be established to protect the company from inadvertent as well as illegal actions by an employee. The policy covering work procedures with the microcomputer system must be thoroughly explained to the workers, and their suggestions or objections should be carefully considered. By doing so you will reduce the risk of employee

FIGURE 47

A bulk eraser used to demagnetize or "erase" the entire disk for security purposes.

fraud and prevent low employee morale. Most computer-related crime is the work of employees, not outside intruders.

Security Education of Personnel

To educate personnel, management must be specific in the information it provides to its employees. Management is also responsible for making certain that all employees understand the conditions under which they are working in a computer environment. Here are some general rules:

- All employees should be educated as to security practices that will be followed when using the microcomputer system. They should be encouraged to be on the alert at all times and report any irregularities they observe.
- Employees should be notified in advance whether they have access to the microcomputer. It should be made perfectly clear that those not authorized by management to use the computer may not do so without running the risk of being dismissed.
- Each employee who may use the microcomputer should be informed, preferably in writing, as to what resources that employee is expected to protect; what hazards may be expected; what variances to note and report; and what corrective action he or she is expected and/or permitted to take.
- Every employee who uses the microcomputer system should be given a specific user number and/or password (as discussed in Chapter 9). Each employee must be made aware of the need to be responsible for keeping these secret from the other employees. Several years ago, as a national lecturer on computer security for the Association for Computing Machinery (ACM), I found it distressing, but at the same time amusing, to find a computer installation in which employee passwords were posted on the bulletin board. In other installations, the employees pasted copies of their passwords on their terminals. In one military installation, I found that several officers had used a piece of adhesive tape on which they wrote their passwords and then placed the tape inside their hats.
- Employees accessing the microcomputer should be told which programs and/or files they are permitted to use on the system.
- A policy of mandatory vacations for all employees should be enforced. Be wary of an employee who cannot stay away from the company for the entire vacation period. In one company, an employee had modified the payroll file to obtain a higher wage rate and was present whenever the payroll was run on the computer system. In that way no one else was aware of the change, and the auditors did not question why the

particular employee was being paid at a rate higher than others in the same position. The employee made it a point to come to work on the day the payroll program was run even though she was on vacation.

- If an employee is notified that he or she is to be dismissed, that employee should not be permitted access to the computer, any printed records, or the disks or tapes used on the computer. This practice is followed in mainframe installations and should be followed with a microcomputer system.

Operating Procedures

In addition to normal employee practices followed by most companies and the rules just noted, a specific set of operating policies should be established. These rules should be part of an employee manual and should be known by all employees who have access to the microcomputer system. Some recommended procedures, depending upon the size of the company, include the following.

- Access to the computer should be limited to designated employees.
- Responsibility for the protection of each and every resource—the computer, different disk files, manuals, and printed reports—should be explicitly assigned by employee.
- User numbers, passwords, and/or key words for control of programs and files should be changed and reissued regularly, at least on a quarterly basis.
- The user number and/or password of an employee who leaves should be deactivated immediately.
- In the normal course of events, each person performing a sensitive operation should be checked randomly, as well as regularly, by a supervisor.
- All employees, except some supervisory personnel, should be restricted in their ability to make printed copies of programs and files.
- A log should be kept at the microcomputer to show the name, time on, time off, and purpose of each employee using the microcomputer system.
- Whenever possible, there should be a strictly enforced rule that at least two employees be present at all times when data are entered or processed by the computer.
- Again whenever possible, the data processing tasks should be divided among several employees, each of whom has a specific set of duties and is not knowledgeable about what the others are doing.
- One responsible individual should be in charge of the security and safety of all backup copies of programs and files.

- All employees should be instructed to keep confidential computer printouts in a secure, locked place in or at their desks and not to leave printouts on the top of a desk when they are not present or using the printout. The employees should also be instructed to destroy such confidential data by using a paper shredder, not to throw such material into wastepaper baskets.
- All confidential and special printouts should contain a special note at the top of the printout, such as:

> This material is for *restricted use within the company by authorized personnel.* When not in use, this material should be kept in a secure locked cabinet at your desk, or locked within the desk. When this report is no longer needed, it must be destroyed according to company rules.

- All materials related to a job should be carefully kept together until the processing of the data is complete. The original source material should then be stored.

FIGURE 48

Printouts can be secured by placing them in a desk-top cabinet, which can be locked. (Courtesy of Wilson Jones Company.)

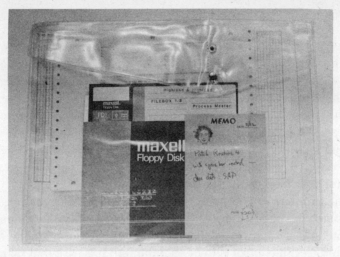

FIGURE 49

A large clip-closed plastic envelope may be used to prevent materials and disks from being lost when work is in progress. Printouts, notes, documentation, and disks can be stored together. (Courtesy of Wilson Jones Company.)

RESTRICT THE USE OF PIP, STAT, AND DDT COMMANDS

These three utility programs, which are part of CP/M, can adversely affect the security of your microcomputer system if their use is unrestricted.

1. **STAT.COM** has several uses, but its primary function is to display information about the programs and files on the disk. The STAT utility aids in security, but anyone knowledgeable about its uses can override its security advantages. Furthermore, a user can determine if there are any files that are not readily available to all users.

2. **PIP.COM** is used to copy files from one disk to another. If you wish to prevent employees from making copies illegally and taking them off the premises, it is necessary to maintain strict control over the use of this utility.

3. **DDT.COM** is used for testing and debugging. It enables a user to display a file or program in various forms, even when it is supposedly protected by different security methods.

It is obvious, then, that the risk of a breach in security is greatly increased if these utilities are provided on a readily available disk. Therefore, it is recommended that none of these utility programs be transferred from the CP/M operating disk to any disk that will be used generally by employees. It is possible to maintain a separate disk with these utilities for use by a supervisor or the individual in the company in charge of security.

MAINTAIN A COMPUTER LOG

One inexpensive and simple part of any security program is the maintenance of a computer log, a record to show who has used the system and for what purpose. This procedure is followed in large computer centers at the computer console. A record of the individuals that use the large computer from a terminal is kept automatically by the computer. However, in microcomputer systems this automatic maintenance of a log is not available as part of an operating system. It can be added by using a specially prepared program, but because of the limited memory and storage capabilities of a microcomputer this method is not really feasible.

One problem encountered with a handwritten log is the resistance by some users who need to access the computer for only a few moments. They find the time needed to sign in and out is longer than their use of the computer. Yet, if control is to be maintained, it is essential that log maintenance be strictly enforced. It does take extra time, but so do other security measures that are used regularly.

There is no standard design for a computer log, but certain elements are common. Modified for use with a microcomputer system, the elements to be recorded are

- Time the individual signs on the computer terminal.
- Name of the user.
- Number(s) of the disk(s) used. It is good policy to number each disk in order to maintain security control and keep track of the location of each file and backup.
- Program(s) and data file(s) used by the individual.
- Task: an update of accounts receivable, preparation of shipping instructions and labels, or others.
- Time the individual signs off the system.

There should be a clock easily visible from the CRT if the system does not have a built-in clock and calendar for display. Also, it is a good idea to start a new log sheet every day.

Computer logs serve several purposes. First, the use of a log discourages unauthorized personnel from using the computer. Second, the log provides management with some indication of computer utilization, not only total time in use, but also use by specific individuals and time for specific tasks. Third, the log indicates an attempt by an employee to browse or perform some other unauthorized act, since the time needed at the computer is greater than that necessary to do the job recorded in the log. In addition, if the time is long, it may indicate that an employee is not doing the job efficiently.

A computer log also helps in determining costs of performing specific operations. One company maintained a running inventory by hand, making adjustments in the shipping room as they shipped orders or received merchandise. When this task was transferred to an employee in the bookkeeping department, who had to make the entries via a terminal, it was found that the time and cost were greater and the records not as current when using automation. In this case, the utilization of the computer was based on a "paper and pencil" system, rather than on rethinking the system based on the computer's capabilities.

FINDING OUT WHAT IS REALLY ON A DISK

From a security viewpoint, it is essential to learn what is on a disk before it is discarded or recycled for other uses. It is also good policy to examine disks periodically to ascertain which programs and files are currently available, which may have been erased from the directory but not from the disk, and whether anyone has tried to tamper with a read/only file.

To obtain a list of programs on a disk, we can use the DIR command that is part of the SYSGEN portion of CP/M. As an illustration of the response to DIR, we use the disk that is used in the next section for the recovery of erased files. We would have the following input and output:

```
A> DIR   <CR>

A: DOCTOR   COM : INSTALL  COM : HELP  : HELP  COM
A: DEHEADER COM : TESTFILE COM : CPU   COM
```

Thus it would appear that there are only seven files on this disk. The name of any file that has been erased has been removed from the disk's directory and would therefore not appear in this printout. If user areas have been assigned, DIR will only give the list for USER 0 area. To examine what appears in each of the other 15 user areas would require 30 additional entries—15 pairs—of which the first of the pair indicates the user area required and the second requests the directory under each.

There are two ways in which we can obtain a quicker and more complete picture of what is on the disk. (Files erased and overwritten are not shown.)

1. We can use one of the programs under **FILEFIX**, which would display the entire contents of the disk. Each file is noted with a user number, and the erased files appear with the letter E preceding the filename, as shown in Figure 50.
2. We could use Ward E of the **DISK DOCTOR** package. This would provide a listing of all the active files, as well as all erased files, which would appear in parentheses.

```
B directory. Press space bar for next screen or <ESC> key to abort.
 Ø PIP     COM    Ø STAT    COM    Ø DDT     COM    Ø ED      COM
 Ø EDIT    COM    Ø PRINT   COM    Ø DISKFILEBAS    E CLOBBER  BAK
 Ø PSWDPGM INT  E ZLOOKUP  BAK    Ø SUPER   BAS    Ø LOOKUP   BAS
 Ø SNOOPCK BAS    Ø HØØ7U   BAS    Ø JOIN    BAS    Ø CREATE   BAS
 Ø HØØ7    BAS    Ø SETUP   PRO    Ø CRUN2   COM    Ø HØØ7A    BAS
 Ø LOOKUP  INT    Ø ZLOOKUP INT    Ø JOIN    INT    Ø HØØ7A    INT
 Ø CREATE  INT    Ø HØØ7    INT    Ø EØØ7    BAS    Ø EØØ7     INT
 Ø OKARA   COM    Ø PATH    COM    Ø PHOTO   COM    Ø PAGE     COM
 Ø SNOOPER FIL    Ø CLOBBER INT    Ø CLOBBER BAS    Ø CBAS2    COM
 Ø SETUP   TRY    Ø KEYPASS BAS    Ø PSWDPGM BAS    Ø ZLOOKUP  BAS
 E HØØ7A   BAK  E ALPHBET  BAK  E ALPHBET  INT  E ALPHBET  BAS

128 total directory entries, 38 in use, 90 remaining

Enter command and <CR>: E
```

FIGURE 50

Printout and/or CRT display showing *all* files stored on a disk using a special module of FILEFIX. An "E" preceding a program or data file indicates that the name has been erased from the directory but the file or program is still on the disk.

HOW TO UNERASE PROGRAMS THAT HAVE BEEN ERASED

If a program or file has been erased accidently or intentionally, it may be possible to restore it. As noted earlier, the name of the file has been removed from the directory, but the file remains untouched until it has been overwritten by material added after the ERA command has been used or it is destroyed by CLOBBER.BAS or a similar program.

It is not possible to restore an erased file using CP/M. It is necessary to use special packages, in this case the same ones used for examining the contents of a disk, **FILEFIX** or **DISK DOCTOR**. The procedure to restore an erased file under **FILEFIX** uses the undelete program, or the U command, as shown in Figure 51.

To verify that the file has been restored, request another directory of the disk using the DIR command.

Using Ward D of **DISK DOCTOR** takes a little more time but produces the same results. These, as well as some other packages on the market, can be used to restore erased files. They are helpful not only when a single-copy file is erased by accident or design, but also when a file that was intentionally erased is needed for some other job.

PROPER DOCUMENTATION IS ESSENTIAL TO SECURITY

More money has been lost by business and government because of the lack of proper program documentation than by computer-related crime. For many years, major computer centers have been aware of the need for efficient and effective documentation, although few have been fully successful in solving this problem. Even in a small organization with a single microcomputer, the development and use of good documentation is essen-

```
Copyright (C) 1982 Alan R. Miller
FILEFIX Version 3.1 for CP/M Ver   2

Options Available:
    A - ALL entries in short form
    B - BLOCK allocation map
    C - CLEAN erased entries
        First character is changed to a $
    D - DELETE filename for given any user
    E - EXIT program
    F - FORGE a link from an existing file to
        another filename or another user number
    L - LONG  display of disk directory
    M - MOVE filename to new user number
    N - make unique NAMES for multiple files
    P - PROTECT or unprotect a file
    R - RENAME a disk file
    S - SHORT display of disk directory
    U - UNDELETE filename
    X - eXamine disk parameters
 or select new disk with A:, B:, C:, etc

Enter command and <CR>:
```

FIGURE 51

List of the options available to the user of FILEFIX.

tial. The manuals obtained with packaged programs are often insufficient for the new user, and too often changes made to meet the needs of the individual user are not included. Even if your organization uses only a few programs, it is critical to prepare good documentation for continual use.

Documentation is essential to the effective development, implementation, modification, operation, and efficient utilization of any system. Books on documentation and chapters in programming books have been published almost since the first program was written. Nevertheless, this is a notoriously weak area in the computer industry. No attempt will be made here to provide all the concepts and techniques of documentation; there is a reading list at the end of the chapter for those interested. It is good programming practice, as well as an aid to security, to have all the programs placed on disks use a common identification procedure with which all employees are familiar. Some of the other more important points are covered here.

Elements in the Documentation of a Program

For each program your company uses, there should be an individual documentation manual (plus backup copies). The complete versions should be available only to authorized personnel, but some parts should be distributed to those who do the data entry and/or run the program. The data entry clerk should have guidelines about the individual items to be entered as part of a program. For example, when an amount of money is entered, omit the dollar sign, $; omit commas between numbers, e.g., 17863, not 17,863; include decimal point and two zeros, if necessary, for cents, even if the amount does not require the cents, for example, 500.00. When preparing input for a payroll program, the data entry clerk should be aware of exceptions. Even if a program is written with built-in controls, some responsibility must be given the clerk.

Likewise, a person running a program and obtaining output should know what the generated reports should look like. A sample copy of a test output report can be used as a guide, and the program can be stopped as soon as an error in form or content appears during printing. It not only costs money, but also hurts employee morale if a report that takes an hour to produce is thrown away because garbage was produced.

A well-documented program manual should contain the following support material:

- The name of the program as it appears on the disk and the disk number on which it can be found.
- A narrative description of the purpose of the program.
- The name of the file(s) used by the program and the disk number(s) on which the file(s) can be found.
- A listing of the self-documented program, including the language in which it is written, the name of the author(s), the date the program was written, and the date of the latest revision.
- A cross-referenced list of all variable names in alphabetical order and an explanation of the meaning and/or use of each. If possible, this list should also include the line numbers in which each variable appears.
- A flowchart of the program.
- Input specifications indicating what variable data are to be entered, if necessary, any upper and lower limits of numeric values, and what to do if any data are missing.

FIGURE 52

Documentation and disks can be kept in an easel binder. A plastic envelope holds the disk and the easel permits reading instructions while you are working at the terminal. (Courtesy of 20th Century Plastics, Inc.)

- A run sheet or operation instructions indicating error and restart procedures that may be needed during the running of the program.
- A set of sample data (including the name of the file and the disk on which it is stored) in order to test the program.
- A sample output of the program based on the test data.
- Equipment needed (e.g., size of memory or number of disk drives) for the running of the program.
- Suggestions for modifying the program—ways to eliminate parts and/ or possible future extensions.
- Procedures for audit control by the supervisor and/or accountant.
- For major programs or a frequently used utility program, a disk with a copy of the program, test data, and the sample output.

NOTE: See CLOBBER.BAS, for a sample documented program.

RECOMMENDED READINGS ABOUT DOCUMENTATION

Because of the importance of this topic as a part of total security, a brief list of specialized books and manuals is included.

Books

1. Marilyn Bohl: *A Guide for Programmers*. Englewood Cliffs NJ: Prentice Hall, Inc., 1978.
2. J. van Duyn: *Documentation Manual*. New York: Auerbach Publishers, 1972.
3. Norman L. Enger: *Documentation Standards for Computer Systems*. Fairfax VA: The Technology Press, Inc., 1980.
4. Max Gray and Keith R. London: *Documentation Standards*. Princeton NJ: Brandon/Systems Press, Inc., 1969.
5. Harry Katzan, Jr.: *Systems Design and Documentation*. New York: Van Nostrand Reinhold Company, 1976.
6. Robert S. Kuehne et al.: *Handbook of Computer Documentation Standards*. Englewood Cliffs NJ: Prentice Hall, Inc., 1973.
7. Larry E. Long: *Data Processing Documentation & Procedures Manual*. Reston VA: Reston Publishing Company, Inc., 1979.

Manuals

1. American Nuclear Society: *Guidelines for the Documentation of Digital Computer Programs*. ANSI N414–1974.
2. National Aeronautics and Space Administration: *Computer Program Documentation Guidelines*. NHB 2411.1/July 1971.
3. National Bureau of Standards: *Guidelines for Documentation of Computer Programs and Automated Data Systems*. FIPS 38/1976.

```
REM     ****************************************************************
REM
REM     PROGRAM:    CLOBBER.BAS              FILE: ANY PROGRAM OR FILE
REM
REM     PURPOSE:    TO SECURE "DEAD" PROGRAMS / FILES
REM
REM                 PROGRAM OVERWRITES EXISTING PROGRAM/FILE THAT
REM                 IS NO LONGER NEEDED WITH * DO NOT SNOOP *
REM
REM     PROGRAMMED IN CBASIC BY ESTHER H. HIGHLAND
REM                 PROGRAMMED:         SEPTEMBER 27,1982
REM                 LATEST UPDATE:      SEPTEMBER 28,1982
REM
REM     ****************************************************************
REM
REM     VARIABLES USED IN PROGRAM:
REM
REM             ANS       Y(ES) OR N(O) TO RESTART THE PROGRAM
REM             FILLS     DATA TO BE WRITTEN IN PLACE OF EACH
REM                       EXISTING RECORD IN THE PROGRAM/FILE
REM             I%        VARIABLE FOR CONTROL LOOP
REM             N%        NUMBER OF RECORDS IN PROGRAM/FILE
REM             NOFS      NAME OF PROGRAM/FILE TO BE "CLOBBERED"
REM
REM     ****************************************************************
REM
REM     PROCEDURE TO USE PROGRAM:
REM
REM       1. INSERT DISK WITH CLOBBER PROGRAM IN DISK DRIVE A.
REM       2. INSERT DISK WITH PROGRAM/FILE TO BE OVERWRITTEN
REM          IN DISK DRIVE B.
REM       3. ENTER   CRUN2 CLOBBER AND PRESS RETURN KEY.
REM       4. IN RESPONSE TO PROMPT: "NAME OF FILE"
REM          ENTER NAME OF PROGRAM/FILE AND PRESS RETURN KEY.
REM       5. AFTER PROGRAM HAS BEEN EXECUTED AND PROGRAM / FILE
REM          HAS BEEN OVERWRITTEN, YOU WILL RECEIVE THE MESSAGE:
REM          "JOB'S DONE .... FILE <NAME OF FILE> CLOBBERED".
REM       6. YOU WILL RECEIVE ANOTHER PROMPT:
REM          "WANT TO CLEAN ANOTHER FILE ... (Y/N) .... "
REM       7. IF YOU WISH TO CLEAN ANOTHER FILE ENTER  Y  AND PRESS
REM          RETURN KEY; PROGRAM WILL START WITH STEP 4 ABOVE.
REM       8. IF YOU DO NOT HAVE ANOTHER FILE TO CLEAN, ENTER  N
REM          AND PRESS RETURN KEY; PROGRAM WILL TERMINATE WITH
REM          "PROCESSING COMPLETE .... PROGRAM ENDED."
REM
REM     ****************************************************************
REM
REM     HOUSEKEEPING AND INPUT OF FILE/PROGRAM NAME, NOFS
REM
REM     ****************************************************************
REM
13      N% = 0
        CLEARS = CHR$(126) + CHR$(28):   REM CLEAR SCREEN
        HIGHS  = CHR$(126) + CHR$(31):   REM HIGH INTENSITY
        LOWS   = CHR$(126) + CHR$(25):   REM LOW  INTENSITY
        FILLS = "* DO NOT SNOOP *"
        PRINT CLEARS:   PRINT HIGHS
        PRINT "This program has been designed to DESTROY any file"
        PRINT "or program by writing over each of the records."
        PRINT LOWS
        PRINT "To abandon this program, enter 0 [zero], otherwise"
        INPUT "Press Space Bar and Return Key. "; ESCS
        IF ESCS = "0" THEN 40
        PRINT: PRINT: INPUT "Name of file ..... "; NOFS
REM
REM     ****************************************************************
REM
REM     PROCEDURE TO DETERMINE NUMBER OF RECORDS IN PROGRAM/FILE,
REM     NOFS, AND THE OPENING AND CLOSING OF THAT FILE
REM
REM     ****************************************************************
REM
        IF END # 1 THEN 20
        OPEN NOFS AS 1
```

```
10        READ # 1; LINE$
          N% = N% + 1
          GOTO 10
20        CLOSE 1
REM
REM       ************************************************************
REM
REM       PROCEDURE TO OVERWRITE EXISTING PROGRAM/FILE, NOF$; EACH
REM       RECORD IS OVERWRITTEN WITH * DO NOT SNOOP *
REM
REM       ************************************************************
REM
          IF END # 1 THEN 30
          OPEN NOF$ AS 1
          FOR I% = 1 TO N%
               PRINT # 1; FILL$
          NEXT I%
30        CLOSE 1
REM
REM       ************************************************************
REM
REM       RESTART/TERMINATION PROCEDURE FOR THE PROGRAM
REM
REM       ************************************************************
REM
          PRINT CLEAR$: PRINT
          PRINT "Job's done .... file "; NOF$; " has been clobbered"
          PRINT: PRINT
          INPUT "Want to clobber another file? ... (Y/N) .... ";AN$
          IF AN$ = "Y" THEN 13
40        IF ESC$ <> "0" THEN 50
          PRINT CLEAR$
          PRINT "Program ABORTED at your request"
50        PRINT: PRINT: PRINT "Normal termination of the program"
          END
```

CHAPTER 14

Contingency Planning

If your microcomputer system is rather new, you may not realize how dependent you will become on smooth and uninterrupted operations. Just a few years ago, in many businesses, it was reasonable to consider recourse to manual operations if automatic data processing became unavailable. But now, the growth of applications leaves few situations in which it is practical to plan on reverting to manual operations during a system breakdown. Thus, contingency plans are necessary to minimize the damage caused by unexpected and undesirable occurrences affecting the microcomputer system.

We have used the term *contingency planning*, rather than the more dramatic *disaster planning* often used in trade publications, to emphasize the fact that although lightning strikes and earthquakes occur, these disasters are much less frequent than are power failures, equipment breakdowns, and other problems that become disasters only if there has been no planning on how to handle the emergency. Data processing operations are disrupted far more often by small problems than by large ones, but in the absence of a good plan, minor damage can cause major losses.

An insurance industry report indicated that fewer than 7% of all companies that experience severe damage to their data processing operations are in business 5 years after the loss. Many users do not understand what will happen if the system fails. They do not appreciate the value of their storage media and often do not even make backups.

A BASIC APPROACH TO CONTINGENCY PLANNING

The development of contingency plans should be an orderly process. The guidelines provided in this chapter have been formulated on the basis of the experience of government agencies, professional organizations, and businesses. Each microcomputer user is different in equipment configuration, applications, personnel, and relative criticality of systems; therefore, one specific plan is not possible. However, the contingency plan for any data processing system, regardless of its size or scope of operations, should, as a minimum, consider the following three elements:

1. *Emergency response:* Procedures to cover the appropriate response to such events as fire, flood, water damage, bomb threat, or natural disaster, to protect lives, limit damage, and minimize the impact on the data processing operations.
2. *Backup operations:* Procedures to ensure that essential data processing tasks can be conducted after disruption to the primary facility. (Backup capability includes such needed materials as files, programs, paper stocks, and preprinted forms, in addition to the more obvious need for compatible hardware.)
3. *Recovery actions:* Procedures to facilitate the rapid restoration of data processing facilities following physical failure or destruction, or loss of data.

To the extent possible, contingency-plan documents should be brief to facilitate their usefulness and acceptance by the users. The plan should be reviewed on a recurring basis and modified as changes in the microcomputer facility work load dictate. Critical applications should be operated on the backup system regularly to ensure that it can properly process the work load.

The development of a successful contingency plan depends on recognition of the potential consequences of undesirable events against which protection is needed. Microcomputer systems use many resources, people, programs, data, hardware, communications facilities, power, environmental control, and even paper forms. All resources are not equally important, nor are they equally susceptible to harm. Therefore, cost-effective protection is heavily dependent on

- an awareness of the facility's relative dependence on each of its component parts,
- knowing, at least in an overall way, what the chances are that something undesired will happen to each component,
- a determination of the effects of undesirable events so that action can be taken to minimize either the chances of their happening, the loss if they happen, or both.

The maximum allowable cost of any safeguard is limited by the size of the expected losses. Any safeguard, or combination of safeguards, must not cost more than tolerating the problem. Clearly, then, a process is needed that will identify and assign a dollar figure to possible losses. Such a process is called *risk analysis*. In addition to providing a cost justification of security

CHECKLIST FOR CONTINGENCY PLANNING

Personnel

	Yes	No	N/A
1. Has one person been given overall responsibility for the contingency plan and for keeping it up-to-date? Has an alternative employee been designated as well?	___	___	___
2. Has responsibility for invoking emergency action and for making decisions been clearly assigned? (This responsibility is best assigned by job title rather than by name, e.g., vice-president or data processing manager.)	___	___	___
3. Is every employee fully aware of individual responsibility in case of dangerous emergencies like fire or flood?	___	___	___
4. Do all computer users have a copy of the "Red Book," giving instructions for coping with processing interruptions? Do they fully understand its use?	___	___	___
5. Is there a complete, up-to-date list of all employees' addresses and telephone numbers off-site, as well as in the office, available to the individual responsible for contingency planning?	___	___	___
6. Are principal points and important employee instructions for emergencies posted on the employee bulletin board?	___	___	___

The Plan

1. Do users and data processing personnel understand and agree on the actions to be taken when processing is interrupted or data are lost?	___	___	___
2. Have all critical computing jobs been identified and assigned priorities for the order in which they will be processed in case of an emergency? Has provision been made to review this list as changing business conditions require?	___	___	___
3. Is insurance coverage periodically reviewed as new types of coverage become available and/or new equipment is added?	___	___	___

4. Are parts of the plan tested periodically, particularly during off-shifts when there are usually fewer employees?   ___ ___ ___

5. Has the backup site been tested to ensure that essential tasks can be run on available equipment? Are there needed supplies located at this site?   ___ ___ ___

6. Do plans for off-site operation include provisions for transportation of personnel and supplies (e.g., disks, paper, and forms) from the office or from backup storage? Have provisions been made for housing employees if the backup site is a considerable distance from the office?   ___ ___ ___

7. Are periodic checks made with rental companies or other potential suppliers of replacement hardware to be sure that the particular equipment you might need is still available?   ___ ___ ___

8. Is a list of people to be notified in case of major delays, including key employees, suppliers, and customers, kept off-site as well as in the office?   ___ ___ ___

9. Is there a formal feedback procedure to encourage signed or unsigned suggestions and criticisms of the plan, particularly after a test has been run?   ___ ___ ___

10. Has provision been made for a periodic review of the risk analysis? Some critical tasks may no longer be so important; others may have been added.   ___ ___ ___

Score Analysis:

- 16 "Yes" answers is great but probably unique.

- 4 "Yes" answers for Personnel *and* 9 "Yes" answers for the Plan is very good. You may get by with 7 out of 10 under Plan, but why add unnecessarily to your risk?

- Less than 4 "Yes" under Personnel or under "Plan" indicates that you are suffering from the "It-can't-happen-here" syndrome. Immediate attention to planning is advised.

measures, a risk analysis provides data on time as a factor in losses of security.

With few exceptions, a large proportion of the microcomputer work load is deferrable for significantly long periods of time before the deferral causes unacceptable hardship. On the other hand, there is usually a small number of tasks that must be completed because delay would cause intolerable disruption. A properly conducted risk analysis will help make the difficult determination of to which category each activity belongs and the maximum tolerable delay for the processing of each deferred activity.

RISK ANALYSIS

The essential elements of this first step in contingency planning are an assessment of the damage that can be caused by an unfavorable event and an estimate of how often such an event may happen. Both these must be estimated, since it is impossible to know absolutely either the impact or frequency of many events. The estimate should be based on a combination of historical data (for natural disasters like tornadoes and earthquakes), knowledge of the system, and experience and judgment. However, rough estimates are sufficiently accurate for the purposes of risk analysis in most cases.

There will be no significant difference in planning if the damage from a certain event is estimated at $1000 or $1500. Assigning values to such events as loss of business to a competitor because of data disclosure, or the damage to employee morale caused by a delayed payroll, is better done in approximate amounts than in exact figures. The time needed for the analysis will be considerably reduced, and its usefulness will not be decreased, if both impact and frequency estimates are rounded, as shown in Figure 53.

Annual Loss Exposure Table [ALE]

I / F	3 Times a Year	Once in Two Weeks (26 Times/Year)	Once a Day (300 Times/Year)	10 Times per Day (3,000 Times/Year)	100 Times per Day (30,000 Times/Year)
$2		$52	$600	$6,000	$60,000
5		130	1,500	15,000	150,000
10		260	3,000	30,000	300,000
50		1,300	15,000	150,000	
100	$300	2,600	30,000	300,000	
300	900	7,800	90,000	900,000	
3,000	9,000	78,000	900,000		
5,000	15,000	130,000			

FIGURE 53

The calculation of the *annual loss exposure* (**ALE**) from a given event is simple when the estimates of *impact* (loss it would cause) and the *frequency of occurrence* (the number of times per year it could happen) have been made.

Annual loss exposure = impact × frequency

or

$$\text{ALE} \qquad = \quad I \quad \times \quad F$$

The table in Figure 53 shows the result of this calculation for many possible values of both I and F. An example will illustrate its calculation and use. The team working on the risk analysis has determined that data entry errors could occur as often as 100 times a day; this could be five an hour for one clerk on three shifts or three clerks on one shift. The cost of correcting each error is $2. The table indicates that the ALE is $60,000, and this is the maximum amount that should be expended to correct the situation.

The calculation was done using $2 for I and 30,000 times per year. (The value of 100 times a day for 365 days would be 36,500, but we have allowed for weekends and holidays, again only approximately.)

$$\text{ALE} = 2 \times 30,000 = \$60,000 \qquad \text{or} \qquad \$60K$$

Actually, it is unlikely that anywhere near $60,000 would be needed once the problem has been identified and possible solutions listed. Can the work environment be improved by better lighting or more rest periods? Can more expert clerks be hired at somewhat higher salaries? Should the programmer include a module in the program that repeats what has been entered and asks whether the entry is correct? This last and most expensive technique would involve programmer and machine time, slow the entry process, and perhaps require an additional clerk, but all these together would probably be much less than $60,000 a year. Even $30,000 or $40,000 may sound like a high price to pay, but not when it is compared with the potential annual loss of $60,000, which was perhaps not even recognized until the analysis was undertaken.

The use of the formula is not limited to the values for I and F given in the table in Figure 53. The risk from occurrences with much smaller frequencies, like natural disasters, have not been included but can be just as simply calculated. For example, for an occurrence with an expected loss of $15,000 that could occur perhaps once in 3 years, the calculation would be

$$\text{ALE} = 15,000 \times \tfrac{1}{3} = \$5,000$$

We have divided the frequency of occurrence F by 3, since we are measuring the frequency of occurrence *per year* of an event that may occur only once in 3 years.

THE CONTINGENCY PLAN

When the risk analysis has been completed there will be a list of company functions that depend on the microcomputer system, classified by whether they can be postponed and for how long, the potential dangers that could affect each, and the maximum amount of money that can be spent for protection. The formalized procedure for dealing with each adverse event, ranging from the common ones that interrupt processing briefly, through the less likely real disasters, must then be worked out. The ordinary interruptions to processing should then be handled differently from disasters like fire and flood.

The Red Book Concept

The ordinary interruptions to processing include a read error when a data file is accessed, a momentary power outage that destroys data on the disk in use, a program that was run before and suddenly cannot be executed, or the discovery that the last clerk forgot to close the file in a program where this is not automatically done by the program or system. The list could go on and still not be exhaustive. Each of these possibilities should be given a separate page in a loose-leaf binder, together with detailed instructions on what to do "in case." It is not adequate, for example, to write, "Get backup." The instruction must be specific: "Look up the disk file directory and determine the number of the backup disk. The backup disks are located in the file cabinet in room 312." Or, "Mr. X will get you the backup." Whether the clerk or Mr. X then makes a new backup must also be predetermined and included with the instruction that the new copy then becomes the office backup.

When the instructions have been completed, the book should be carefully indexed. The illustration also gives the categories under which this emergency would be listed in the index. I suggest a *red* binder, although this is obviously not an essential part of the procedure, because it would make the binder quickly identifiable if it is kept with manuals and other documents, and the color suggests "stop and read." A copy of the book should be kept readily available at each terminal and the appropriate employees instructed in its use.

The Red Book must be kept up to date to reflect changes in the system and the addition of new problems that may not originally have been included. If a new problem is encountered, it must be thoroughly analyzed, a page added to the book, and a change made in the index. Some events may have to be deleted, such as, what to do if a tape cartridge will not fit the machine when you are no longer using tapes. Have better solutions become available since the original work was done? For example, does the company now have Disk Doctor or FILEFIX (see Chapter 7) available for recovering crashed disks or for locating bad sectors on disks? This job of maintaining the Red Book should be the responsibility of a particular employee and each incident should be reported to that individual, in writing, so that he or she can determine whether a change in the Red Book is necessary.

Disaster Plans

Emergencies like natural disasters and man-made malicious events are characterized by low rates of occurrence and high levels of uncertainty. Effective strategies for coping with such emergencies require early detection and planned containment. Detection systems for smoke, fire, intruders, and flood are discussed in earlier chapters in this book, and the planning we suggest now starts with the assumption that such basic systems are in place.

The backup plan aims at the maintenance of critical portions of the work between the loss of computer services and its restoration at the original site. In Chapter 7, we indicated that a complete set of off-site backup disks was essential, and if this procedure has been followed the next steps in maintaining essential operations can now be taken. The risk analysis will have identified which jobs are critical and which are discretionary and can be postponed for some time. For some jobs it may even be possible to revert to manual procedures for a short time. But generally, if there has been a major equipment failure or destruction, it will be necessary to obtain the use of replacement hardware and, in some cases, a new temporary site for essential operations.

The emergency plan must identify each employee's function, and each employee must know what that function is. Who, for example, will make the decision on whether to evacuate the area and under what conditions? Some are obvious, like fire; some less obvious, like a power failure of undetermined length.

As with the instructions in the Red Book, the plans for action in case of disaster should be in writing, with one page for each possibility, indexed, and kept up to date. However, it is not necessary to keep a copy at each terminal, but one should be within easy reach of the individuals responsible for making critical decisions.

ALTERNATIVE PROTECTIONS

The proliferation of microcomputer systems has been so rapid that the security measures available have not kept pace. In mainframe computing, backup procedures have developed to the point where there are fully configured "hot sites" available as backup for hardware and sites. The possibilities for microcomputer systems depend on location, dealer, and manufacturer, and a thorough investigation of available protections should be done by each user before breakdowns occur.

Insurance: Coverage offered varies greatly, and no generalization can be made. Discuss with your insurance broker whether coverage is for damage to hardware or only destruction of hardware. Does the company offer disk insurance, and what precautions must be taken to maintain that coverage? Does the insurance cover the cost of maintaining operations and renting equipment or only the cost of replacing the destroyed hardware?

Duplicate Hardware: This is an expensive alternative, and the duplicate hardware must be kept off-site for security. Individual peripherals can be duplicated without too much cost, however, For example, an inexpensive matrix dot printer could be kept available, or quickly purchased, depending upon your location, to substitute temporarily for a better daisy wheel in an emergency. A well-designed microcomputer network should have some duplicate facilities built in.

Service Contracts: An increasing number of manufacturers of CPUs and printers are developing national service organizations. Some offer service through the dealer who sells you the equipment. These contracts may be quite expensive, running as high as 15 to 20% of the purchase price of the equipment per year. There are, in addition, two cautions to bear in mind when considering a service contract. If the dealer offers service and states that the repairs are done locally and quickly, verify whether this applies to minor repairs only. In many cases, all but the simplest repair work must go back to the manufacturer or central service area, which makes the repair neither local nor quick. If the contract specifies replacement of equipment during a long repair period, be sure the dealer or manufacturer will supply fully compatible equipment, including disk type and size and type of microprocessor.

Equipment Rental: There are companies, and their number is growing, that specialize in renting electronic equipment and components. So far, most of these companies offer a limited number of brands and may not have one exactly compatible with the equipment you own. Individual dealers and manufacturers may also rent equipment. Rental costs are usually high, about 12 to 18% of the equipment cost per month. As in the case of backup equipment, the investigation of this possibility must verify that completely compatible equipment will be available if and when you need it.

Reciprocal Agreements: This possibility exists if a nearby company has a similar configuration. If such an agreement is considered, be sure it is in writing and can be legally enforced. In mainframe computing, agreements between users to make facilities available to each other on an emergency basis were quite common some years back. The government agencies in Washington, D.C., for example, assumed that since they had similar configurations, they could depend on each other for emergency operations. It was then found that many of the agencies might have to run critical work at the same time or that the slack time available was insufficient to run the required work.

In an agreement of this type, between a unit of the State University of New York and a nearby commercial company, the agreement worked to the benefit of the company but to the detriment of the college. The company's system broke down on a Friday morning when the payroll had to be run. If this work was not completed before noon, the employees would not be able to cash their checks before the weekend. They called the college and asked for just about an hour on their computer. Ordinarily, this would not have been a problem, but just at that time the school was running grades and transcripts, a long job, with a long start-up time, but the agreement was honored. The payroll was run, and the employees at the college worked until 2 o'clock the next morning instead of leaving at 8 o'clock in the evening.

Reciprocal agreements have not been tested in microcomputer systems. If one is available in your area, remember that you are offering time, as well as providing yourself with a backup.

Off-Site Processing: Businesses with a large enough volume of data processing work, and particularly those with microcomputer networks, may find it practical to have backups of disks automatically made by a service organization by means of telecommunications. General Electric Information Services Company is one of many companies that offers this service. It may also be possible to arrange for emergency processing with such service organizations.

CHAPTER 15

Microcomputer Network Security

In this chapter we examine more complex microcomputer systems and their concomitant security problems. In the beginning, microcomputers were used as stand-alone units, a single terminal (CRT and keyboard) interfaced with a central processing unit (CPU). Recently, many manufacturers have introduced multiuser, multitasking microcomputer systems in which a single but larger CPU is capable of supporting more than one terminal. These systems support anywhere from 4 to 64 users, each with an independent terminal.

Some businesses using microcomputers have found it advantageous to interface their microcomputer with a large mainframe computer. In the simplest form of connection, the microcomputer serves as a *dumb terminal*. This is a primitive mode of operation, since the power of the microcomputer is not fully utilized when it is on line. The ability to transfer files between the microcomputer and large mainframe is a more sophisticated level of operation.

We have now reached a level of interfacing microcomputers by setting them up as *networks*—physically separated sets of points (CPUs, terminals, and communications devices) that are interconnected by communications channels so that there is at least one continuous path between any two points. Mainframe networks have been around for many years, and the security of these systems has been developed over the years. Mainframe security is still far from ideal. The joining of microcomputers in networks is in its early stages. As noted earlier, the security found in the operating systems of large mainframe computers is not as yet found in any microcomputer. The security in microcomputer networks, likewise, is far from that found in mainframe systems.

In order to understand the security problems in microcomputer networks, we will examine the various designs and the protocols or procedures needed in a network. It will then be possible to assess the security inherent in microcomputer networks and consider additional security measures that can be implemented.

PURPOSES OF NETWORKS

In its simplest terms, a computer network varies from the interconnecting of several terminals with a single computer to the joining of one or more computers by some communications channel, such as a telephone line. Computer networks have many uses in the business and professional world, and they exist in many forms. Some networks are public, like that of the General Electric Information Services Company, to which anyone may subscribe for a monthly fee. Other networks are private, such as those used by major corporations for the internal transmission of data. Some networks are specialized, like *SWIFT* (Society for Worldwide Interbank Financial Transactions), an international network for banks for the transfer of funds.

In the microcomputer field, the development of networks permits the following.

Sharing of Expensive Resources: A remote microcomputer may have a greater CPU capacity necessary to run a program you need and that is unable to run on your own machine. Specialized storage media, such as large data storage hard disks, may be shared by several users. Furthermore, unnecessary duplication of data files and programs may be avoided by having several users in the network share the same software. It is also possible for network users to share special output devices, such as a plotter or specialized printer.

Transferring Data: A network makes it possible to have almost instantaneous sharing of data within a company or to speed the exchange of information between the sales office in one area and the production plant located in another community.

Backup Support: Depending upon the design (topology) of the network, it may be possible to continue processing data even if one CPU is down and awaiting repair.

Improved Communications: A microcomputer network can be used for electronic mail to obtain replies to letters and memos in a very short time. The network can also be used for *computer conferencing,* which can be seen as something halfway between a conference and a very rapidly published newsletter.

NETWORK COMMUNICATIONS TERMINOLOGY

Asynchronous transmission	The interval between each character or block of characters is determined by the frequency of the input rather than any internally generated timing; this method is sometimes called "start-stop" transmission. The maximum speed of transmission is far below that provided by synchronous transmission.
bps	Maximum number of coded character elements that may be generated per second by a communications device; with current equipment, the number of *bits per second* varies from ten to two million.
Channel	A path, or *line*, for the flow of data between devices. • *Simplex channel* permits transmission in one direction only. • *Half-duplex channel* provides for transmission of data in either direction. • *Full-duplex channel* provides for data transmission in both directions simultaneously.
Communications protocol	A set of standards defining the procedure and information content for an exchange of data between different parts of a network.
Concentrator	A device that allows data transmitted over a number of lower speed lines (bps) to converge and be immediately retransmitted over a single, higher-speed line; in some respects, a high-level multiplexer.
Full-duplex	Refers to communications equipment capable of transmitting simultaneously in two directions.

ELEMENTARY NETWORKS

The most elementary network is a microcomputer with several output devices. A single microcomputer is interconnected by a multiport switch to two different printers—a matrix dot printer for inexpensive, fast printouts, and a daisy wheel printer for quality letters. Using a multiport switch, which is controlled by hand, with three outputs instead of two, we can connect a modem to the system and be able to communicate over telephone lines with another microcomputer or mainframe computer.

Another elementary network is a microcomputer interfaced with a mainframe computer. In simplest form, the microcomputer acts as a dumb terminal and permits the user either to operate on the mainframe *or* the microcomputer.

Half-duplex	Two-way, nonsimultaneous transmission of data.
Interrupt	Temporarily suspending sending or receiving data because a higher-priority task must be executed; once the higher priority task has been completed, the sending or receiving is resumed.
Modem	An acronym for *modulator/demodulator*, this is a device that transforms electrical impulses from a computer into a form suitable for transmission over telephone lines, and vice versa.
Multiplexer	A device that modulates and/or demodulates data between two or more input/output devices over a common transmission link.
Polling	Inquiring whether a communications device sharing a common circuit has data to transmit or is currently receiving data.
Private line	A communications circuit, either telegraph or voice grade, reserved for the use of a subscriber, also known as a *tie line, leased line,* or *dedicated line.* The monthly rental cost within the continental United States ranges from about $2.00 per mile for a 30 bps line to about $25.00 per mile for a 56,000 bps line.
Synchronous transmission	In this transmission method, the sending and receiving units are kept in step with each other by a special timing device, say, 100 ticks or pulses per second. The data are transmitted as a signal along with this timing pulse at a fixed rate that does not depend upon the structure of any character or blocks of characters.
Voice grade line	A telephone circuit for transmitting audio signals, suitable for speech and digital communications.

The next level above this is to use the microcomputer as an *intelligent terminal*, so that we are in fact linking two computers. It is possible to maintain data files on the mainframe computer system and use these files for computation and modification on the microcomputer system. Some of the computer service bureaus currently offer the communications software and even the microcomputer hardware to enable anyone to interface with their system. An important advantage is that the microcomputer user can easily produce an off-site, backup copy of data files and programs by storing files on the service bureau's system.

THE DESIGN OF COMPUTERS INTO NETWORKS

There are four main topologies (designs) of local microcomputer networks: star, loop, ring, and common-bus. Each network topology controls terminal-to-terminal communications or computer-to-computer communications in a different manner, and each has its advantages and disadvantages and offers different security protection levels.

A Star Network

A multiuser, multitasking microcomputer system is an example of a *star network*, in which connecting cables rather than telephone lines are used for communications (see Figure 54). There is only one central controller—a message traffic cop. All messages are to and from the controller. Thus, if one terminal wishes to communicate with another, the message must pass through the controller first before reaching the receiver terminal. In some of the poorer systems, it is very awkward for two users to communicate with each other.

The main advantages of a star topology are that the design is well understood and the hardware and software necessary for its operation are fairly well established. One disadvantage is the "weak link" of the central controller, or CPU, which if inoperative, closes down the entire system. In addition, the joining of additional nodes (terminals, printers, and storage devices) tends to degrade the performance of the system. The CPU in such networks is often overworked. It must control the switching among the terminals, the various input/output devices, sequentially perform computations and logic operations for each of the jobs being run, time-share access to disks for each drive, operate the output devices connected to the system, and access the memory in sequence for control and operations.

Until recently, there was greater security in a star network than in a single, stand-alone microcomputer system because the operating system

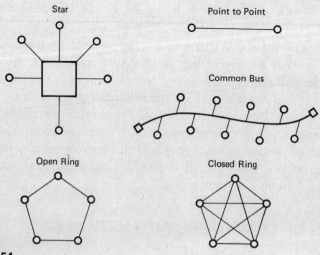

FIGURE 54

Communications network designs.

had several enhancements not found in single-unit operating systems. In addition to user ID and password schemes, ensuring that only authorized users may sign onto the system and gain access to the files, it is possible to lock certain files and records for use by specified users in a star network. The newer version of CP/M has greatly narrowed this difference.

A Loop Network

Like the star network, a *loop network* has a central controller. This network is a circular configuration of nodes (e.g., computers and terminals) that includes the controller, often as a dedicated CPU, as one of the nodes (see Figure 54). All messages travel to the controller first, which then routes them over the line to the destination node. In some loop networks, data transmission follows a single path, say, clockwise around the loop. Thus, if two nodes next to each other wish to communicate, the message might go through the entire ring until it reaches the controller and then proceed to the receiving node.

One of the loop's advantages over a star network is that it can support a greater number of nodes. Loops, however, suffer from the same weak-link disadvantage as the star design; a controller breakdown causes the entire system to fail. Another disadvantage is that loops are generally slow and are controller bound.

A Ring Network

The limitations of a microcomputer loop network may be overcome by joining several independent microcomputers in a ring network in which there is no central controller. Message control is distributed among the different nodes.

In an *open ring* (see Figure 54), messages on the ring travel indirectly through other nodes to reach the destination node.

The main weakness of the open-ring configuration is that the breakdown of any one node degenerates the system if communications travel in both directions, or there is a complete system failure if communication is one-way. It is sometimes possible to patch the communication ring by bypassing the downed computer(s) with special wiring panels, but this is costly and requires human intervention. A *closed-ring* network, on the other hand, eliminates the need for patching and provides for greater security during data transmission than the open ring because data can be sent directly to the receiver by the sender. It is, however, considerably more costly, requiring a more complex protocol and two-way communications lines.

In an open-ring system, all but unclassified transmitted data should be encoded, since other "listeners" are along the path. In a closed ring, which permits direct transmission from sender to receiver, with no other node in the path, a lower level of security may be adequate.

A Common-Bus Network

It is possible to join two or more stand-alone microcomputers and/or micro-computer star networks into one major network using the common-bus topology (see Figure 54). All the nodes are fully connected to each other along a common communications medium. Messages do not travel from node to node but are broadcast over the entire communications line simultaneously. There is no central controller, but instead is fully distributed.

Because of its design, the failure of equipment at any node does not affect the operation of the remainder of the network. This *distributed network*, as it is technically known, permits several microcomputers and many users to share different output devices and hard and floppy disk storage, as well as specialty devices, such as light pen digitizers and/or card or optical readers.

Access to the network is shared equally among the nodes on a first-come, first-served basis. This equality and the efficiency and stability of the network is maintained by sophisticated technology. Since all messages are broadcast over the communications line, it is obvious that this type of network requires data encryption. Even if the line is privately owned within a company's own building or property complex, encryption should be used for all but unclassified data.

MICROCOMPUTER COMMUNICATIONS SOFTWARE

To understand the complexity of the problem of network security, let us first examine briefly the question of *protocol*. A communications protocol is a set of rules that communicating computers and components have to follow. Rather than being technical, we will look at these rules as if they governed a committee meeting.

Communications Protocols

First, there is the committee meeting, with a chairperson who controls all communications. The chairperson polls each committee member in sequence to determine if the member has anything to say to anyone else. Only when the individual member wishes to speak is permission given. If the member elects to pass, that member must wait until the next time the chairperson calls, and the chair polls each committee member before returning. All messages are "relayed" through the chairperson. This is the method commonly used in star and loop networks.

Second, there is a committee meeting in which the chairperson controls all communications by recognizing a speaker who has indicated a wish to speak. If several members wish to speak at once, the chair assigns priorities to each, and each member speaks in turn. Once an individual speaks and wishes to speak again, that member goes to the "end of the line." This method is often used in loop networks and less frequently in the star topology.

Finally, there is a committee meeting with no chairperson or controller. Each individual may speak to anyone else whenever the member wishes, provided that the other receiver is not speaking or listening to someone else. There may be a waiting list to speak to a receiver who is engaged, or there may not be, so that the speaker has to call again, hoping not to get a busy signal. It is possible to give particular committee members priority status, so that they can interrupt any nonpriority communication in progress. This system is used with ring and common-bus networks.

Inherent in the protocol are the method of polling, and some other features that affect security, including

- techniques used to detect errors in transmission,
- the method used to recover lost data or to correct erroneous messages,
- the procedure used to interrupt ongoing transmission for priority messages,
- authentication of the message source, and
- verification that the message will be transmitted to the proper receiver.

Communications Topology and Security

Several microcomputer communications software programs or packages are available for use with different network topologies. Some of these are in the public domain; they are available from the CP/M Users Group or from various publications. Other communication software is available from microcomputer manufacturers, and packages can be purchased from software producers. Let us look at some networks and evaluate the communications software available.

Microcomputer to Mainframe

Many larger users have complained that there is no standard package to interface a microcomputer with a computer mainframe. Some users have developed their own software or have modified public domain packages. Yet in almost all of these, the level of security depends upon the mainframe, not the microcomputer.

A microcomputer interfaced with a mainframe as a dumb terminal has the mainframe's security when acting as a terminal and its own operating system's security when working as a microcomputer. Once the micro-computer system is interfaced as an intelligent terminal so that data files and programs can be transferred between the microcomputer's disks and the mainframe, the level of security for the microcomputer is governed by the mainframe's security, but the security of the mainframe may be weakened.

Multiuser, Multitasking Star Network

The multiuser, multitasking microcomputers, which permit the use of several terminals with a single CPU, depend upon the operating system, such as Digital Research's MP/M, to handle communications and opera-tions. These systems did offer more security than the multiuser, single-microcomputer system before the newer version of CP/M was released. With that new release, however, there is not that much difference between the security systems.

The star networks, in which the CPU is the controller for several terminals and output devices, can offer a *linked-block structure* for security of the system, ranging from access to the system to individual file protection. The linked-blocks, or layers (see Figure 55), provide for

- access control by user identification number,
- user password authentication,
- device identification number and matching against the user password,
- access control to files by verification of all previous entries,
- password verification for use of specific file subgroup, and
- file "conditioning" or operations that may be performed by the user:
  - write control—cannot read file, only enter new data,
  - read control—can read but cannot modify,
  - modify control—can modify but cannot delete any record, or
  - delete control—full control over the file.

One method of furthering the security of star networks, as well as ring and common-bus networks, is through the use of special input/output devices with built-in hardware encryption. Computer Transceiver Systems' EXECUPORT SHERLOCK terminals can provide a security system that is double locked. First, the CPU has the same master key for encryption as the terminal, and that key can be different for the various terminals. Second, a randomly generated key, known as a session key, is encrypted by the terminal's master key and passed on to the CPU. The session key not only reinforces the data encryption but also authenticates the source of the

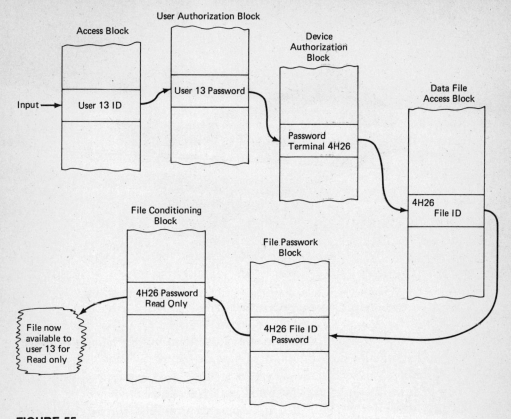

FIGURE 55

Design of a linked-block structure for security.

message. No two session keys are ever encrypted in the same way by the input/output terminal.

Point-to-Point Network: Two Microcomputers

It is possible to interface two single-terminal CPU microcomputer systems as a single network using public domain software or software supplied by the computer's manufacturer. The more successful marriages of this type, without using a mainframe, have involved using identical model microcomputers from the same producer.

Some producers have introduced special interface devices and software so that their brand microcomputer can be interfaced with another brand. One of the more significant interface techniques provides the ability to have an 8-bit microcomputer communicate efficiently with a 16-bit microcomputer. This permits a user to operate with the many packages and programs written for the 8-bit machines and at the same time upgrade newer purchases by obtaining 16-bit hardware.

FIGURE 56

Portable terminal with built-in modem can provide security with automatic encryption and decryption using a randomly generated session key for the NBS Data Encryption Algorithm. (Courtesy of Computer Transceiver Systems, Inc.)

With a point-to-point system it is possible for either computer to use the other's disk files and/or memory. Software security of such systems is not much different from that available for a single-microcomputer, multiuser system. The software and hardware interface devices for point-to-point systems still offer far less security than that provided when both microcomputers are interfaced via a mainframe computer. Therefore, many of the software security methods included in this book should supplement the operating system's security protection.

Major Networks

A major microcomputer network is defined here as the joining of two or more multiuser, multitasking computers with or without some single-terminal microcomputers, without any interfacing with a large mainframe computer. The communications software developed for such networks is still limited, and most support a common-bus topology. Many of these are known as "development packages" to be used by professional systems designers.

The interface of two relatively small microcomputer systems, for example, two CPUs each with four terminals, compared with one CPU handling eight terminals, has the added security of some on-site backup capability. Even if not all work can be performed on one of the systems, it is very likely that essential tasks can be managed without loss.

Although we may know the levels of security offered by two individual microcomputers or microcomputer networks, we cannot be sure of the level of security achieved if the two are interfaced. In this case it is not even safe to assume that the security of the combined system will be better than either one alone; it may even be poorer. It should certainly not be assumed that the individual security levels will add up to give the new network a much higher security level than either component.

At this stage in the development of microcomputer networks, it is necessary to include many supplementary security measures in support of those of the operating and communications systems. Although many of the techniques are time-consuming during operation, thereby reducing system response time, and also require storage space, they are necessary, since none of the network packages for microcomputers provide a sufficiently high level of security.

COMMUNICATIONS HARDWARE AND SECURITY

The usual links between nodes in a microcomputer network are telephone lines and/or coaxial cables, although it is also possible to use satellite or microwave communications systems. Telephone lines, most typically used, may be either dial-up (switched) or leased (dedicated). In a dial-up line, the data are sent over the telephone company's regular voice lines and switched circuits. Noise and interruptions on these lines can make data communications difficult. On a leased line, the line is "conditioned" to reduce noise and distortion.

Modems, special communications hardware, send and receive data over the telephone lines in one of two ways. If transmission is *synchronous*, a series of precise timing pulses accompany the data over the lines to tell the receiving device when to read each incoming bit. *Asynchronous* transmission does not include the timing pulses, but instead adds extra bits to mark the beginning and end of each character during transmission. Asynchronous transmission is simpler and less expensive than synchronous but also less efficient; synchronous modems are typically much faster.

Modems come in two types: stand-alone units or fully integrated boards. A stand-alone unit consists of a single-board microprocessor and is interfaced with the microcomputer by using a RS-232 cable and a connector to the telephone lines. The newer type is a fully integrated board placed directly inside the computer, thereby eliminating an extra piece of equipment; only a wire to the telephone jack is necessary.

Most microcomputers interfaced with a mainframe, and many smaller networks of microcomputers use modems for asynchronous communications. In addition to the modem it is also necessary to have communications software. One of the more popular packages is Dynamic Microprocessor Associates's **ASCOM**, an asynchronous communication control program, which is menu-driven and can be customized.

When several computer terminals and CPUs are transmitting and receiving simultaneously, it is necessary to have a modem between each device and the telephone line. If the data from many terminals could be combined on one communications line without the loss of information or significant delays, the savings in the cost of transmission would be large. *Multiplexers* do exactly that; they combine several individual messages so that all can be sent over the same communications line simultaneously, providing improved line utilization. There is also the possibility of using *concentrators*, which like multiplexers combine several lines but are capable of then transmitting the data at a much higher speed.

The type and quality of the hardware used in the network will, in part, determine the level of security the system achieves.

- If a four-wire, *full-duplex* leased line is used, the probability of data loss or transmission error is reduced compared with a voice-grade line. For short distances, depending upon the type of microcomputer used, coaxial cable will provide the same level of transmission security.
- It is preferable to have communications hardware, such as modems and multiplexers, with built-in diagnostics to help detect line and equipment errors and isolate their cause.
- With a large network, if the volume of transmission is great enough, a multiplexer or concentrator is valuable, since only a single encoding and decoding device and a single line are required for the communications link.
- The modem, multiplexer, and/or concentrator should be quality products capable of enabling the user to select specific circuits to detect data errors caused by elementary malfunctions of hardware.

FIGURE 57

A fully integrated auto-answer/auto-dial, full-duplex, direct-connect 300/1200 baud modem slips into a single expansion slot of a 16-bit microcomputer. (Courtesy of Ven-Tel, Inc.)

APPENDIX

Selected Sources of Hardware and Software

The following is a list of addresses for companies whose products are included in this book. For product tradenames see *Acknowledgments* on page xiii.

Advanced Micro Techniques
    1291 E. Hillsdale Blvd.
    Suite 209
    Foster City, CA 94404

Blat Research & Development
    Corporation
    8016 188th SW
    Edmonds, WA 98020

Columbia Data Products, Inc.
    8990 Route 108
    Columbia, MD 21045

Computer Transceiver
    Systems, Inc.
    P. O. Box 15
    East 66 Midland Avenue
    Paramus, NJ 07652

Consolink Corporation
    1840 Industrial Circle
    Longmont, CO 80501

CPMUG
    The CP/M Users Group
    1651 Third Ave.
    New York, NY 10028

Cryptext Corporation
    P. O. Box 425
    Northgate Station
    Seattle, WA 98125

CyberSoft Incorporated
    P. O. Box 151
    Waterloo, Ontario
    Canada N2J 3Z9

Digital Marketing Corporation
    2670 Cherry Lane
    Walnut Creek, CA 94596

Digital Research
    P. O. Box 579
    160 Central Avenue
    Pacific Grove, CA 93950

Dynamic Microprocessor Associate
545 Fifth Avenue
New York, NY 10017

General Semiconductor
Industries, Inc.
P. O. Box 3078
2001 West Tenth Place
Tempe, AZ 85281

Gould, Inc.
Electronic Power Conversion
Division
2727 Kurtz Street
San Diego, CA 92110

InfoDevices
78 East Industry Court
Deer Park, NY 11729

Maxell Corporation of America
60 Oxford Drive
Moonachie, NJ 07074

Merritt Software, Inc.
P. O. Box 1504
Fayetteville, AR 72702

Microsoft Corporation
10700 Northup Way
Bellevue, WA 98004

MPPi, Ltd.
1126 Adirondack
Northbrook, IL 60062

Okara/KIAI Systems
5453 Manila Avenue
Oakland, CA 94618

Okidata Corporation
111 Gaither Road
Mt. Laurel, NJ 08054

Peachtree Software, Inc.
3445 Peachtree Road, NE
8th Floor
Atlanta, GA 30326

Pemall Fire Extinguisher
Corporation
39A Myrtle Street
Cranford, NJ 07016

Perfection Mica Company
740 North Thomas Drive
Bensenville, IL 60106

Phase One Systems, Inc.
7700 Edgewater Drive
Suite 830
Oakland, CA 94621

Public Key Systems Corporation
P. O. Box 1504
Fayetteville, AR 72702

SofTech Microsystems, Inc.
16885 W. Bernardo Drive
San Diego, CA 92127

Software 2000 Inc.
1127 Hetrick Avenue
Arroyo Grande, CA 93420

Sola Electric
1717 Busse Road
Elk Grove Village, IL 60007

Standard Software Corporation
of America
10 Mazzeo Drive
Randolph, MA 02368

Starside Engineering
P. O. Box 18306
Rochester, NY 14618

Supersoft, Inc.
   P. O. Box 1628
   Champaign, IL 61820

Sutton Designs, Inc.
   Sutton Building
   Interlaken, NY 14847

Systems Furniture Company
   2727 Maricopa Street
   Torrance, CA 90503

TII Industries, Inc.
   1375 Akron Street
   Copiague, NY 11726

Ven-Tel, Inc.
   2342 Walsh Avenue
   Santa Clara, CA 95051

Western Telematic, Inc.
   2435 South Anne Street
   Santa Ana, CA 92704

Wilson Jones Company
   6150 Touhy Avenue
   Chicago, IL 60648

3M
   3M Center
   St. Paul, MN 55144

20 Century Plastics, Inc.
   3628 Crenshaw Blvd.
   P. O. Box 30231
   Los Angeles, CA 90030

Index

USER'S NOTES

USER'S NOTES

USER'S NOTES

USER'S NOTES

USER'S NOTES

USER'S NOTES